Henry James Coleridge

The Return of the King: Discourses on the Latter Days

Henry James Coleridge

The Return of the King: Discourses on the Latter Days

ISBN/EAN: 9783743397439

Manufactured in Europe, USA, Canada, Australia, Japa

Cover: Foto ©Lupo / pixelio.de

Manufactured and distributed by brebook publishing software (www.brebook.com)

Henry James Coleridge

The Return of the King: Discourses on the Latter Days

Quarterly Series

THIRTY-EIGHTH VOLUME

THE RETURN OF THE KING

ROEHAMPTON
PRINTED BY JAMES STANLEY

[*All rights reserved*]

THE RETURN OF THE

DISCOURSES ON THE LATTER

BY

HENRY JAMES COLERIDGE

OF THE SOCIETY OF JESUS

LONDON
BURNS AND OATES
GRANVILLE MANSIONS W
1883

✠

ET FACTUM EST

UT REDIRET

ACCEPTO REGNO

(*S. Luc.* xix, 15)

PREFACE.

THE present volume is made up of a collection of Sermons, which were written and preached at various times and with long intervals between them. The first, the second, the third, the tenth, and the seventeenth, were preached in the December of 1868, and have already been published in the first volume of the *Sermons by Fathers of the Society of Jesus*, which has long been out of print. The fourth, fifth, sixth, eighth, and ninth were preached in the Advent of 1881, and the twelfth, thirteenth, fourteenth, fifteenth, and sixteenth, in the Advent of 1882. The seventh, which was partly occasioned by a particular attack on the Church, was preached on the Sunday before Advent, 1874, and was published at the time; the eleventh was preached on the same Sunday a few years later; and the four Sermons which close the volume were preached on the Sunday afternoons in February, 1879.

The reader, therefore, must not expect to find in these Sermons that connected and systematic treatment of the great subject to which they refer, which would be natural in the successive chapters of a well-planned work on that subject. The Sermons have now been arranged in the order of ideas, and they have the unity and continuity which will usually belong to the productions of the same mind on the same subject. Nor is there any great department of the subject which has been altogether left untouched.

I fear also that it has been impossible to free them from occasional repetitions, such as would be inevitable under the circumstances of their composition and delivery. I have in two cases separated a single sermon into two parts, and I have supplied here and there some connecting paragraphs, for the sake of giving the whole more cohesion. But the same ideas will still be found recurring here and there, to an extent greater than might be the case if I had had the time to recast the whole series, and for this defect I must apologize beforehand.

H. J. C.

London, Feast of the Patronage of St. Joseph, 1883.

CONTENTS.

SERMON I.

Anticipations of the Last Days.

"But Mary kept all these words, pondering them in her heart" (St. Luke ii. 10).

	PAGE
I. The Church blends the two Advents	1
Spirit in which the subject should be studied	2
II. Scripture on the two Advents	4
Our Lord's reference to the Judgment	6
Language of the Apostles	7
III. Conscience anticipating Judgment	8
The early Christian converts	10
IV. Succession of Fathers and Saints	11
Grounds of their anticipations	12
St. Jerome, St. Chrysostom, St. Gregory the Great	14
St. Vincent Ferrer	14
V. Conclusion	16

SERMON II.

Prophecies of the End of the World.

"Unless there come a revolt first, and the man of sin be revealed, the son of perdition" (Thess. ii. 3).

	PAGE
I. The Thessalonian Christians	19
Advantage to us of their difficulties	20
St. Matthew's words misconceived	21
Explanation by St. Paul	22
St. Paul on Antichrist	24
II. Early Christians instructed on Antichrist	25
The apostasy	26
"He who holdeth"	27
Explained of social order	28
The providential signs	28
III. Principles now at work	29
Successive results	31
Attacks on order	31

SERMON III.

The Decay of Faith.

"But yet the Son of Man when He cometh, shall He find, think you, faith on earth?" (St. Luke xviii. 8.)

	PAGE
I. Meaning of our Lord's question	35
Remarks on interpretation	37
II. Scriptural passages	38
Decay of faith	40
St. Paul on the last times	41
III. Speech at Athens	42
Opening of the Epistle to the Romans	43
Description in the Epistle to Timothy	45
The two passages almost identical	45

	PAGE		PAGE
IV. Good element in heathenism	46	No hold left on which to fasten truth	81
Natural element	47	VI. Conclusion	83
Satanic element	49	NOTE to page 71 (from the *Creed of Science*)	86
Not to be entirely restored	50		
V. Revival of heathenism in our times	51	SERMON V.	
VI. Conclusion	54	*The Decay of Charity.*	

SERMON IV.

The Creed of False Science.

"Take heed that you be not seduced" (St. Luke xxi. 8).

"Because iniquity hath abounded, the charity of many shall grow cold" (St. Matthew xxiv. 12).

I. Signs of the Judgment	58	I. Our Lord's words	89
Indifference to them, how marvellous	59	Decay of charity belongs to Christians	97
Our Lord's warning	60	An objection suggested	92
II. Two elements in the prophecy	61	II. Full meaning of our Lord's language	93
Their relative importance	61	What would destroy charity	95
Characteristics of men of the last day	63	What our Lord expected from it	96
St. John on Antichrist	64	Our Lord's work complete	96
III. False creed the foundation of insensibility	65	And that of the Holy Ghost	97
Such a creed in our time	66	One thing more wanted	97
Misuse of the name of science	67	What our Lord expects from charity	98
Truths at the foundation of the doctrine of Judgment	68	Conditions of the work of the Church	99
IV. Modern and ancient "philosophers"	70	Charity the cause of charity	100
Creation "unknowable"	70	Of heroic labours	100
The Darwinian "Creator"	71	Of continual prayer	101
Doctrine as to man, the soul, the future	72	III. Triumphs of the Church	102
This "creed" prepares for blindness	73	Defects in charity from the beginning	103
V. Its destruction of morality	74	Christians outside the Church	104
Its sweeping character	75	Separation has become normal	104
Its attractiveness	76	Treatment of the Holy See	106
Its deceptiveness	77	Easterns and Anglicans	107
Its hopelessness of correction	80		

	PAGE
IV. Doctrine of opportunities	109
The history of the Church	110
Rise of Islam	110
The discovery of America and the Cape of Good Hope	112
Present state of the world	113
Conclusion	114

SERMON VI.

The National Spirit.

"Nation shall rise against nation, and kingdom against kingdom" (St. Matthew xxiv. 7).

I. Strangeness of our Lord's words	116
The early Church and Jewish nationalism	118
We are accustomed to the spirit of nationalism	119
II. Usefulness of the consideration	120
Nationalism in modern literature	121
Nationalism as perpetuating hatred	122
It can only be restrained by charity	123
III. What is good in national feeling	125
God's designs in the system of nations	126
Principles underlying that system	127
Rights of national allegiance	129
Patriotism and the law of God	131
IV. Christian and Pagan patriotism	132
Contrast	133
Restraints on Nationalism in ancient times	134

	PAGE
The work of the Church	135
Dangers from a false creed	135
Modern "Unities"	136
V. Our present dangers	138
Positive and negative side of patriotism	140
Conclusion	141

SERMON VII.

The Abomination of Desolation.

"You shall see the abomination of desolation ... standing in the holy place" (St. Matthew xxiv. 15).

I. Interpretation of prophecy	142
The text can apply to our times	144
Continual fulfilments	145
II. The abomination of desolation at Jerusalem	146
Meaning of the explanation	148
The secular power in the sanctuary	149
III. Three relations between the two powers	150
The Christian system	151
The un-Christian system	153
The anti-Christian system	154
Cause of persecution	156
IV. Attack on the Church in England (1874)	157
Conclusion	159

SERMON VIII.

The Days of Noe.

"As it came to pass in the days of Noe, so shall it be also in the days of the Son of Man" (St. Luke xvii. 26).

I. Recapitulation	162
Some remaining features	163

	PAGE
Engrossment in material enjoyment	164
The days of Noe	165
The Cities of the Plain	166
II. Points of comparison	168
Great advance in material comforts	169
Comparison with ancient times	170
Progress of the age favours the popularization of physical enjoyment	171
Deep moral corruption	172
Old and modern Catholics	173

SERMON IX.

The Loosing of Satan.

"The last state of that man becomes worse than the first" (St. Luke xi. 26).

I. Features of the last days	175
Their connection	176
II. These are human elements	179
Activity of Satan fettered by our Lord	180
The return of the evil one	181
The future loosing of Satan	182
III. Absurdity of supposing him idle	184
"Spiritualism"	185
It is very widespread	186
Human testimony	186
Internal evidence from "Universalism"	188
Satan detected	188
Reception of the system by the world	189
IV. Conclusion	190

	PAGE

SERMON X.

The Man of Sin.

"I am come in the name of My Father, and you receive Me not; if another shall come in his own name, him you will receive" (St. John v. 43).

I. Our Lord speaks of Antichrist	194
General law of Providence	195
Scriptural prophecies concerning Antichrist	196
II. Antichrist a single person	198
Like other men	199
His character	200
Persecutor of the Church	202
Enoch and Elias	203
End of Antichrist	203
III. Extraordinary features in his history	204
He will be the man of his time	205
Welcomed by the world	206
Fascination of his success	208
Analogous triumphs in history	209
IV. Satanic action discerned by the saints	211
Conclusion	212

SERMON XI.

The Church in the Last Days.

"Wherever the body shall be, there the eagles also shall be gathered together" (St. Matt. xxiv. 28).

I. Our Lord's words enigmatic	214
Recapitulation	215
II. The last prophecy of our Lord	216
His presence manifested in two ways	218

	PAGE
As the lightning	210
As the prey to the eagles	210
III. The notes of the Church	221
These are external evidences	222
Internal evidences also	223
The unction spoken of by St. John	225
IV. Need of both witnesses	225
Conclusion	227

SERMON XII.

Reasonableness of the Judgment.

"And God indeed having winked at the times of this ignorance, now declareth unto men, that all should everywhere do penance, because He hath appointed a day wherein He will judge the world in equity, by the Man Whom He hath appointed, giving faith to all by raising Him from the dead" (Acts xvii. 30, 31).

	PAGE
I. St. Paul at Athens	229
His audience	230
His address	231
Sternness of the doctrine	232
II. St. Paul guided by the Holy Ghost	233
Truths of natural religion	234
Truths of revelation	236
Two parts of the doctrine of the judgment	237
General and particular judgment	237
Contrast between the two	238
III. The early Christians full of the thought of the judgment	239
Considerations concerning the judgment	239
The particular judgment known only to ourselves	241
It is not only to be repeated at the general judgment	242
Evil and good done by men after their deaths	243
IV. The providence of God is to be manifested	244
Correction of public opinion needed	246
Conclusion	247

SERMON XIII.

Particular and General Judgment.

"But with me it is a very small thing to be judged by you or by man's day, but neither do I judge my own self. For I am not conscious to myself of anything, yet am I not hereby justified, but He that judgeth me is the Lord" (1 Cor. iv. 3, 4).

	PAGE
I. Three tribunals mentioned by St. Paul	248
His estimate of them	249
The judgment of men	250
The authority and accuracy of conscience	251
The tribunal of God	253
II. The two judgments of God stages in the rectification of our thoughts	254
Our gradual preparation by the three tribunals	255
Revelation to ourselves at the particular judgment	257
Its circumstances and conditions	259
III. A new range of knowledge then opened to us	260
The rewards of faithfulness	262
The particular judgment prepares us for the general	263
Magdalene in the Pharisee's house	263

	PAGE
Revelation implied in the resurrection of the body	265
The consequences of sins revealed	266
IV. Conclusion	268

SERMON XIV.

The ways of God manifested.

"What I do thou knowest not now, but thou shalt know hereafter" (St. John xiii. 7).

	PAGE
I. Our Lord's words to St. Peter	271
He did disclose some things	272
Manifestation of the ways of God	272
II. Delight of contemplation of the works of God	273
Beauty of the spiritual world	274
The symmetry and harmony of God's works in this order	275
Wonderful manifestation in this respect at the last day	276
Action of God on the soul	276
Both in saints and in sinners	277
III. We can now gather certain great principles of God's action	278
Many difficulties always remain	280
Answer of St. Paul	281
A number of questions	282
III. These are instances of the difficulties to be solved	283
Answers to some	284
Conclusion	286

SERMON XV.

The Book of Life.

"And I saw the dead, great and small, standing in the presence of the throne, and the books were opened, and another book was opened, which is the book of life, and the dead were judged by those things which were written in the books according to their works" (Apoc. xx. 12).

	PAGE
I. The first book in St. John	288
What is the second book?	289
Analogy of human justice	291
II. The book of life is the life of our Lord	292
Purpose of our Lord's life	293
What God has done in giving us His Son	293
Our Lord's life the norm of judgment	296
III. Instantaneousness of the judgment	297
The light will remain for ever	298
Manifestation of the interior of our Lord	298
And of those who resemble Him	299
Conclusion	300

SERMON XVI.

The Saints of God.

"And when the Son of Man shall come in His majesty and all the Angels with Him, then shall He sit upon the throne of His majesty, and all nations shall be gathered together before Him, and He shall separate them one from another, as the shepherd separateth the sheep from the goats, and He shall set the sheep on His right hand and the goats on His left" (St. Matt. xxv. 31—33).

	PAGE
I. Salvation may appear difficult	302

		PAGE
II.	Difficulties do not deter us in worldly things	304
	Descriptions of our Lord not discouraging	305
	The perfection of our Lord frightens us	306
III.	The world will always be the same	308
	Our hopes at the death-bed of our friends	308
	Salvation is the undertaking of God	310
	He became Man for that purpose	310
IV.	Great numbers of the saints	312
	From all classes and conditions of men	312
	Saying of St. Augustine	314
	The saints had the same difficulties with ourselves	315
V.	Thought of the particular providence of God	316
	The saints have had the ordinary means of grace	318
VI.	Conclusion	319

SERMON XVII.

All things made new.

"And I heard a great voice from the Throne, saying, Behold the Tabernacle of God with men, and He will dwell with them, and they shall be His people, and God Himself with them shall be their God. And God shall wipe away all tears from their eyes, and death shall be no more, for the former things are passed away; and He that sat on the Throne said, 'Behold, I make all things new'" (Apocalypse xxi. 3—5).

		PAGE
I.	The beginning of the new creation	321
II.	Unfulfilled prophecy	323
	Circumstances of the end of the world	327
III.	Terrible character of the Second Coming	328
	But also joyful	330
	Life from the dead	331
	Blessedness of soul and body	333
	Greater than in the state of innocence	334
	The merits of the Passion	336
IV.	The renovation of the universe	337
	Holy companionship	338
V.	The things that shall not pass away	339
	Conclusion	342

SERMON XVIII.

The Greatness of Death.

"He killed many more at his death, than he had killed before in his life" (Judges xvi. 30).

		PAGE
I.	The last exploit of Samson	344
	Opportunities of Christian death	345
II.	Greatness of death in what it shows us of God	347
	Destruction of the union between body and soul	350
	Questions settled at death	352
III.	Death the great dispeller of illusions	353
	And the great revealer of truths	354
IV.	Ennobling power of death	356
	Conclusion	356

SERMON XIX.

The Sacredness of Death.

"And for them do I sanctify Myself, that they also may be sanctified in truth" (St. John xix. 19).

I. Meaning of sanctification, as applied to death 359
Natural witness to the sacredness of death . 361
II. Death is sacred as belonging to God alone . 362
And as bringing us into the presence of God . 364
III. Death gives great glory to God . . . 366
It shows the truthfulness of God . . . 367
It punishes all rebellion against Him . . 368
It enables us to make Him the greatest of sacrifices . . . 369
Immense merits to be gained by death . . 371
IV. Conclusion . . . 373

SERMON XX.

The Happiness of Death.

"To me to live is Christ, and to die is gain" (Philip. i. 21).

I. The happiness of death included in the foregoing considerations . 377
It may be merciful even to the wicked . . 378
II. Misery of perpetuating a bad life . . . 380
Mercy to the impenitent 381
Mercy to the human race 381
III. Our Lord speaks of death as a going to the Father. . . 383
St. Paul in the Epistles of the captivity . . 384

IV. The three motives of happiness in death . 387
Conclusion . . . 393

SERMON XXI.

Our Lord and Death.

"Behold we go up to Jerusalem, and all things shall be accomplished which were written by the prophets concerning the Son of Man. For He shall be delivered to the Gentiles, and shall be mocked and scourged and spit upon, and when they have scourged Him they will put Him to death, and the third day He shall rise again" (St. Luke xviii. 31—33).

I. What has our Lord done for us by dying? . 395
Passages from St. Paul . 397
II. What is meant by our Lord dying for us . 398
Difference between His case and that of the martyrs . . . 399
He could do nothing for Himself . . . 400
St. Paul on the fear of death 401
Our Lord's destruction of death . . . 402
He is Lord of death . 403
He leaves it for awhile in His Kingdom . 403
III. Our Lord always turns evils into goods . . 406
The world beyond the grave 407
Penalty of death changed into an occasion of merit 408
IV. More than this, our Lord has taught us how to die 409
Value of the Passion in this respect . . 409
Conclusion . . . 410

SERMON I.

ANTICIPATIONS OF THE LAST DAYS.*

Maria autem conservabat omnia verba hæc, conferens in corde suo.

But Mary kept all these words, pondering them in her heart.

(Words taken from the 19th verse of the 2nd chapter of St. Luke's Gospel.)

I.

THE Church at this time, my brethren in Jesus Christ, is training us to prepare ourselves more particularly to celebrate with joy and thankfulness the great feast of Christmas, the commemoration of our Lord's first coming into the world, in poverty, in suffering, in gentleness, in benignity and humility. But she is led by a heavenly instinct to do this, in great measure, by means of considerations concerning our Blessed Lord's future coming in glory, majesty, and power. These two thoughts seem, as it were, to require, each the other, as its own fitting and natural supplement. It seems as if from Bethlehem and Nazareth we were to be continually looking on to the end of all things, and reminding ourselves that that sweet and gentle Child, around Whose opening days are clustered so many tender thoughts of thankfulness and

* Preached on Advent Sunday, 1868, which fell that year in the Triduum of Preparation for the Feast of the Immaculate Conception.

B

hopefulness and love, is to come hereafter, terrible to His enemies, a fire going before His face, Heaven and earth rolling up like a scroll before Him, "with the voice of an Archangel and the trumpet of God "* calling on the dead to arise and come to judgment. It seems as if, on the other hand, we were not to look forward to the great and terrible day of the manifestation of the Son of Man as our Judge, without remembering that it is our own blessed and most loving Jesus Christ, the Babe of Bethlehem, the Boy of Nazareth, He Who drew all hearts around Him in Galilee, Who is to sit on that great white throne, and call His people before Him. And again, the Mother is put before us as well as the Son. As if to carry out still further the blending of the two advents, Providence has arranged that just at this time we should be called on to keep the great feast of our Lady's Immaculate Conception, and to be helped by the thought of that perfect sinlessness and purity, which alone in all the world was worthy to receive Jesus Christ when He came, to prepare ourselves to stand before the tribunal of her Son, the Lamb of God, the Judge of all the Earth.

And therefore, my brethren, let us begin our consideration of these awful subjects by placing ourselves under her special protection and patronage. It has been the lot of this great subject of our Lord's second coming, that it has been inquired into and thought about in very different ways. The prophecies, direct and indirect, concerning it, which are to be found from one end of Scripture to the

* 1 Thess. iv. 15.

other, are very numerous, and in some cases very minute, and even intricate in detail. In consequence, they invite from those who are not animated by great reverence and diffidence in their own discernment, what must be called a presumptuous and intrusive method of treatment. We find men who are not guided by the analogy of the faith and the instincts of the Church, drawing out schemes of what is to happen before the end of the world, and fixing the precise year of that event of which our Lord said, "Of that day and hour no one knoweth, no, not the Angels of God, but the Father alone."* They tell us when this or that is to come about, and the end of all things is to take place. This is not either reasonable or Catholic—not reasonable, for no prophecy can be expected to be read in all its details beforehand, and, as a matter of fact, some of these interpreters are foolish enough to fix such dates as fall within their own lifetime, and thus are themselves enabled to prove their own folly. It is not Catholic, because, although the Church has always set her face steadily to the contemplation of the future, although she knows well the blessing that is to be gained by the devout study of God's warning notes, still it is her spirit to confine herself in her explanations to certain great outlines, certain prominent and distinguishing facts, which are marked unmistakeably on the pages of Scripture, and, for the times and seasons, she leaves these in the obscurity in which the same Scripture has veiled them. That is the way of the Church in the interpretation of

* St. Matt. xxiv. 36.

all prophecy as yet unfulfilled, and pre-eminently of these prophecies of the end of the world. And, my brethren, we shall have enough to do for all practical purposes if we can define these few most prominent features of the latter days, which shall precede the coming of the Son of Man. And we shall consider them best if we pray our Blessed Lady to obtain for us a share of that humble, reverential, thoughtful, and tranquil spirit, which was her own characteristic when she studied the Holy Scriptures before the Incarnation, and when she kept on considering mystery after mystery of the Incarnation as it came about, comparing one portion and feature of God's wonderful dealings with another; that characteristic tone of mind which made the holy Evangelist, who so seldom leaves his simple narrative to speak of the qualities of persons, to write of her more than once, "Mary kept all these words, pondering them in her heart!"

II.

When we read in the pages of Holy Scripture the several prophecies which relate to the coming, or the comings, of our Blessed Lord, we are struck by a fact quite in harmony with what I have remarked on as to the close union between the two events in the mind of the Church. Not only is the second coming of our Lord to judge the world, the article which we profess every time we recite the *Credo*, spoken of from one end of Scripture to the other, so that we may almost say, that there is no one thing so constantly foretold and dwelt on as the last end of

all things; but also, when Prophets are speaking of
the first coming of our Lord, of His advent in gentleness, in love, in meekness, in humility, and in poverty
—when He would not break the bruised reed nor
quench the smoking flax, when He would have
nothing to do with judgment, and would not condemn
even the poor woman who had been taken in adultery
—I say, when they speak of our Lord's first coming,
they seem unable to restrain themselves from adding
particulars which belong to His second advent in
power, majesty, and wrath. The famous passage
in Malachias the Prophet,* is a case of this kind.
We know that it refers to our Lord's first coming,
because it is a part of the prophecy about His
precursor at that time, St. John the Baptist. And
yet when the Prophet has spoken of our Lord's
coming, "The Lord Whom ye seek, and the Angel
of the Covenant Whom ye desire, shall come to His
temple," he breaks out, "Who shall be able to think
of the day of His coming, and who shall stand to see
Him? for He is like a refining fire, and like the
fuller's herb." And it was just the same with St. John
the Baptist himself. When he spoke to the Jews
about our Lord's coming so immediately after him,
his words were full of the future judgment. "The
axe is laid to the root of the tree," he says; " Every
tree that doth not yield good fruit shall be cut down
and cast into the fire;" "His fan is in His hand, and
He will thoroughly cleanse His floor, and gather His
wheat into the barn, but the chaff He will burn with
unquenchable fire."† It is as if the light of the

* Mal. iii. 6.   † St. Matt. iii. 10, 12.

fires of the great judgment day made everything else pale and faint in comparison, to the eyes of those who saw the future of God's doings with the world; as if the figure of Jesus Christ coming in the clouds of Heaven, with all His holy Angels, to judge mankind, was so grand and fearful as to draw to itself their gaze from everything else, even from the prodigies of love of Nazareth, Bethlehem, and Calvary.

We may remark also, my brethren, that as the second coming of Christ was so frequently in the mouths of His Prophets, so also was it spoken of frequently by Himself and by His Apostles, and this at the most solemn and critical times of all His and their ministry on earth. Thus, when He closed His public preaching on one of the days of Holy Week, and sat down on the way to Bethany, to look for the last time, as it was to be, on the Temple and City which He had done so much to save, He uttered His great prophecy about their destruction, but in such a way as to blend and mingle with the description of their destruction that of the signs of His own coming, and of the end of the world.* Again, at the very moment of His condemnation, when Caiaphas adjured Him by the living God to say whether He were the Christ or not, our Lord at once spoke of the day of judgment. He was as a lamb before His shearers, dumb, not opening His mouth, till this adjuration came to force Him to speak, alone, forsaken, betrayed, reviled, slandered by false witnesses, denied by His Apostle, ill-treated even at the very tribunal

* St. Matt. xxiv.

of justice, and yet He calmly said the words, "Thou hast said it. Nevertheless I say to you, hereafter you shall see the Son of Man sitting at the right hand of the power of God, and coming in the clouds of Heaven." *

So it is all through the New Testament history. When the Apostles are looking up after their ascended Lord, they are reminded of this by the Angels— "Ye men of Galilee, why stand you looking up to Heaven? this Jesus Who is taken up from you into Heaven shall so come as you have seen Him going into Heaven." † And when St. Peter first opened the course of Apostolic preaching on the day of Pentecost, he spoke of the second coming of our Lord; when he wrought the first Apostolical miracle, he spoke of the second coming of our Lord; when he received the first of the Gentiles, Cornelius, into the Church, he spoke of our Lord as appointed to judge the world.‡ In the same way, when the Apostles bore testimony to Jesus Christ even before the heathen, who knew nothing of the Old Testament, they preached the doctrine of the judgment. St. Paul, when he spoke to the philosophers of Athens about the unknown God, told them that He Whom they ignorantly worshipped had appointed a day to judge the world by the Man whom He had appointed; and when the Roman Governor sent for him to hear him discourse, he spoke of the judgment to come.§

* St. Matt. xxvi. 64. † Acts i. 11.
‡ Acts ii. 19, 20; iii. 20, 21; x. 42.
‖ *Ibid.* xvii. 31; xxiv. 25.

III.

Now this reference of the chief Apostles to the great Day of Judgment, when they are addressing themselves to the heathen, points to a great truth which may be mentioned now, though I shall have to dwell on it more fully hereafter. This truth is that the doctrine of the Judgment of man by God is not one which could be recognized by those only who had received a special revelation on the subject. St. Paul shows in his argument in the Epistle to the Romans, that this truth about the future judgment is one which has its witness in every human conscience, and cannot be quite obliterated, either by the presumptuousness of infidelity or by the corruptions of superstition. St. Paul speaks of the Gentiles as showing the works of the law written in their hearts, "their consciences bearing witness to them, and their thoughts between themselves accusing or else defending one another;" and then he speaks of the day in which God "will judge the secrets of men by Jesus Christ, according to my Gospel."* I shall have to draw out at some length, before these discourses close, what may be said as to the entire reasonableness of this assumption on the part of the great Apostle, that the truth of the final judgment of man by God is a truth to which reason and conscience bear sufficient testimony. For it is a truth on which we shall have to dwell more particularly when we come to consider by itself this great judicial act of God, which may be altogether distinguished, in idea, from the simple

* Romans ii. 15, 16.

truth of the second coming of our Lord, of which it formed a part in the minds of the first Christian generations. For the present I only observe that it is so—that whether in prophecy, or in the language of the writers of the New Testament, these two things are so blended into one, that to speak and think of the one is to speak and think of the other, though there are many passages in the New Testament in which the one may be the direct subject of thought rather than the other. But why is it not to be said that the doctrine of the future judgment is one of those truths which require a special supernatural revelation to imprint them on the mind of man? This truth is founded on man's own consciousness. It is because we must never consent to think and speak of man otherwise than as God has made him, a free intelligent being, conscious both of his freedom and his intelligence. Man knows that he is free, and that freedom implies responsibility, and an account to be given to his Maker; and he bears within himself an unsleeping judge, the voice of his conscience, which may be disobeyed but will not be silenced, which always speaks with authority, and appeals in every heart, Jewish, Christian, or heathen, civilized or barbarian, pagan or atheist, to a judgment to come, which shall confirm its sentence and vindicate its right. To this simple truth St. Paul confidently appealed, as I have said, before the philosophic idlers of Athens, and again, a few years later, when the Roman Governor Felix had him in his keeping, and was willing to listen to his words, he "treated of justice and chastity and of the judgment to come," so that "Felix was terrified," and his evil conscience would not allow him to hearken to the Apostle any longer.

This truth, moreover, which found its echo even in the minds and hearts of the heathen, was a part also of the elementary teaching imparted by the Apostles to their converts. They were all trained, as St. Paul words it to the Thessalonians, who had at that time been but a few weeks in the light of the Christian faith, "to wait for God's Son from Heaven, Jesus, Whom He raised up from the dead;"* and so entirely did the great truth of His coming fill their minds, that they had to be warned by the Apostle who had taught it them not to expect it too soon. For to them, my brethren, as it would seem, there was but little thought of the long future of the Church upon earth—no picture of hope and expectation of so marvellous a history as that on which we now look back over the length of so many centuries, of the conquest of the world, of the leavening of society, of the triumph of Christian civilization and philosophy, of the unravelling of the mysteries of nature and the subjugation of the physical elements to the uses of man under the guidance of the Church. Prophets had spoken of such glories, but these Christians dwelt rather on the great end and crown of all prophecy, which was to be the beginning of the new kingdom of God, the coming of the Son of Man in power. And so we find among them the clearest evidence of such an expectation as that against being engrossed by which St. Paul had afterwards to warn them,†

* 1 Thess. i. 10.   † 2 Thess. ii.

that the second advent was immediately at hand. Our Lord had said, "The end is not yet,"* and still there was this expectation in the minds of the early Christians.

IV.

Nor was this hope in their minds only, my brethren, but in the minds of those who came after them in successive generations. I find the same expectation in St. Cyprian in the third century, in St. Chrysostom and St. Jerome in the fourth, St. Gregory the Great witnesses to it in the sixth, St. Bernard in the twelfth, St. Vincent Ferrer in the fourteenth and fifteenth †— all were looking continually for the appearance of the Man of Sin, whose coming was to go before that of our Lord. In this, my brethren, how different, we may say, from the generality of men in our time! who seem, in their indifference and incredulity, to bring before us the fulfilment of the prophecy of St. Peter, and thereby most truly to indicate the actual drawing nigh of the end by their very forgetfulness of it: "In the last days there shall come deceitful scoffers, walking after their own lusts, saying, Where is His promise and His coming? for since the time that the fathers slept, all things continue as they were from the beginning of the creation." ‡

St. Peter seems to say, in these and some following words, that men will be led to this unbelief by their

---

* St. Matt. xxiv. 6.
† St. Cyprian, *Ep.* l. iii. 1; l. iv. 6; St. Chrysost. *in Joan.* xxxiii.; St. Hieronym. *de Monogamia ad Ageruchiam;* St. Greg. Mag. *Ep.* l. iv. 38; St. Bern. *in Qui Habitat,* Serm. vi.
‡ 2 St. Peter iii. 4.

own confidence that they have ascertained the unchangeableness and absolute necessity of the laws of the physical universe, and that they will have put aside as an exploded tale the record of Scripture as to the great interference with those laws which has already taken place once in the history of the world by the Deluge. Yes, surely this temper of forgetfulness and self-confidence is an even more significant mark of the approaching end than the anxious expectation that our Lord was to come at once which prevailed among the early Christians and the Saints ; and it explains also our Lord's prediction that He is to come at a time when He is not looked for. There are to be signs in the sun and in the moon and in the stars ; the powers of the heavens, the very laws of the universe in which these men are to put so much trust, are to be shaken. And yet, as it was in the days of Noe before the Flood, and in the days of Lot before the destruction of Sodom and Gomorrah, so also shall it be in the days of the coming of the Son of Man.* That is, all these signs shall be addressed in vain to the majority of mankind, and the last day shall come upon them as a snare.

Now it may not be without profit to us, my brethren, if before we leave this subject we consider a little more closely how it may have been that the saints of God, such as those whom I have mentioned, had so strong an impression on their minds as to the near approach of the last days, an impression which we know to have been at once most beneficial to them and to others, and at the same time, as to the actual

* St. Luke xvii. 26—30.

history of the world, in one sense, premature. In the first place, we may see little difficulty in the fact that the Fathers of the earliest centuries, such as St. Cyprian, before the declaration of the liberty of the Church on the part of the first Christian Emperor, should have been in perpetual expectation of the advent of the last days. As long as the supreme power of the Imperial throne was at the disposal of pagan Emperors, however virtuous some of them might have been, there was always the possibility, and constantly the recurrence, of the most savage persecution. And we know that this persecution frequently had a kind of miserable success, in almost stamping out the Church here or there, and that, if it generated martyrs by thousands, it did not the less generate apostates and compromisers by tens of thousands. The heroism of the martyrs lives on in the history of the Church, but the students of her history know also that there were other pages in the annals of those days which were not filled by the heroism of the martyrs. And again, the Roman Emperors, as was shown only too clearly when the Empire became Christian, were the possessors of an amount of irresponsible power such as the world had never seen before, and will perhaps never see again till the days of Antichrist. Thus it was not difficult for the leaders of Christian thought and the devout contemplators of the prophetic writings, to see, in men like Nero or Domitian or Decius or Diocletian, figures very nearly approaching to the form of the Man of Sin as sketched in the inspired volume. The last time might well have been looked for in those days of persecution.

If we pass to the age in which St. Jerome and St. Chrysostom lived, the age which succeeded the peace of the Church as secured by the first Christian Emperor, we find ourselves at once in the age of the great heresies, of the beginnings of the schism which afterwards tore the East from the West, an age in which, again, the Imperial power played but too frequently the part of the old persecutors. That was the age of the decay of charity, as it had been foretold by our Lord, and we find the great Chrysostom giving this as the reason why the end was at hand, because charity had waxed cold. Thus, if the Fathers, like St. Cyprian, had one kind of evidence of the approach of the latter days, in the virulence of the persecutions, the Fathers of the fourth and fifth centuries had another kind of evidence of the same approach, in the decay of Christian love. If we pass on to the time of St. Gregory, we find other reasons for the opinion to which that great Pope gave utterance. For then the Empire had broken up under the blows of the Northern barbarians, ruin and desolation were rife everywhere over what had been the realm of the great Roman Peace, and the miseries of the populations had been aggravated, as St. Gregory tells us, by a change in the seasons and by very frequent visitations of the anger of God by pestilence, and earthquake, and famine. The great Fathers, then, had abundant reason for seeing, in the features of their own times, the lineaments of the last days.

But the most remarkable of the saints of whom I have made mention in this connection is the great preacher of penance, St. Vincent Ferrer, the first of a succession of great missionary saints to whom Christian Europe owed it that she was prepared against the great chastisement and desolation of the Reformation of the sixteenth century, and perhaps saved from being overwhelmed by the aggressive power of the unbelievers, who were already making themselves the masters of the former capital of the Eastern Empire, where they still remain. St. Vincent Ferrer was specially commissioned to preach the approach of the Day of Judgment, as immediately at hand, though we have his sermons remaining to us to show that his ordinary teaching was of the plain practical truths of Christian faith and morality. Of the two great missionary preachers who followed on his track, St. Bernardine of Siena and St. John Capistrano, we have the sermons of the first only preserved to us, and they, like the sermons of St. Vincent himself, are on the ordinary great truths of morality and of religion. It may well have been the case with them, as with St. Paul, when he tells us of himself, after speaking of the judgment, "Knowing the fear of the Lord, we use persuasion to men,"* and that a part of the power which they wielded over the hearts and minds of their contemporaries came from the impression which they produced and shared, that the Day of Judgment was at hand. And well indeed might the saints of the time of the great Western Schism see, in the wickedness and scandals around them on every side, as good a reason for their conclusion as that which made St. Gregory speak as he did, or St. Chrysostom speak as he did. The world is always provoking the judgments of God,

* 2 Cor. v. 11.

and when the scandals by which saints are terrified are found in the sanctuary itself, as well as in the world outside the Church, it may well indeed be thought that the end is nigh.

V.

I gather two conclusions from what we have been considering, and with them I will end to-day, though the truths on which they are based will be constantly before us in the course of these sermons. The first of these is, that we can seldom find an age, in the life of the Church, in which she has not to contend with the evils which will rise to their highest expression in the last days. The last times have really been upon us from the beginning of the history of the Church, as St. John says in his Epistle. They have been upon us from the beginning, for this reason, that the principles which, in their full and final development, will produce the state of things on which the last judgment will fall, have been always at work in the world and always countermining the holy and saving influences of the Church of God. The last struggle is already begun, and will continue until the end on the same lines and with the same conflicting forces. Each generation of Christians thus has its part to play in this holy warfare, for it has to fight in its own day against the principles which will assail the Church with the greatest fury in the days of the end. And each generation, according to its faithfulness and watchfulness, or its slothfulness and laxity, will either help on the Church in the years which are to succeed its own tenure of life to stand firm against the final assaults, or it will make her weaker in her resistance to those final assaults. Thus it is that the descriptions and characteristics of the last days are always full of interest and instruction, and it is always well that men should be reminded of the truth, on which our Lord and His Apostles insist, that if we are not watchful and sober, our loins girded, and our lamps burning, the day will take us unawares, and we may have to bewail our folly as long as eternity lasts. No mistake can be more pernicious to ourselves, or render our influence on those who come after us more pernicious, than that false persuasion in which we are so often inclined to fold ourselves to sleep, that we have nothing to do with the perils of the last time.

There is another reason also which may account for the urgent vigilance and ever wistful expectation in which the lives of the saints have always been passed. This reason is contained in that true view concerning the end which underlies all the thoughts and language of the saints on this subject. We can see almost at once why it was that, at so early a period, and again later on, the disciples of the Apostles, and, indeed, the generality of Christians, were literally, as our Lord bade them be, like men waiting for Him. With them, the last time was not so much the end of the world, the close of the long conflict of the Church, the great day of account, as *the coming of the Lord*. Their eyes and hearts strained forward to see Him Whom some of them had seen and known, and Whom all had heard of and loved. Now, as to this, we are all on a level, because, to each one of us, the coming of our Lord, the end of the world, the day of account, is the day of his own death. I do not mean to say that the particular judgment by which each man is judged at the moment at which he dies, is the same as the judgment of which we are speaking. But still, after the moment of death the world closes to us, with all its interests, all its events, and all its history, and we have no more to do with it until we are summoned to stand before our Lord at the Day of Judgment. Our part is played, the latter days are come to us, the Judge is at the door, we meet Him at our death. This is the one true view of our condition here. The stream of human life may be flowing on for many centuries yet, or for few, and as long as it flows on, the life of the Church on earth will last. But to each drop of that seemingly endless stream the last moment comes, whenever it passes from between the river's banks into the mighty ocean of eternity.

SERMON II.

PROPHECIES OF THE END OF THE WORLD.

Nisi venerit discessio primum, et revelatus fuerit homo peccati, filius perditionis.

Unless there come a revolt first, and the man of sin be revealed, the son of perdition.

(Words taken from the 3rd verse of the 2nd chapter of the Second Epistle to the Thessalonians.)

I.

IT must often strike you, my brethren in our Lord, as you study the writings of St. Paul and the other Apostles, how much we owe to the occasional, and as it seems to us, to the accidental character of the questions or difficulties which were put to them, or with which they had to deal. These Thessalonian Christians, who had not been very long admitted to the privileges of the Church, happened, as we should say, to have misunderstood some words of the Apostle, or of some other Christian teacher, concerning the end of all things for which they were told to be always ready, to which they were bidden always to look forward. In consequence of their mistake the blessed St. Paul had to write to them a second epistle, mainly with the object of setting them right on the subject of the time of the approach of the end of the world. The more we study this great Apostle, the more do we become aware of the truth that, even by his own natural disposition and character, and apart from the spiritual charity and zeal of which he was so filled by Divine grace, he was one of those who are always ready, on every subject on which they are interested, to pour out a great stream of information and thought, even when less would be enough for the occasion before them. And it was in the Providence of God, Who guided his hand and his mind in the composition of this and other epistles, that short as is the passage from which these words of the text are taken, it should contain, at least in germ or in sum, the chief features of what is the subject of many prophecies both in the Old Testament and in the New, the subject on which our thoughts are engaged for the present, the end of the world, and what shall take place before that comes about.

St. Augustine tells us that the hesitation of St. Thomas about the truth of the Resurrection of our Lord has been of more benefit to us than the ready belief of others of the disciples, because it was in consequence of that hesitation that we have the beautiful incident of the manifestation to that great Apostle of the proofs of the Resurrection, with a fulness and completeness of evidence which might otherwise have been wanting in the Gospel narrative. And so we may say of this mistake of the Thessalonian Christians that it has turned out to our benefit and to the benefit of the whole Christian world, for without it we might not have had, in the pages of the New

Testament, so clear and full a statement of the doctrine of the Apostles on this important subject of the revelation of Antichrist and of the state of the world before that revelation, or at least at the time when it shall be made. And although some lines of the picture of the last days, as it is drawn in the sacred writings, are not to be found in this short passage of St. Paul, it is still sufficiently full for our purpose to-day, and I shall therefore use it as a text from which I may state to you the chief features of that general picture, on which we shall have to dwell more particularly one by one, before we can part from this wonderful subject.

I must begin by reminding you that, as I said just now, the Thessalonians may have mistaken some former words of the Apostle to them, and this may have been the occasion of the necessity under which he found himself of correcting their error. It seems that they had been so impressed by what he had told them about the second coming of our Lord, as to think of it as imminent, to have been so persuaded that it would happen very soon, as to be surprised at the death of some of their own brethren before it came about, and to have been perplexed at the thought that these, who had died prematurely, as they imagined, might have missed their share with the rest in the glories and triumphs of that second coming of our Lord. The great Gospel document on this subject, with which they were perhaps familiar, seems to be that which is contained in the Gospel of St. Matthew, the only Gospel, probably, which was within their reach at that time. And, if you will study that account of the words of our Lord on this subject in His last prophecy on the Mount of Olives, you will see that He says nothing at all about those of the elect who may have died before the second Advent. So the Thessalonians had the reason for their difficulty that is to be found in this silence of Scripture in the great passage to which they would naturally have turned in their researches on this matter, and it is very likely that St. Paul, and the teachers whom he had left behind, or sent to complete his work among them, had not thought it necessary to touch on the question concerning the dead in Christ at the time of the second Advent. Thus there was a gap to be supplied in the information of the Thessalonians on this subject, and it was supplied by St. Paul in his first epistle to them. "If we believe that Jesus died and rose again, even so them who have slept through Jesus will God bring with Him. For this we say unto you in the word of the Lord, that we who are alive, who remain, unto the coming of the Lord, shall not prevent them who have slept. For the Lord Himself shall come down from Heaven with a commandment, and with the voice of an Archangel and with the trumpet of God, and the dead who are in Christ shall rise first, then we who are alive, who are left, shall be taken up together with them in the clouds to meet Christ, into the air, and so shall we be always with the Lord."

In this passage, as you see, St. Paul dwells mainly on the answer which was required in order to set at rest the troubles of the Thessalonians. He tells them how it shall be at the Last Day with the dead in Christ.

He forbears to mention many things which we know will take place at that time of which he speaks, notably the judgment itself, and the separation of the good and the bad which is to last for all eternity. On the other hand, it is characteristic of him that he gives us quite a picture, so to say, of the coming of our Lord, the commandment, or shout of command, the voice of the Archangel, the trumpet of God, and the catching up into the air of the Saints. Now, in the passage from which the text before us is taken, St. Paul takes quite another feature of the latter days, for the purpose of removing from the minds of the Thessalonians another false conception which may have arisen from a misunderstanding of his former words. He had spoken of the elect who were to be found alive at the second Advent, and as he and those to whom he was writing were, of course, among the living, he spoke of them as included in that number. He had said nothing of what he knew very well, that an untold number of generations of Christians might pass away one after the other before the coming of that great day. Thus the Thessalonians, in their literal manner of understanding all that he said or wrote, appear to have taken it for granted that, at all events, the end of all things for which they were taught to long, and the prospect of which was to be their sufficient reason for abandoning all the good and pleasant things of this world which they had before enjoyed and loved, was to take place in such a space of time as would be covered by their own lives. A false conception of this kind might be mischievous, both as encouraging a tendency to recklessness and idleness and neglect of duties, to which they were somewhat prone, and also, when its falsehood was discovered and proved by lapse of time, it might tend to cast discredit on the teaching of which it was supposed to have formed a part.

For this reason St. Paul, in the passage before us, takes the pains to disabuse them of their mistake. And he does this in the same way in which he had removed their former mistake. He insists mainly on the one great point which was important, that certain things were to happen before the manifestation of Antichrist, which was to be, so to say, the last scene in the great drama of humanity, the scene which was to be immediately succeeded by the coming of our Lord. And, as in the other passage, he had dwelt on the particular features of the picture which he had sketched, of the coming of our Lord, so in this passage he enlarges on certain particulars as to the person and actions of Antichrist, which are not absolutely necessary for the information of the Thessalonians, and on certain features also of the generation which shall be ready to welcome Antichrist, when he comes in all the power of delusion possessed by his master Satan. For Antichrist will be what he is and be as successful as he is to be, mainly on account of the disposition of the generation to which he will address himself. He will be the child of the time, the man of the age, the personal expression and outcome and summary of the ruling characteristics and propensities and tastes and ideas of that generation. If we may so use the Divine words, he will come unto his own, and his own will gladly receive him.

II.

The passage before us, then, enables us to set before ourselves the chief features of the great Scriptural prophecies of the last time. It is our business to-day to consider them in general, later on one by one. In the first place—I do not mean first in point of time, but most conspicuous—we may place the revelation, as St. Paul calls it, of the Man of Sin. Before the second coming of our Lord, that one great enemy of God, who is called in Scripture Antichrist, is to appear, and for a short time to reign and cause himself to be worshipped. When St. Paul warns the Thessalonians that the day of the Lord is not to come at once, he says it will not come "unless there come a revolt first, and the Man of Sin be revealed, the son of perdition, who opposeth and is lifted up above all that is called God, or that is worshipped, so that he sitteth in the temple of God, showing himself as if he were God."* Another day I hope to explain what the Scripture tells us concerning him; for the present it is enough to have named him as one of the prominent figures in the prophecies of the latter days. Now you may remember that both St. Paul and St. John, when they speak of him, do so rather by way of reminding those to whom they write of what they already knew than as instructing them afresh. St. Paul says: "*Remember you not*, when I was with you, that I told you of these things?" and St. John: "'Little children, you *have heard* that Antichrist cometh."† And we may surely

* 2 Thess. ii. 4.   † 1 St. John ii. 18.

conclude that the Apostles had some good reason for teaching their converts at once concerning this servant of the evil one—such a reason, for instance, as would be contained in the working in the world around them of that very spirit of antagonism to our Lord, of which Antichrist is to be the fullest and most conspicuous embodiment.

In the next place, we may mention, that great apostacy—as it would seem, from the Catholic Church—which St. Paul mentions under the name of the "revolt." Our Lord warns the Apostles and their followers against the extreme seductiveness of evil,* and it seems to be clearly foretold that there shall be in the latter days a great falling off—altogether or for a time—of a great number from the Christian faith. In this same passage to the Thessalonians already quoted, St. Paul mentions this expressly further on, when he speaks of the success of the wicked one, "whose coming is according to the working of Satan, in all power and signs and lying wonders, and in all seduction of iniquity to them that perish, because they received not the love of the truth that they might be saved. Therefore shall God send them the operation of error to believe lying."† Of this apostacy, too, I shall speak hereafter, and so I pass on from it now.

Then, in the third place, there is mention made of a certain power existing in the world, which, for the present, hinders the manifestation of Antichrist, and which is to be taken away and overcome by him. We find this again in St. Paul—"And now you know

---

* St. Matt. xxiv. 5, 24.   † 2 Thess. ii. 9, 10.

what withholdeth, that he may be revealed in his time. For the mystery of iniquity already worketh, only that he who now holdeth do hold, until he be taken out of the way."* And, my brethren, this I need not leave for future treatment, but I pause for a moment to explain what it means, according to the most received interpretation of the Fathers and Catholic commentators. Antichrist, then, we are told, is peculiarly and specially the lawless one, who shall trample under foot all laws, human as well as Divine. The apostacy of the latter days will worship him as a god, and will follow his example and spirit in all manner of lawlessness. On the other hand, the power in the world which hinders and prevents his full manifestation, is said by the Fathers to mean the temporal government of the Roman empire. Their language sounds strange to us, but this is the case more from the words which they use than from the ideas they intend to convey. When they speak of the Roman Empire, they mean, as we should put it now, the principle which in those days was embodied and represented by that Government, the principle of law and order and right and obedience, the rule of conscience and of the natural law, as represented in the fabric of human society, which cannot stand for a moment without this principle of law and order and power and justice, to hold it together and to support it. Now, by this it seems to be meant that, as faith is founded on reason, and grace built upon nature, so the supernatural society of the Church pre-supposes, and thus in a certain sense rests upon, the civil

* 2 Thess. ii. 6, 7, 11.

society. And if any power of evil can utterly subvert and undermine the latter, it will go far towards obtaining a momentary victory over the former. This power then, as it seems, kept and keeps back the full manifestation of Antichrist, and when it is taken out of the way he will appear. Now this consideration enables us to see that the ancient interpretation of which I speak need not, after all, seem to us so very strange. We are quite sufficiently accustomed to hear of dangers which are supposed to be undermining, not this or that monarchy or state, or the Church or the throne in any particular country, so much as the whole order of civilized society itself. And surely the fear and the anticipation of these dangers are ripe enough in all reflecting minds at the present day, and it would be easy to collect from public writers and philosophers sayings startling enough as to the height to which this evil has risen or may rise. It is hardly an exaggeration to say, that this fear is the dominant feeling in the minds of large masses of men in modern Europe, and that it makes them ready to accept almost any one as a political leader or ruler who promises them what is called the "salvation of society." The power of conscience and of religion is no longer great enough, as they fear, to secure the very foundations of social order, and they look nervously and piteously to any one who seems for the time to be strong enough to do it. This is enough to make the commentary of the Fathers on these words of St. Paul perfectly intelligible to us.

And once more, we may place, as the fourth great feature in the prophecy of which we are speaking, the strange fact to which I have already alluded, that, on the one hand, God shall warn mankind concerning the coming of the judgment in the most marked manner, by signs in the sun and moon and stars, by earthquakes, by incursions of the ocean—by "the confusion of the roaring of the sea and of the waves,"* and that, on the other, these warnings shall pass unheeded by the great mass of men. And there shall also be other signs, not in the physical universe, but on the face of society, marking, by new and wonderful events, the history of mankind, the chief of which we may consider to be the blossoming of the barren fig-tree, according to the mystical meaning attached to that prediction by ancient writers. The blossoming of the fig-tree is the conversion of the Jewish nation to the faith of Christ by the preaching of Enoch and Elias. "From the fig-tree learn ye a parable," said our Lord to His Apostles, who had heard Him shortly before curse and wither the fig-tree close to the spot where they were sitting; "when the branch thereof is now tender, and the leaves come forth, you know that summer is nigh."† And St. Paul, speaking of his own nation, reprobate for a time from Christ, says: "If the loss of them be the reconciliation of the world, what shall the receiving of them be, but life from the dead?"‡

III.

And now, my brethren, I say that the mere enumeration of these chief features in the prophetic

* St. Luke xvi. 28.   † St. Matt. xxiv. 32.   ‡ Rom. xi. 15.

vision of the days before our Lord's second coming goes far to explain how it was, and how it always must be, that God's watchful servants seemed and seem to find themselves in the presence of these signs, and to see the light of the coming of Christ breaking through the clouds. I shall have to say this over and over again in the course of these Sermons. It is because these elements of the prophecy are the embodiment of principles and movements which have been at work in the world from the beginning, and which will only work more powerfully, more conspicuously, more successfully, at the end. As to Antichrist, I repeat what St. John says—"Children, you have heard that Antichrist cometh, and even now there are become many Antichrists, whereby we know that it is the last hour."* And he goes on to speak of the heretics and false teachers of his own time. And as even in St. John's time there were many Antichrists—forerunners, and foreshadowers of the great Man of Sin, the enemy of God—so the keen and true instincts of the Church have always felt the working against her of the spirit of Antichrist, the temper of disobedience, heresy, schism, falsehood, deception. Then, from time to time there have arisen conspicuous instances, men who have had so bad and baneful a pre-eminence over their fellows in the evil work of oppressing the Church, persecuting the faith, opposing the Holy See, and corrupting Christian doctrine and Christian manners—men like Julian, or Mahomet, or Luther, or some of the tyrannical Emperors—as almost to

* St. John ii. 18.

seem to fulfil in their character and history the personal conditions of Antichrist himself.

So also with the apostacy of the latter days. This too has always had its forerunners and its anticipations. The whole history of the Christian centuries is marred by the stains of certain great apostacies, more or less complete, from the Catholic faith and from the unity of the Church. There were apostacies in St. John's own time, of the heretics who denied Christ; then there were the apostacies of Arius and of Nestorius, then the complete apostacy of Mahomet, the departure of the Oriental Churches from unity, the fall in the sixteenth century of a great part of northern Europe from Catholicism. In our own day there are apostacies almost without number, new religions professing either to improve upon the religion of Christ, or to supersede it, or to deny it altogether and leave nothing in its place. Nor in our own time, nor in the times of the early apostacies, have there been wanting dealings with Satan, lying wonders, or the professors of mysterious intercourse with the other world, capable enough, as St. Paul says, of deceiving those who do "not love the truth to believe it."

And so, also, with regard to that other great lever of evil, the attack on the principles and foundations of social life and civil society, which is to be at last, in the days of Antichrist, successful in overthrowing it and casting it out of the way—this also has always had its anticipation in every age. The mystery of evil, working towards the destruction of the human race, as always been active. Even before the fall of

Jerusalem the empire was so convulsed by civil wars and the claims of rival candidates to the throne, that men might need the warning that "the end was not at once." And then again, later on, the whole Roman civilization and the fabric of the world-wide empire seemed to be tottering to destruction under the blows of the northern barbarians. Who could then have foreseen how the Church would tame the savage conquerors of Europe, and raise up out of the ruins of the world the new civilization and the new fabric of Christendom, to supply, and far more than supply, the place of the empire, to be the refuge and home of the principles on which the stability of society rests,—and which again, in our own days more than ever before, are made the mark of the fiercest attacks of the agents of the Evil One, who now all but openly proclaim that their object is as much to destroy social order and right as it is to subvert the Church of God? And if you will turn to the acts of him who of all men has the surest instinct as to the evils of our time, because he is the successor of St. Peter, *Fidelis servus et prudens, quem constituit Dominus super familiam suam ut det illis cibum in tempore*—if you calmly and, as I may say, with the eye of an historian, look to what the Church has specially lifted her voice to speak about by means of the Holy Pontiff in this day, you find much indeed about sacred dogmas, much about ecclesiastical right, much about the privileges of the Church as invaded by the secular power; but, not less than all these, you will find that Pius IX. has had to warn the world as to things which are the very foundation of Christian and even of natural society, the sanctity of marriage, the parental right of education, even the natural right of law and property and justice, which the secret sectarians of our own times are doing their best to undermine. And if in a year's time we are to see,* what has not been seen for so many centuries, the Bishops of the Catholic Church assembled in a General Council around the Vicar of Jesus Christ, it is not only and not entirely for the needs of the Church and of religion as such, but for the needs of human society and civil order, the very foundations of which are being sapped by the enemies both of God and man.

IV.

These three things then, the persecution of the Church by the spirit of Antichrist, the seduction and apostacy of many by means of the delusions of evil, and the subverting of human society by the instruments of Satan, are, indeed, particularly marks of the latter days, but they are also marks of all days that have been since the beginning of the Church. And therefore the true sons of the Church, those who have her instinct and her spirit of watchfulness against the common danger, have ever been ready to utter loud notes of warning to the men of their generation, that Antichrist was at hand, and that the end of all things was approaching; and, as St. John says, "because there are many Antichrists," and because there is much apostacy, and because there is much plotting against the very foun-

* Preached in the Advent of 1868.

D

dations of society, "therefore we know that it is the last hour." And so, my brethren, though we know not whether in our times, or a century hence, or ten centuries hence, the end of the world may come, we know, as the earliest Christians knew and divined so well, our duties and our true wisdom. The mystery of iniquity is all around us, and, besides, men are turning away their eyes and trying to persuade themselves that the world is so uniform that it had no beginning, and that its laws are so stable that it can have no end. But whether the days in which we live be the latter days or no, it is our business, first of all, to fit ourselves to meet our Lord, who will come to each of us "as a thief in the night," not unprepared for, as we hope, but suddenly at last, as we know. And beyond this, it is our duty to fight for our Lord's cause in the world, to throw all our little weight into the scale against the powers of evil—against the spirit of heresy, schism, lawlessness, sensuality, disregard of all sanctions and obligations, human and Divine, which is in the air all around us, and which breathes destruction to the Church and to that Christian society which the Church has founded and sustained. "Blessed are those servants, whom the Lord when He cometh shall find watching. Amen, I say to you, He will gird Himself and make them sit down to meat, and passing He will minister unto them. And if He shall come in the second watch, or come in the third watch, and find them so, blessed are those servants!"*

* St. Luke xii. 37, 38.

SERMON III.

THE DECAY OF FAITH.

Veruntamen Filius Hominis veniens, putas, inveniet fidem in terra?

But yet the Son of Man when He cometh, shall He find, think you, faith on earth?

(Words taken from the 8th verse of the 18th chapter of St. Luke's Gospel.)

1.

THESE words of sad foreboding were uttered by our Blessed Lord when He had been exhorting His disciples never to faint or grow weary in prayer. He told them how the unjust judge had avenged the poor widow's wrong, simply because, in her importunity, she gave him no peace till he did so. He feared not God, and did not regard man, yet he was forced by her continual prayer to do justice. "Hear what the unjust judge saith; and will not God avenge His elect, who cry to Him day and night, and will He have patience in their regard? I say to you that He will quickly revenge them. But yet the Son of Man, when He cometh, shall He find, think you, faith on earth?" His Elect will cry to Him day and night, and He will certainly come quickly to avenge them. The persecution of Antichrist will be very severe, and his seductions very powerful, so as to lead astray, if it were possible, even the Elect. But, by the mercy of God, it is not possible. About this same time He said to the Jews, "My sheep hear My voice, and I know them, and they follow Me, and I give them life everlasting; and they shall not perish for ever, and no man shall pluck them out of My hand. . . . No man can snatch them out of the hand of My Father."* And so we may venture to say, Yes, Lord, Thou shalt find faith upon earth, though it may not be the wide, the intense, the universal faith which Thy mercies and Thy love have deserved of us. There shall be wise virgins then, with oil in their lamps, good and faithful servants, whom their Lord, when He cometh, shall find watching! But at the same time, my brethren, we must say, if we look to the account of the latter days which is given us generally in the writings of the Apostles, that there will have been great ruin and havoc made among Christians before our Lord cometh. There is to come the great apostacy—as it seems, a greater and more calamitous loss to the Church, for the moment, than the schism of the East, or the perversion of the North of Europe. This is our subject this afternoon, this is the "revolt" of which St. Paul spoke in those words to the Thessalonians which formed our text last Sunday. So to-day I take this as the first great and general feature of the last days, a feature which, as we examine it closely, we shall find to unfold more than one points of detail on which it will be well for us to dwell.

* St. John x. 27—29.

Before I proceed to count up what indications are given us of the falling off of the latter days, let me make one or two remarks on the manner in which we must interpret the words of the holy Apostles who seem to speak of this. In the first place, we must remember that, to the Apostles and the writers of the New Testament generally, the life of the Church is one and continuous. With God, one day is as a thousand years, and a thousand years as one day. The Apostles and Prophets see the future, to some extent, in the view of God Himself, and they speak of the last days as imminent, and even present to the men of their own generation, for this reason, among others, that the same Church which existed in their days will have to meet the storms of that last outbreak of evil. I have already pointed this out, but it must be insisted on again and again. St. Paul knew perfectly well that the days of Antichrist were far distant, and he even warned the Thessalonians not to think them close at hand; and yet he seems to speak of those who are to be alive at the Day of Judgment as if he and those to whom he wrote might be among them. In the same way, while describing the many evils of the last ages of the Church, the Apostles spoke of the special forms in which the mystery of iniquity would work in the generation which was rising up around them, as they themselves drew near to the end of their course. The same principles of evil with which we have to contend, and with which those after us will have to contend in different developments, were already sending forth those evil shoots which sprung up into the heresies of the first and second centuries; heresies to which the men of our day are not likely to return in every particular, though they have sometimes imitated them with wonderful exactness. Thus, in examining what the Apostles tell us of the evils of the last days, we may sometimes find a distinct and particular prophecy of a form of error which is now either dead and gone, or at least living only in some remote development. For instance, there is a distinct description given in the Epistles of the Manichean heresy. In these prophecies, then, we must seek chiefly the roots and seeds and sources of the future apostasy, which are the same, more or less, in all ages and in every generation. In them we shall learn what to expect in the times to come, and what we are all to do battle against in our own time.

II.

And now, when we turn to the Sacred Scriptures, and ask them what they have to tell us about the evil principles which shall rule the world to so large an extent in the latter days, we find that this prophecy, like that about Antichrist, fills a large space in the sacred pages, and is to be found in the Old Testament as well as in the New. Daniel tells us "that many shall be chosen and made white, and shall be tried as in the fire, that the wicked shall deal wickedly, that none of the wicked shall understand, but the learned shall understand."* Now this, you see, corresponds to what St. Paul tells us of the delusions of the latter times, that because people

* Dan. xii. 10.

receive not the love of the truth, God shall send upon them the operation of error, "to believe lying." What Daniel says about the blindness of those times our Lord Himself says about their lawlessness: "Because iniquity shall abound, the charity of many shall grow cold."* St. Peter, and St. Jude who follows him, tell us about the scoffers and mockers, the disdainful despisers of revealed truths, those who "walk according to their own desires in ungodlinesses,"† and laugh at the expectation of Christians as to the fulfilment of the prophecies as to Christ's second coming. In these passages, my brethren, we seem to have a faint though definite picture of men who will suppose that they have made themselves perfectly masters of the secrets of the physical universe, who have to their own satisfaction disproved the truths of the holy narrative of creation, and so think they have nothing to fear from anything as to the future which Scripture records by way of prophecy. I have already said that St. Peter tells us that these men will willingly forget the fact of God's one greatest interference with the physical order of things since the creation, within the range of human history, I mean the chastisement and almost entire extinction of the human race by the waters of the Flood.

If we put these descriptions together, my brethren, without proceeding further in our examination of the prophecies, we have a picture the chief features of which may thus be described. There is to be in the latter days a great disregard of all law, moral and social, human, natural, and Divine; there is to be a

* St. Matt. xxiv. 12. † St. Jude 18; 2 St. Peter iii. 3.

great decay of charity in the largest sense of the term, of the natural charity which binds man to man, the tie of natural kindliness which should keep together the different members of the various unities which God, Who "maketh men to be of one mind," has established in the world, the family, the country, the race—as well, alas! as of that supernatural charity by which the children of God are bound together in Jesus Christ. There is to be a great blindness to truth, though witnessed to by evidence incontrovertible and luminous in the highest degree, and this blindness to, and dislike of, truth is to be accompanied by a strong and fanatical belief in debasing and corrupting delusions. This hatred of truth, and this love of ungodliness, are to be further punished by great intellectual pride, an arrogant reliance on supposed acquirements and false knowledge, which again is naturally to issue in contempt for the simple faith of Christians in the Divine revelation, in the words of Scripture, and in the teaching of the Catholic Church.

You will observe, my brethren, that here we find no mention made of distinct heresies or false doctrines. There is rather to be a general decay or denial of all faith, and a sort of practical paganism. And thus we are prepared for what some old Christian writers tell us on this very subject of the future restoration of heathenism. There is a mysterious vision in the Apocalypse,* of a beast that was wounded, and, it seemed, slain, but which is brought to life again by the power of the false prophet, and adored by all

---

* Apoc. xiii. 3, 12.

on earth whose names are not written in the Book of Life. This vision is interpreted, by the writers to whom I allude, of heathenism, which has been, as it were, put to death by the Christian religion, but which will hereafter revive and reign for a short time. Now I say that, whether this old interpretation be certainly true or not, it is at least wonderfully confirmed by St. Paul's account of the latter times. I have as yet hardly alluded to this great Apostle, because his words are so clear and full that I have kept them for the last. St. Paul, if we may so say, is that one of the Apostles and of the writers of the New Testament who seems to have been commissioned to speak with a special force and authority both on the subject of the latter days and on all that concerns the heathen world. He, who had begun his life by being so exceedingly zealous for the traditions of Judaism, so that he had gone beyond all others in his care for them and in his hatred to the Church, which he looked upon as supplanting and subverting them, had afterwards, by the providence of God, to turn himself with a singular devotion, with a peculiar gift of intelligence and depth of sympathy, to the heathen world, for whose conversion he laboured so long and with so much blessing from God. We call him, my brethren, the Apostle of the Gentiles, not only because he preached so much among them, as other Apostles also preached, but for this reason also —that he had a gift and grace of his own to understand them, to penetrate the system which reigned among them, to put his finger upon its weakest points and the sources of its misery, and to apply to the special wounds which it had inflicted upon the human race the gentle medicines of truth and grace. And it may be said, without fear of contradiction, that if St. Paul were to be considered simply as a Christian philosopher commenting upon the evils and general tendencies of his own age, and of the system of the world under which he lived, he would have to be placed at the very head of all philosophical writers, for the analysis and description which he has given us of the heathen world.

III.

We have this description chiefly in two great documents—in St. Paul's speech at Athens to the philosophers,* and in his account of the miseries of heathendom in the Epistle to the Romans.† I shall speak presently of a third great passage which I mean to compare with these, in which, years after his Epistle to the Romans, he describes the men of the latter times. Let us first deal with the account given by the Apostle of the heathenism among which he lived and worked. In his speech, then, at the Areopagus, St. Paul describes in brief God's ways of dealing with the world. He tells the Athenians, as you know, of the "unknown God," Whom they worshipped in ignorance, Who, nevertheless, was the Creator and the Father of all. He had made of one blood, of one stock, of one nature, all nations on the face of earth. He had given them, as is implied in this, one moral law, one promise, one primeval tradition, one common hope of future salvation. Then

* Acts xvii. 22—31.   † Rom. i. 18—32.

He had, as it were, withdrawn, and left them to themselves, though still His providence ruled them, appointing the whole course of what is called the world's history, the rise, and fall, and character, and vicissitudes of nations and empires, and giving to all men, as St. Paul had said before at Iconium, abundance of good gifts, "Giving rains and fruitful seasons, filling our hearts with food and gladness."* And the Apostle tells his hearers how the heathen had, as it were, to grope, like blinded men, after God, although He was all the time so near to them, as to all of us—"for in Him we live and move and be." And he speaks in the same place, though gently and reservedly, of those terrible and lamentable errors into which the nations left to themselves had fallen, touching upon the crown and consummation of them all, the idolatrous worship of false gods.

And now we must turn to the other great passage, which must be compared with this of which I have been speaking, where, at the beginning of his Epistle to the Romans, the same Apostle gives what we may call a companion picture to the former, describing the manner in which the heathen nations had in return treated God, and the consequence to themselves in which that treatment had issued. He speaks of the inexcusable ingratitude of the heathen to so good and wonderful a Creator, of their refusal to acknowledge Him, notwithstanding the strong evidences concerning Himself which He had imprinted on the face and on the course of nature ; of the punishment which fell on them—that of being given

* Acts xiv. 14—17.

over to idolatry: and then again of the further punishment of this judicial delusion, by which they became the slaves of lusts which in their abominable degradation went even beyond the extreme indulgence of all natural animal appetites. You may remember, my brethren, that fearful picture, on the details of which it is not necessary that we should linger for any space of time this afternoon. The character of heathendom, as he describes it, is based, of course, on intense selfishness, working itself out in an eager grasping after all the objects of concupiscence, and so in avarice, in the reckless pursuit of pleasure at whatever cost to others, in the passionate love of earthly honour and position ; then rising, as was only natural after this, into intense pride and haughtiness, into unbending stubbornness of will and judgment, and, further still, wreaking itself on all who came across its path, in envy, contentiousness, violence, contumely, in malignant craft, or insolent and reckless cruelty. By the side of these savage features of debased humanity, we find placed, as is always the case in reality, a voluptuousness and licentiousness that knew no bounds. And these two great passions of lust and pride combine in the character of the heathen world, as drawn by St. Paul, to smother and destroy all those instincts of natural piety and goodness which are implanted in man by his Creator, to which his conscience witnesses, and which animate and sustain all that social and domestic life which is the fundamental condition of our being and our happiness as men. Hence we find in St. Paul's description of heathenism a number of traits which point to the want of all natural affection. The tie which binds parents to children, and children to parents, was dissolved; so again, the law of faithfulness and truthfulness, which is essential in order that we may trust one another in the common intercourse of life, was set aside, as also the rule of gratitude and honesty, the law of respect for the characters of others in men's language, the observance of obligations, the habit of peaceableness, the practice of kindness, even the instinct of mercy to the conquered, the weak, the helpless, the afflicted—mercy, the one provision of God for the numberless and otherwise inconsolable miseries to which the world is given up!

Such, in brief, is this great description of the heathenism of his own time given us by St. Paul. And now I come to the point of our argument concerning the latter days. This same great Apostle, as I have already said, has dwelt in more than one place on the characteristics of the men of those future times, as he has so often dwelt on the characteristics of the old heathen. We have already had occasion to examine what he has said in some of these passages; but one great description remains, written, moreover, as I have said, at the very end of St. Paul's life, on the eve of his martyrdom, in his last Epistle to his beloved child Timothy.* This is the longest and most particular description given us by the Apostle, and striking as it is in itself, it is perhaps still more striking when it is compared with the earlier passage in the Epistle to the Romans, to which I have referred. If you will take that passage, in which

* 2 Tim. iii. 1, seq.

the vices and degradation of the unconverted heathen world are described with so much indignant severity, and yet with a certain discriminating tenderness and largeness of sympathy, and if you will put it side by side with the other account which, by way of prophecy, St. Paul gives, so many years afterwards, of the corruptions of the latter days, you will find that with one or two striking differences, which I shall point out, the two passages tally exactly. The differences that exist are important in themselves, as we shall see ; and they are precious also on another ground, because they show us, if that be needed, that St. Paul has weighed his every word, that he has nowhere indulged in any mere expletives of invective, nowhere made one single charge, either against the ancient heathenism or against its modern revival, without the fullest knowledge and the calmest deliberation. Bear with me, then, if I dwell for a few moments on the points of agreement and of difference between the two.

IV.

In that old heathenism of the Roman world, into which it was the will of God that the Christian religion should be introduced by the Apostles, there were three diverse and often conflicting elements. There was a good element, which came from God ; there was a thoroughly bad element, which came from Satan ; and there was a corrupt element, which was the fruit of the workings of unregenerate human nature upon society, and upon the objects of sense and intelligence with which man is placed in relation.

The good element we see embodied in great part of the laws and institutions of the ancient world, as also in much of the literature, the poetry, the philosophy of Greece and Rome, which literature consequently—after having been purified and, as it were, baptized—has always been used by the Christian Church in the education of her children. This element, I say, was originally the gift of God, the Author of nature, to man, the offspring of reason and conscience, the tradition of a society of which God was Himself the founder. It enshrined whatever fragments of primeval truth as to God, the world, and man himself, still lingered, in whatever shape, among the far-wandering children of Adam. St. Paul alludes to this element in the first passage on which we dwelt to-day, and his words altogether seem to imply that God watched over it, supported it, and fostered it, as far as men were worthy of it, and that it might even have been expanded into a perfect system of natural religion and of reasonable virtue, had men been grateful enough to earn larger measures of grace from God, Who left not Himself without witness in His daily providence, and was "not far from" any one of His children.

But now we come to another element, which just now I placed the last of the three, the workings of which we may distinguish in the heathen world. All flesh had corrupted its way upon the earth, and man had shut out the knowledge of God from his soul, and had let his passions lead him instead of his conscience. The unregenerate instincts of nature gradually overpowered the moral law in the heart of man, and their victory reflected itself in the rules of society, in the customs and maxims by which human life was guided. In proportion as man became more and more the master of the world, as wealth and power, and knowledge and experience increased, as civilization (so to call it) and means of communication advanced, there grew up that great system of cruelty and immorality, of the godless pursuit of pleasure and worldly ends, which we call paganism. For paganism is not properly a religion, so much as a system of human life and human society, according to the impulses and unbridled lusts of the natural man, checked only by what remained of strength in the law of right as written in men's hearts, in the voice of conscience, and in the old traditions of better days, and also by the law of necessity which made it imperative that society should in some way or other be kept alive and held together. St. Paul, in the passage to the Romans on which we have dwelt, has described to us, my brethren, what sort of men they were who were penetrated by this pagan spirit. And now, as I have already said, when the same Apostle comes to describe the men of the latter days, he paints them, as to all moral degradation, in the same colours as the pagans of his own time. The two passages correspond as to this word for word; the latter text is almost a repetition of the former. Thus far, then, we have St. Paul's authority for saying that the apostacy of the latter days will be a return to heathenism, understanding by the word that godless system of life and manners which is the fruit of the unrestrained development and reign of the lower instincts of human nature.

These thoughts bring us to the third element of paganism—that which I call the work of Satan, the enemy of God and man. As to this, also, we have St. Paul's authority, in that passage where in a few short words he tells us that the gods of the heathen were devils.* We, my brethren, are often inclined to look upon the personages of which the heathen mythology is made up, as a number of poetic creations, as the powers of nature symbolized, or perhaps, at the worst, as great men and famous heroes of fabulous times raised by a sort of natural canonization to the thrones of a higher world. This is the human part of the heathen religions, skilfully used by the authors of evil to disguise their own work for the delusion of men. But there was more behind the forms of apparent grace and beauty than the imagination of earthly poets. This might have been seen, we might truly say, by the base impurities in which they were steeped. No, my brethren, unless St. Paul is mistaken, unless thousands of Christian Martyrs were mistaken who treated the heathen idols as the forms under which the apostate angels were adored, the gods of the heathen were Satan and his associates, permitted by the just judgment of God to draw to themselves the adoration which men had denied to Him; and taking care to deify in themselves every shape of human vice and passion, and to exact from their worshippers impure rites and filthy mysteries, that man made in the image of

* 1 Cor. x. 20.

God, might learn from them to degrade himself even beneath the level of the beasts of the field. Or, if we want a still more clear proof of the Satanic agencies which underlay the pagan religion, we may find it in that other kind of worship which it exacted in the ancient world, and is still found to exact— I mean the frightful tribute of human sacrifice, a custom widely spread and almost universal among pagan nations, some of whom have astonished even their Christian discoverers by their mildness and gentleness, their courtesy and simplicity, and yet have been found to be penetrated to the core by corruption, and to be in the habit of honouring their gods by the frightful homage of hecatombs of human victims, a homage enough of itself to proclaim as its author the hater alike of man, and of God Who created him!

Here, then, my brethren, we have come to that part of the comparison as to which it need not be said that St. Paul's two descriptions are identical. We need not exaggerate the miseries of our own time, nor draw in darker colours than St. Paul the evil features of the last great apostacy. The Son of God, as another Apostle tells us, was "manifested that He might destroy the works of the devil,"* and I do not find, in any of the prophetic descriptions of the restored paganism of modern days, that the system of the worship of false gods is to revive, with its abominable rites of blood and its mysteries of licentiousness. Wherever the Cross has been once firmly planted, we may surely hope that the world has seen

* 1 St. John iii. 8.

the last of the public worship of Satan. In St. Paul's description of the latter days, I find the blasphemy of the true God substituted for the worship of devils. But, my brethren, the Son of God was not manifested altogether to destroy the works of man. He came to raise man, change him, regenerate him, sanctify him, by uniting him to Himself. He did not come to take away man's free will, or to tear out of his nature those seeds of possible evil which produced all the human part of the paganism on which we have been reflecting. The empire of Satan has been overthrown, but alas! man is still his own great enemy, and though our Lord has armed him against himself, He has still left him the power to mar the work of God in his own soul, and this power, which each one of us possesses in his own case, is always fearfully active in the corruption of the Christian society, the character of which is the result and the reflection of that of the parts of which it is made up.

V.

And now, my brethren, what need have we of any subtlety of inquiry or refinement of speculation to tell us that this modern heathenism of which the prophecies speak is around us on every side? Mankind are in many senses far mightier, and the resources and enjoyments at their command are far ampler, than in the days of old. We are in possession of the glorious but intoxicating fruits of that advanced civilisation and extended knowledge which has sprung up from the seeds which the Church of God has, as it were, dropped on her way through the world. Society has been elevated and refined, but on that very account it has become capable of a more penetrating degradation, of a more elegant and a more poisonous corruption. Knowledge has been increased, but on the increase of knowledge has followed the increase of pride. Science has unravelled the laws of nature and the hidden treasures of the material universe, and they place fresh combinations of power and new revelations of enjoyment in the hands of men who have not seen in the discovery increased reasons for self-restraint or for reverence for the Giver of all good gifts. The world, the home of the human race, has been opened to civilised man in all its distant recesses, and he has taken, or is taking, possession of his full inheritance; but his onward path is the path of avarice and greed, of lust and cruelty, and he seizes on each new land as he reaches it in the spirit of the merchant or the conqueror, not in that of the harbinger of peace, the bearer of the good tidings of God. At home, in Christendom itself, we hear, as our Lord said, of wars and rumours of wars, nation rising against nation, and kingdom against kingdom. In the Apostles' time, it was an unheard of thing that the majestic peace and unity of the Roman Empire should not absorb and keep in harmony a hundred rival nationalities. In our time it is not to be thought of that the supernatural bond of the Christian Church should be able to keep nations which are brethren in the faith from devouring one another.

Or, again, my brethren, let us turn from public to private life. Look at social life, look at domestic manners; consider the men and women of the present day in their amusements, their costumes, the amount of restraint they put upon the impulses of nature; compare them at their theatres and their recreations, compare them as to their treatment of the poor and the afflicted classes; compare them, again, as to the style of art which they affect, or the literature in which they delight, with the old heathen of the days of St. Paul. I do not say, God forbid! that there is not a wide and impassable gulf between the two, for that would be to say that so many centuries of Christendom had been utterly wasted, and that the Gospel law has not penetrated to the foundations of society, so that it is not true that our Lord rules, as the Psalmist says, "in the midst of His enemies,"* even over the world, which would fain emancipate itself from His sway. But I do say, that if a Christian of the first ages were to rise from the dead, and examine our society, point by point, on the heads which I have intimated, and compare it, on the one hand, with the polished refined heathen whom he may have known at the courts of Nero or Domitian, and, on the other, with the pure strict holiness of his own brethren in the faith, who worshipped with him in the catacombs, he might find it difficult indeed to say that what he would see around him in London or Paris was derived by legitimate inheritance rather from the traditions of the martyr Church than from the customs of the persecuting heathen. He would miss the violence, the cruelty, the riotous and ruffianly

* Psalm cix. 2.

lust, the extraordinary disrespect for humanity and human life which distinguished the later Roman civilisation; but he would find much of its corruption, much of its licentiousness, much of its hardness of heart. The unregenerate instincts of human nature are surging up like a great sea all around us, society is fast losing all respect for those checks upon the innate heathenism of man which have been thrown over the surface of the world by the Church. It is becoming an acknowledged law that whatever is natural is right, and by nature is meant nature corrupted by sin, nature unilluminated by faith and unassisted by grace—that is, the lower appetites of man in revolt against conscience, looking for no home but earth and no satisfaction but in the present, "having no hope of the promise, and without God in this world."*

VI.

I conclude, my brethren, with one or two considerations which naturally rise to the mind in the presence of such thoughts as these. First, all these dangers with which we are beset, which have their roots in human nature, and whose growth is fostered by the condition of the world, have been met by our Lord Jesus Christ, and are provided for in the Church. We are apt to marvel at what we may deem the superfluous richness and profusion of what we may call the armament of the Church, the variety of the means of grace, the multiplied channels by which heavenly strength is conveyed to fainting and

* Ephes. ii. 12.

wounded souls. And yet not one of all these is needless; the whole strength and all the weapons of the Church will be strained to the utmost in her final struggle. The whole might of unregenerate nature, in its undying repugnance to submit to the restraints of the law of God, is bearing down upon the Christian bulwarks of society with a weight as immense, and as relentless in its pressure on every part, as the tide of a whole ocean, which is swung in its daily flow against the rocks and cliffs of a far-stretching continent. What can resist it? One force alone, the force of God, Who sets bounds to the sea, and can check the raging passions of a whole race. We hear little in the latter days of heresies and schisms, of isolated communities and partial forms of Christianity. These things will have had their day and have done much evil in it, but they are too frail and miserable in themselves to live on the surges of that last tempest of humanity—the Church alone can ride out the storm.

But again, my brethren, how does the Church deal with such assaults as those we are contemplating? She works, no doubt, by the sacraments and the other means of grace, by the word of God preached and taught in the sanctuary, and the like. But the strongholds of the Church are in the family and the school. Her battlefields are those on which such questions as that of the sanctity of marriage and that of the purity of Christian education are fought out. Give her the forming of her children, and she will train up the Christian youth and maiden, she will join them in a holy bond to form the family, of

Christian families she will compose Christian communities, Christian nations, and out of Christian nations she will build up Christendom, a Christian world. She can cure nature, and nothing else can. Give her free scope, and you will hear little of that long list of heathen vices of which you have heard to-day; little of men being covetous, contentious, slaves of avarice and licentiousness, there will be no complaints of the decay of mercy, or of natural affection, of human kindness, honesty, faithfulness.

So then, in these our days, can we too often remind ourselves of the points of attack chosen by the enemies of faith and of society? Can we forget with what a wearisome sameness of policy the war is waged year after year, first in one place and then in another; how certain it is that as soon as we hear that some nation hitherto guided by Catholic instincts has become a convert to the enlightened ideas of our times, the next day will bring the further tidings that in that nation marriage is no longer to be treated as a sacrament, and that education is to be withdrawn from the care of the Church and her ministers? And, indeed, my brethren, we know not how soon we ourselves may be engaged in a deadly conflict, on one at least, of these points. Up to this time we, at least in England, have been able to train our children for ourselves. And, to give honour where honour is due, we have owed our liberty in great measure to the high value which certain communities outside the Church set upon distinctively Christian and doctrinal instruction. But we know not how soon the tide of war may come to our homes. We hear a cry in the air—it says that the child belongs to the State, and that it is the duty of the State to take his education to itself. The cry is false; the child belongs to the parent, belongs to the Church, belongs to God. In that cry speaks the reviving paganism of our day. Surely it should teach us, if nothing else can, the paramount importance of Christian education. If we give in to that cry we are lost. Train up your children, my brethren, in the holy discipline and pure doctrine of the Church, and they are formed thereby to be soldiers of Jesus Christ in the coming conflict against the powers of evil. Train them up in indifference to religion and Christian doctrine, and if they are not at once renegades from their faith, at least they are far too weak and faint-hearted in their devotion to the Church, to range themselves courageously among her champions in her terrible battle against the last apostacy.

SERMON IV.

THE CREED OF FALSE SCIENCE.*

Videte, ne seducamini.
Take heed that you be not seduced.
(Words taken from the 8th verse of the 21st chapter of St. Luke's Gospel.)

I.

WE have heard, both to-day and last Sunday, my brethren in Jesus Christ, of the description given by the blessed Evangelists of the signs which are to go before the second coming of our Lord. As St. Luke puts them before us, they are terrible enough—there are to be signs in the sun and in the moon and in the stars, and more than these, "distress of nations by reason of the confusion of the roaring of the sea and of the waves, men withering away for fear and expectation of what shall come upon the world." And indeed we can imagine nothing more fearful for the dwellers upon the earth, than that those natural elements and bodies which seem to us to be the most stable and immutable of all things, the orbs of heaven and the forces and foundations of the natural world, should be changed and shaken before their eyes and under their feet. It is easy to understand

* Preached on Advent Sunday, 1881.

that such a falling to pieces of the whole fabric of the universe as we see it around us must fill the hearts and minds of men with the utmost terror and consternation. It is terrible enough to read of a ship sinking or burning in the midst of the howling ocean, but in such cases all is in accordance with the laws of nature, and one element at least remains by means of which safety may be hoped for. But what hope can possibly remain when the world itself is dissolved?

And yet, my brethren, there is one thing which is here foretold by our Lord which seems in many respects to be more wonderful than any of these changes in the heavenly bodies themselves, and in the physical order of the universe. It is a wonderful thing, though no man can pretend to say it is impossible, that the "sun shall be turned into darkness, and the moon into blood," as one of the old prophets tells us, before the great and terrible day of the Lord. It is a wonderful thing to hear, though we cannot deny its possibility, that the stars shall be seen to fall from heaven, and the powers of the heavens, the physical forces and laws by which the whole visible creation is ruled, should be shaken. And, if such things are to happen, it is not a matter of surprise that the whole world should be filled with awe and consternation thereby. But the most marvellous thing of all is that it should be necessary for our Lord, in His Divine foreknowledge of the future, to add to the prediction of these great and most appalling signs the further warning, "take heed that you be not seduced," as if in the face of all these divinely ordained signs of the end of the world men would still be in danger of seduction.

Surely, we might say to ourselves, if God is so good as to vouchsafe all these signs beforehand of the second coming of our Lord, this time not to save the world but to judge the world, it is not likely that men should deceive themselves any longer as to the meaning of these signs. The signs themselves will be enough to awaken the most obdurate and to startle the most inattentive. But our Lord seems to tell us that it will not be so. He went on to say, as St. Luke tells us, that heaven and earth shall pass away, and then he added the further warning, "take heed unto yourselves, lest perhaps your hearts be overcharged with surfeiting and drunkenness and the cares of the world, and that day come upon you suddenly, for as a snare shall it come upon all that sit on the face of the whole earth." These words contain a twofold warning, one against delusion, another against worldliness and engrossment in the pleasures and interests of this life. And our Lord seems to say to us that, with the universe as it were crumbling to pieces about their ears, and with all these signs of terror flashing about them, and even notwithstanding the agonies and alarms which they cannot help experiencing, men will not understand the meaning of these signs ordained by God for their salvation and conversion, and that the apparent ruin of the universe will come upon the eyes of a dull and senseless and heedless generation, just as the warnings which were sent before the Flood fell on a generation of men who had no power of understanding them. And if this is again to be, then the most marvellous and the most inexplicable of all the signs before the end of all things will be the dulness and delusion of the men in whose time they are to come.

II.

My brethren, if the blindness of the men of the last age is to be the greatest of all the marvels that shall be then to be seen, it is also the one marvel of them all which it may be most important for us to study, especially if it be true that we can find the explanation of this blindness in a series of thoughts which will not take us beyond the experience of our own times. You may know that in the range of predictions concerning this last time which we have given to us in the Sacred Scriptures, of which the words of our Lord on the occasion of His last prophecy on Mount Olivet form the most important, though by no means the only important part, there are two main elements on which our Christian consideration may profitably dwell. There is, in the first place, the description of the state of the world such as it will be at the time of the last Advent of our Lord, and there is the description of the signs and portents by which, in the good providence of God, that last Advent will be heralded and announced. The description of the state of the world, morally and intellectually and religiously, is a different thing from the description of the physical signs which are to go before the face of the coming Judge.

Neither of these subjects can be a matter of indifference to us. We do not know when the end may be, and our Lord bids us always be on the watch, and these two things constitute a sufficient reason why we should be students of all that can enlighten us as to these most momentous points. But of the two, if we are to make our choice, it cannot be doubtful which should be the subject which it most concerns us to study and to make ourselves familiar with. It is most important that we should be able to recognize the signs when they come, but whether we do so or not depends on this other question—whether we are free from the influences of the state of humanity and society which will make the men of that day, as a mass, fail to see what those signs mean. The signs are the work of God, and are in the hand of God, but the failure to recognize them will be the fault of men. The signs may come in our time or not, but the state of the world is a matter with which we all have much to do, and which interests and concerns us all nearly, for it is a matter as to which we all have our responsibilities and our duties. We must first of all be men such as our Lord would have us be, men of whom He speaks as having their loins girded and their lamps burning, watchers and waiters for their Master whose coming they are to be expecting. Such it is our business, and it is not beyond our power, to be. And if we are such men as these, then it will not be a matter of overwhelming importance whether we live or not in the days when these signs shall be vouchsafed to the world. We shall then have guarded ourselves from the evil elements, as rife in our time as in any other, by the influence of which the world will be plunged into that state of dulness and apathy, which even the most marvellous physical commotions will fail to rouse.

And again, the day of the coming of our Lord is to be the day of our death, whether that happens generations before the end of the world or not. If the signs are not to come in our time, at all events it will be no vain speculation, no useless occupation of mind and heart, to train ourselves, morally and spiritually, to discern them whenever they do come, because that preparation of ourselves will enable us to resist all evil influences, and to be fit to stand, as our Lord says, before the Son of Man. This then is a study which can never be thrown away, and it will reveal to us, if I am not mistaken, a truth of which many of us have but little suspicion—that there are now prevalent and visible in the world around us many of those very features which are predicted by our Lord and by His prophets as the features of that last and most miserable generation, which is to be so insensible to its own danger, and so blind to the merciful warnings of God, that it will be asleep on the very brink of the abyss which is to open and engulf it, deaf to the voice of God in conscience, to the cries of agony of a dying world, and to the thunders of the approaching doom.

It cannot but be of immense importance to us, my brethren, if on examining what we can gather from the sacred writings concerning the characteristics of the men of that last and most senseless generation of the children of Adam, we should be able to find that there are among us and around us now many of those characteristics. The signs of the last day may not be yet, but the state of mind and of heart which will make those signs fruitless for the warning of so many is not wanting now. Again recall what St. John says in his Epistle as to Antichrist, " Little children, you know that Antichrist cometh, and even now there are become many Antichrists, whereby we know that it is the last hour." And he goes on to speak of the heretics who had even then begun to go forth from the unity of the Catholic Church. He, the inspired Apostle, the seer of the Apocalyptic vision, did not mean to foreshorten the time which was to elapse between his own days and the end of the world. He did not mean, in particular, to make his disciples believe that the coming of the Man of Sin, of whom St. Paul had written, was to be immediately. He meant to say that the Antichristian leaven was already at work in the Church, and the elements of the character of the great enemy of God were already to be discerned in the heretics and schismatics of the apostolic age, as they have been discernible in the heretics and schismatics of all succeeding ages. Now what St. John teaches concerning the spirit of Antichrist may very well be asserted concerning the spirit of the men of that last generation who are to be the ready dupes and servants of Antichrist when at last he is revealed to the world. The elements which will produce, or which are sufficient to produce, the utter blindness and dulness and hardness of the men of the last times are already to be seen among ourselves, in the Europe and in the England of the last quarter of the nineteenth century. I do not say whether the end of the world is at hand or not, of that day and that hour no man knows, and the Father hath placed it in His own power. Not even the Angels of Heaven know it. But I do say that there are the features in the present generation which make it very fit indeed to be the last generation of the world, and that when that last generation comes it will not be very unlike the generation in which we live. There are now at work, in the most influential societies in the world, principles and elements which have only to be strengthened and developed, in order to bring about that state of things and that temper of human society which will, if one may so say, bring on the last day, and which, when the last day is imminent, and when all its signs have been brought about by God, will make men gaze at them with stolid indifference, and have no capacity at all for reading them or interpreting them.

III.

I suppose, my brethren, that all will agree with me in thinking that the men of that or of any other generation would be blinded to the recognition of the marvellous signs which are to precede the day of judgment, if they had learnt to disbelieve altogether in its possibility, and if they had come to think that they could explain all such phenomenas as those of the signs of which I speak, in a way which would satisfy them that signs at least of a coming judgment they could not be. Such men might be shaken by fear and consternation, some of them might even be, as the rest would say, foolish enough to be driven back by them to the old traditions of faith in natural or revealed religion which they had long abandoned. But the generality of such a people would look on such phenomena as interesting or as appalling, as requiring an explanation, even though they might not be able to find one, or as even signifying that a great physical catastrophe was at hand, for which they must make up their minds and from which there was no escape. Such a temper of mind would be possible enough, and yet it would be very far indeed from that, to the intelligence of these alarming natural phenomena in the only way in which they could be of use as warnings of the coming judgment. It might engender a philosophical resignation and tranquillity, it would not make men repent or strive to make their peace with God.

Well, my brethren, a creed of this kind, if creed it can be called, which consists mainly in the denial of everything that can be matter of what we commonly call belief, is fast spreading among us, and bids fair to be the popular doctrine of the day. For the present it is mainly confined to the educated classes, but in our times education has made very rapid progress indeed, and it is fast becoming the truth that there is very little difference between one class of the community and another in the level of general knowledge. The creed of which I speak will soon get hold of the masses of the population, and indeed we are told by those who study most intelligently the thoughts and ideas of the masses, at least in the large towns which are the characteristic products of the age in which we live, that it has already spread among the lower orders to a degree little suspected by those who are not familiar with the facts. It is called the creed of modern science, and its articles are formulated almost with the same precision as those of the Christian doctrine of which they are in the main a categorical denial.* Now, when I speak of this as the creed of science, I am not giving it a name, but using the name which it already has obtained, and I am bound to say has obtained without right. It is not the creed of true science, but the creed of scientific imposture. At the name of science I am inclined to bow my head, as to the name of one of the greatest gifts of God to man. I revere, as I am bound to revere, and to give thanks to God for, the revelations He has allowed us to receive of the true science of the universe in which we live. For they help us to know Him better, they make our life in many ways brighter and more beautiful, nobler and more elevated, and in the hands and mouths of those who are true philosophers—alas! how few—they shed a light even on the next life and on revelation itself in the true sense of the word, a light which comes from Him and for which all His children should thank Him. And when I see a Christian philosopher and man of science, I honour him as the one true interpreter of a class of verities which God desires to be made known, for His own glory and for the support and consolation of His creatures. And I honour such a man all the more, because in our times he is like the angel of whom the poet sings as

     Faithful found
  Amid the faithless, faithful only he.

* See Note at end of this Sermon.

For it is with science, as it has been with that other great gift of God to His children in this world, a gift which is His because He is the Author and Defender of human society as such, the gift of liberty. And as the poor Girondin lady on her way to the guillotine cried out to Liberty, so we may say of this great name of Science, " O Science, gift of Heaven, what follies and what falsehoods and what mischiefs are palmed off on us in thy name!"

My brethren, it would require many long discourses if it were necessary for us to go through, article by article, the creed, as it is called, of modern science, which, as we are told, has already a great multitude of adherents, and is likely, as far as we can see, to lay hold more and more powerfully every day of the public mind for many obvious reasons. But it is enough for us, in view of the subject immediately before us, to speak of those elementary points which are concerned especially with that great act of God to which we look forward when we anticipate what we call the Day of Judgment, which, as our Lord tells us, is to be ushered in by these marvellous signs which are yet to fail to rouse the generation to which they are immediately addressed. And here I must repeat more at length what I have already in some measure set before you in a former Sermon. This truth of the judgment of God on man is a truth partly of natural religion and partly of revelation. I mean it embraces the truth that God is the Creator and Lord of the whole universe, that it is God Who has given to human nature the faculties which it possesses, that it is His right to call men to an account, at the end of their probation, for the use they have made of their liberty, and that this judgment and this rendering of account to Him are the just foundation to them of the eternity which is to follow, and which is to be for them an eternity of reward or of punishment in accordance with the sentence which shall then be pronounced upon them and enforced by the power of God. So far this doctrine contains nothing that is not practically witnessed to by the conscience of every child of Adam, and therefore it may be called a part of natural religion. Thus we find that St. Paul fearlessly appealed to it in his famous speech to the Athenian philosophers on the Areopagus, and he would not have done so if he had not known that there were in the minds of those to whom he spoke, the germs and rudiments of the truth of which he so confidently spoke. He told them that the Creator of all things had left the nations of the world in great measure to themselves in times past, but that now He called on them all everywhere to do penance, because He had appointed a day in which He would judge the world in equity by the Man Whom He had chosen.

Thus, St. Paul went on to add points which are no part of natural theology, so to speak, that is, that the judgment was to be by a Man, Whom God had chosen, and that God had given all men a proof of this new truth by raising Him from the dead. Now here were new things certainly, and we find accordingly that these heathen philosophers took objection to what was new and not, as far as the Scripture narrative tells us, to what was old. When they heard of the Resurrection of the dead, some of them mocked, as St. Luke tells us—he does not say that they mocked at the doctrine of the responsibility of man to his Creator, or of his having to give an account of his use of his liberty to the God Who made him free, and so responsible. This is enough to show us what elements of truth must exist in the mind or in the teaching of men, in order that they may have some kind, at least, of intelligence or capacity of intelligence, of the truth of the coming judgment, and so of the signs by which that judgment is to be preceded.

IV.

Well, my brethren, the philosophers of the age in which we live have gone far beyond the sages of the Athenian schools in the first century in their negation of truth. If St. Paul had made his speech in a learned society in London, instead of at Athens, he would have been stopped at the very outset of his discourse by the jeers and mockery of his audience. These men of whom I speak are not courteous in their treatment of what had been the common belief of the wisest of mankind for ages before they appeared in the world. For the doctrine of the creation of all things by a God Who is far above the natures which He has made out of nothing, they have invented a new word, for no old word is strong enough for the measure of their unbelief. The doctrine of Creation is not to them only improbable, or unproved, or untrue, or uncertain, it is *unthinkable*. The most courteous and civil in his language of the men of whom I am speaking is the greatest among them, the writer to whom is owing the theory, as it is called, of Natural Selection. This doctrine is not, to ordinary minds, very far removed from the simple doctrine of chance, as the explanation of all phenomena. But, anyhow, this writer, we are told, "postulates" a Creator of some sort, at the beginning of the countless ages which are required for the evolution of the present forms of life. And if the word Creator were enough, we might thus find in the theory of this famous man some acknowledgment of the fundamental truth on which the Christian doctrine of the Judgment is built.

But, as we all can see at once, the word is not enough, and the teaching of this philosopher—at least as it is explained and developed by his followers—leaves very little room for what we Christians call a Creator—a God Who not only creates all things out of nothing, but Who is continually active in support of the creation which He has called into existence, a free intelligent personal God, Who, besides being thus active, is a free intelligent personal conscious God, Who has a purpose and a design in all that He does and has done.* The Creator of this theory is one who may be necessary for the first existence of the rudiments out of which the whole world has been developed, but He stands by inactive, while the laws which He has established work themselves out. He has no purpose in His creation, and He is not the kind of Being of Whom even the idea can be entertained that He will ever be

* See Note at the end of this Sermon.

the Judge of human souls and call them to account for the use of their liberty. Souls and liberty are words which these men use, if at all, in no more Christian a sense than they use the word Creator. After the very idea of God has been got rid of, it is not much more to destroy the idea of the separate and indestructible existence of the souls of men. The Judge is first removed from the sphere even of possible thought, and then, of course, those whom He is to judge follow Him into nothingness. The modern creed is not unanimous in its decision as to the existence of the soul, but it generally denies the freewill of man, and thus cuts away the truth of his responsibility. And as to his future existence, it is quite certain with them that man cannot survive the world in which his lot is cast, and this world they acknowledge must eventually come to destruction, though there may be an immense series of centuries to pass before that consummation takes place. So the Judge is gone, and the persons to be judged are gone, and the subject-matter of the judgment is gone, and that future eternal existence, the happiness or the misery of which alone makes it a matter of importance whether man owes the account he is supposed by Christians to have to render to a most just and severe Master. Man is not truly free, and at the most his responsibility lies in some kind of obligation under which he lies to the society of which he forms a part, and even his responsibility is subordinated to his self-interest. And of course if the soul does not survive the body, the very foundation of the whole doctrine of the Judgment is removed.

My brethren, I do not say whether this creed of modern science will last till the great day of account itself. For the fancies of the philosophers of modern times are like the bubbles which children blow, and very few of them last long before they burst. But what I have told you is only a part of a very large range of false doctrines linked together, more or less, by a kind of identity or continuity, and this is the creed which is fast taking possession of large portions of the educated communities of modern Europe and America. It is a very destructive, a very degrading, as well as a very foolish creed, and if it were to the purpose to-day to draw out its details, and to tell you what it makes of duty, what account it gives of virtue, how it treats all that is most noble and great in what the intelligence of man has acquired or stored up during so many painful centuries of toil in the life of our race, if I were to tell you what is the Gospel of this new religion, what are its promises, what is its social creed, and how it purposes to deal with religion and with morality, the family, the home, the dearest rights of men, I should have to shock you far more than I may have shocked you already. But I am now only speaking of this creed as a most adequate preparation for that state of utter blindness and hardness which we are taught to expect in the days of Antichrist, in the men of that last age of the world, and surely it is evident that little more can be required than the prevalence of the creed of which I speak to produce that insensibility to the phenomena of the last age which seems to us so marvellous. And so, my brethren, we may say, as

St. John says in the passage which has already been quoted to you, " Even now there are become many Antichrists, whereby we know that it is the last hour." In any case, my brethren, there is enough in this creed to account for the phenomenon of which we are speaking, that is, the dulness of the men of the last generation to the warnings of God, and therefore it represents to us the sufficient cause of that greatest of all calamities, against which our Lord is so anxious that we should be on our guard. And therefore it is worth our while to examine it a little more closely, not indeed in its details, but in its effects and in the characteristics which may make it so dangerous to the men of our own time, whether it last beyond that time or not.

V.

Now, out of many things that might be said of a creed like this, I must select just those few which it may be most important for us now to note. In the first place, then, let us consider the great though superficial attractiveness of a belief like this. It is indeed a sad thing to have to speak of the attractiveness of a form of falsehood which makes man blind to the existence of God, to the spirituality of the soul, to the liberty with which he is himself endowed, in short, to all that constitutes in him that Divine image which is his greatest glory. It is a mournful thing to think that, after so many centuries of the boasted progress of humanity, it should have come to this, that the very highest achievement of the intelligence of man is to find out that he is no better than the beasts that perish, that he has no future, that he has no true moral responsibility, that he is incapable of virtue and of merit, and that his truest wisdom is to follow his animal appetites. What further degradation to an intelligent being can be imagined I do not know. Yes, this is a mournful creed, and one can only wonder that those who think they have discovered it to be true, do not hide their discovery from very shame, and let the rest of mankind go on believing the fair dream that they are made for Heaven and are the children of God. But it is not easy to fathom the depths of the degradation of which men become enamoured when their hearts are set on the enjoyment of temporal goods, and yearn, above all things, for freedom from the uncomfortable restraints of conscience and of the moral law.

What is attractive in this pernicious creed, besides its promise of immunity to all kinds of foulness and corruption, is the sweeping and thorough-going character of its so-called doctrine. It is written of the wisdom of God that "it reaches from end to end mightily and orders all things sweetly,"* and of this sensual and devilish wisdom, to use the words of the Apostle, we may say that it reaches from end to end boldly and orders all things speciously. There is an attractiveness to our poor weak minds in large and magnificent generalizations, in neat and exact laws, in theories which account in a few words for everything, in easy panaceas, and in the demolitions of old creeds by a single blow. This doctrine of false science in our day has a kind of arctic grandeur and even

* Wisdom viii. 1.

beauty of its own. Thus it is not necessary to suppose, or to assume, that those who have built it up are conscious of any formed desire to get rid of religion, of freewill, of morality, of responsibility, of duty, of a future state. For, even without this, it has, like so many of the results of mathematical investigation, a symmetry and a glitter of its own which is pleasant to the intelligence, even if it freezes up the heart. There are men whose lives have in them no prayer, no exercise of the mind on spiritual things and the unseen world, who are as dead to all active charity as the rich glutton mentioned in the Gospel, though they belong to a more intelligent and speculative class than he, and to these men of keen minds and hard hearts there is, as I say, a charm about such theories as this which others can hardly understand.

But then, when we speak of the attractiveness of a creed such as this, we must in the first place consider, not what charms it may have to the man of science and the student in his closet, but how it will affect the masses when it is popularized, what its influence will be when it comes, as it soon may come, to be taught in Board Schools, to be instilled into the minds of the people in penny newspapers, to be tacitly assumed as true and as the foundation of all truth, in the whole shallow literature of a world incapable of serious thought or reflection. Then it will certainly reveal charms which address themselves, quite in a different degree of attractiveness, to the secluded and refined student on the one hand, and, on the other hand, to the hearts and wills and passions of multitudes, who care nothing for the possible millions of ages outside their own short span of existence in this world, and to whom this creed will be simply the Gospel of a new era of fearless and unbridled liberty, far more effectively such than that liberty in the name of which so many horrors have been perpetrated in the most civilized countries of the world, since the latter half of the last century. In all human societies, except that of the Catholic Church, the many are ruled by the few, and not always for the sake of the many rather than for the sake of the few. In our times the masses have learnt their strength, and they can only be kept from exerting it by law, by religion, by conscience, by the fear of God. Which of these checks on brute violence will remain, in the face of the prevalence of this new creed? And can it be doubted then, that when it comes to be the creed of the great mass of mankind, their faithfulness to its ghastly precepts will be written in letters of blood and destruction on every community and society of man in the whole world?

But, in the next place, my brethren, if this creed is so attractive, is it not also equally deceptive? We are told in the Sacred Scriptures that the Antichrist shall come on the men of those days "in all the seduction of iniquity," that they shall have lost and set aside the love of truth, that they might be saved, and that, in consequence, God shall send upon them an operation or working of falsehoods, that they may believe lying. Now it might almost be said that the prophets, so to call them, of the new faith, confess this themselves, that they believe lies. This is a startling thing to say, but let me explain what I mean. Of course I do not say that they confess that they believe what they know to be false. But they do confess what makes this possible. They do confess —they say it one of another—that they very frequently indeed set at nought the laws of logic and of reasoning in the manner in which they build up their conclusions, which nevertheless they hold as most certain truths, and with a firmness of conviction like that, as they think, with which Christians hold the truths of revelation. I do not go for the proof of this to the enemies of science, but to the teachers themselves, who are continually exposing one another for the want of observation of some of the simplest laws of reasoning, in their haste to arrive at the conclusion on which they had set their heart. The process begins well enough in a great number of cases. A man of ability and industry gives himself, perhaps for years, to the investigation of some part of the great realm of nature. He extracts a number of results, and then he at once leaps to a generalization. This generalization, though founded, after all, on imperfect knowledge, and liable to be overthrown, or greatly modified, by new discoveries which may follow, becomes a theory, and then we find this theory developed into a law, the application of which is insisted on far beyond the field of the original research, and then the law becomes a truth and a principle from which a large number of other conclusions are drawn, and thus a whole Philosophy of the Universe is raised and set up, like the statue of Nabuchodonosor, to be worshipped under pain of a new kind of persecution for all who hesitate. My brethren, it is more like the statue of which the same poor King dreamed, gold and silver and brass and iron, and resting on feet of clay.

Thus the deceptiveness of this new creed lies in this, that its adherents rush to conclusions the premisses of which rest on uncertainties, and it is not too much to say that they know this all the time, yet so enamoured are they of these conclusions that they will not practically acknowledge that they can be no more certain than the uncertainties on which they are are built. Now, these are the men of all others in the world who exercise most efficiently the critical faculty, and who insist most strictly on the requirements of exact logic in everything else. See them when there is a question of the evidence of a miracle, or a revelation, or of a Divine messenger, or of a Church which claims to speak in the name of God! Put a faulty syllogism or an incomplete induction before them then, and mark their severity! But when the question is as to some physical theory which may cast a doubt on revelation, or Scripture, or the authority of conscience, or the spirituality or immortality of the soul, and then these false men of science are children. They will reject the evidences of the religion of Jesus Christ, severe as the argument may be, but they will have their own theories, hatched yesterday and perhaps to be discarded by themselves to-morrow, accepted at once as so certain that they may be reasoned from as accepted and prolific truths. And when this kind of credulity becomes the case with masses of men in their acceptance of such a system, is it unfair to say that this **system** is allowed, judicially, as St. Paul tells us, to have a power of deceptiveness which is without a parallel in the history of human thought? And this is the same thing as to say of it that it may well enough be the creed of that last generation, on which, because it would not retain the love of truth that it might be saved, God will send an operation of delusion, that it may believe lying.

And now let me add one more characteristic of this new creed of science, which, if that new creed ever comes to be dominant, will greatly add to the difficulty which will prevent men from parting from the illusion, and which will certainly hinder them from recognizing the signs by which the last coming of our Lord is to be announced. This creed is not only very attractive and very deceptive, but it is a creed which will give to those who adopt it the fewest possible chances of ever laying it aside for the truth. This statement only requires a short explanation to make its truth obvious. The world has been full from the beginning, and it may be full unto the end, of various forms of false belief. Since the Church was placed in the world by our Lord, the multitudinous brood of heresies and schisms which have gone forth from her in rebellion against this or that point of her teaching, or against the rule of unity by which her faith and her charity are defended, have added by scores and by hundreds to the shapes of falsehood by which mankind was before oppressed. Since the abandonment of Catholic unity in this country alone, who shall count the religious sects which have sprung up in the Anglo-Saxon race in England and in

America! Well, my brethren, some of these sects and religions are very far indeed from the Catholic faith, while others have retained considerable portions of the Catholic truth. Something of the same kind may also be said of the false forms of religion outside the Christian pale. There is hardly one of these that we know of, however wild, extravagant, and degraded, which does not retain some portions at least of the primitive truths which were the inheritance of our race from the beginning of time. It is by these fragments and shadows of truth that all false religions live; it is by these fragments and shadows of Catholic truth that the sects live which have gone forth from the bosom of the Church. Even Mahometanism has the principle of the unity of the Godhead; even the wildest modern Spiritualism has the principle of the existence of an unseen world of spirits. These fragments of truth are not merely the life of all these false systems. They are also the handles, so to say, which the teachers of the truth in its Catholic perfection can lay hold of in their attempts to lead into the light of the Church those of the disciples of the sects who have adopted them and hold them in good faith. We have far enough to go sometimes, but we can mount up at last to some truth which the sectarian or the misbeliever holds in common with ourselves, and then, as all truth is a harmonious whole, we can lead him along the path of truth from the point at which he, or the poor soul who founded his sect, began to diverge from it.

I do not suppose, my brethren, there is any race

of the children of Adam, however savage and degraded, even to the level almost of the beasts of the field, in which there is not some glimmer of a natural law, some idea of a God, some anticipation of a future, and, even if such a case were to be found, we might say of them, at all events, that they have lost in the lapse of ages, in their misery and isolation, the remains of their primeval treasure, but they have not deliberately thrown it away and trampled it under foot. And if that be true, then, surely as the Queen of the South and the men of Ninive shall rise up in the Day of Judgment and condemn the Jews of our Lord's time, so surely will these poor benighted savages rise up in that same great day and condemn the false disciples of science, who, in the full light of Christianity, have cast out of their own hearts and minds the truths which they once possessed. Where is the handle in their system which they have left us to lay hold of, that we may rescue their disciples from the misery in which they are plunged? What contact has any part of the system of God's truth with this so-called creed? Is there any wild creature to be found in the interior of Africa or in the half-discovered recesses of Borneo, without any idea of civilized life at all and of the intellectual treasures of the human race, who, as far as concerns religion and the idea of God and of the soul and of conscience and of judgment and of a future life, is more brutalized by the centuries of degradation which have passed over his ancestors than are those votaries of science, one may almost say, by their own free choice and the deliberate perversion of their understandings? True, the one thing in which they do believe, that is, the immutability of the laws of nature, will be shattered to pieces before their eyes. And so it may be said that God in His mercy will address them, so to speak, on their own ground. But how will this catastrophe of nature revive in them the thoughts which it is an axiom with them to consider unthinkable, and lead them to the knowledge of Him Whom they banish from His own creation as unknowable? How will it wake up in them the moral sense, the idea of duty, the consciousness that they are something more than bundles of impressions or automata, or that they have immortal souls, and that they are called to stand before their Judge? The fear, the terror, that falls on them will fall as well on the beasts of the field and on the fowls of the air. But it will not make them feel themselves to be men in the Christian sense of the word, any more than it will make the birds of the air set their consciences in order, or move the beasts of the field to contrition, compunction, and prayer.

VI.

Surely, then, my brethren, it is not an exaggeration to say that Satan has seldom been permitted to invent, for the seduction of mankind, a more pernicious, a more degrading, or a more inaccessible creed than this which falsely goes by the name of the creed of science. It is true that the delusion may pass away, like other delusions, for it is certain that the progress of scientific researches will continue, and that nature must have many more secrets to surrender to the immense thirst of man for such discoveries.

As the true progress of science continues, it may be said, the fancies and absurdities of the earlier pioneers die away, and the result is to leave us in the possession of a number of new truths, which sober men soon come to see in their consistency and harmony with what has been the possession of our race from its beginnings. It may be that the intoxication of our generation will pass away, like the intoxication of the generation which lived in the days of what we look back on as the "Renaissance," when for a time it seemed to some as if the Christian elements in society were to be overwhelmed by the revival of paganism. The religious and Christian instincts of the children of the Church were strong enough to overcome the venom which had been infused into society, and to assimilate that part of the new learning which was cognate to themselves. So it may be with what seems to us the madness of false science—so it certainly should be, when we consider its unreasonableness and its inconsistencies.

So, then, what the future will be is the secret of God, and I am far from saying that it may not please Him once more to restore the world, by a new generation of saints, or by other new provisions of His inexhaustible wisdom and power. But it must be remembered that the end will come at its appointed time, and that God will not for ever defer the chastisements which He has so often threatened. That which makes one time worse than another in the decline of the world and the resistance of the waywardness and childishness of men to the truth and to the Church, is not so much the existence at any given time of one of the predicted signs of the coming judgment, as the concurrent existence in any one generation of all or most of these predicted signs. The arm of the Lord is not shortened, and our Lord has used a remarkable word in that saying of His, so often quoted, in which He rebuked the curiosity of the Apostles themselves as to the features of the latter days. "It is not for you," He said, "to know the times or the moments, which the Father hath put in His own power."* He did not say His own knowledge or wisdom, but His own power. As if He were speaking of something which depended, above all things, on the free choice of God, independent of any ordinary laws or general rules by which He conducts the government of the world. It is written of Him in the Sacred Scriptures, that "He made the nations of the earth for health"—*Sanabiles fecit nationes terræ*,† and as long as it pleases Him to continue to mankind the blessed presence of the Catholic Church, the world possesses in her a fountain of fresh health and a remedy against every ill. But God will not always interfere to prevent the world from rejecting the Church. It is our business, all the more, as the Apostle says, "as we see the day approaching," to take our part in the conflict on the side of truth and of God, and a part of the discipline of our warfare is to be able to discern the signs of the times in which we live. This creed of pretended science is one of these signs—one out of many which concur in the world now around us. It is a sign which, when taken in conjunction with others, of which I shall

* Acts i. 7.   † Wisdom i. 14.

have hereafter to speak, may well make us echo the words of the beloved disciple, that from what we see before us "we know that it is the last hour."

NOTE TO P. 71.

SOME of the statements in the text with regard to the Darwinian theory may seem to require confirmation or explanation. But I must content myself with a few quotations from a book which may be usefully consulted on the general results of the system, and of others cognate to it, even though there may be here and there conclusions from which some of the disciples of the new philosophy might perhaps dissent, I mean the *Creed of Science*, by William Graham, M.A. (London, 1881.)

With regard to the statement that to ordinary minds there is little difference between the Darwinian selection, and chance, the following passage may suffice:

> What strikes us most in reading this marvellous story of the origin and process of manufacture of Nature's living forms, is the seemingly chance affair it all was. We are not permitted, on Darwinian principles, to suppose that there was any prevision, or forecast of what was to come, in Nature's blind bosom. There was no conception, not even the vaguest dream, on the part of Nature, in the commencement of the cosmic process, of the forms of life that should emerge in the sequel. Nature did not know what she did, for there was no principle of knowledge within her. Still worse, there was no constant purpose in view, and no controlling power governing the process of evolution. ... What has resulted need not have resulted, for Nature neither knew or cared nor directed. Things might have taken a wholly different course, on the earth at least, with a slight accidental alteration of conditions at a critical moment in the history of any one of the species. In particular, man, himself, the crown of creation, might not have appeared at all. And after his appearance, it was only owing to the chapter of accidents unusually favourable that he emerged victor from the general battlefield of existence. ... On the Darwinian hypothesis, man is the child of chance, as from the evolution hypothesis, in its full generality, all life is the result of chance (pp. 25—27).

The writer goes on to combat the implied statement of Professor Tyndall that this is not so.

A few pages further on the author says:

It is extremely difficult or wholly impossible to trace the operation of mind in this process. There is no room allowed for it. The more we read the story of Darwin, the further and further the notion and possibility of mind recede. The species in the organic worlds are brought into being in much the same fashion as the physical worlds in the system of Democritus, namely, by chance. In this system, after many unsuccessful trials and momentary adhesions of the atoms, after ephemeral worlds had been born and dissolved again in the course of a day—at length a particular combination of the atoms occurred, which, as the event turned out, had permanent cohesion in it, from which resulted the solid universe, and in a like fashion all that is therein. In a manner not dissimilar the species of animals and plants were begun, and survived, while some quickly disappeared, on Darwin's theory, and there seems on the whole as little room left for a shaping intelligence (according to our old notions) in the origin of species according to Darwin, or rather Darwinism, as in the origin of the world according to Democritus (pp. 37, 38).

On the question of the meaning of the Creator in this system the following passage may be quoted:

We are entitled to consider the system, whether Darwin himself would accept all the consequences involved in it or no. For it is the system as a whole that really concerns us; it is there that the important and far-reaching consequences of the whole doctrine of Natural Selection and Evolution are most clearly manifested. But Darwin himself is only responsible for the conclusions drawn by other Evolution philosophers so far as they are logically contained in his principles and methods of reasoning. Now, in Darwin's *Origin of Species* a Creator is placed at the commencement of the process of organic evolution—and an intelligent Creator, other than the plastic powers of nature—which, however, his most eminent followers have set aside. The question arises, are they justified in so doing, on Darwinian principles? and the still graver question, are they justified on true and universal and philosophical principles? The former question I am inclined to answer in the affirmative, for the Creator of the *Origin of Species* seems introduced, more for ornament than for any serious work that He has to do, or at least, rather to conciliate the mass of hostile theological prejudice, certain to be aroused by the other doctrines, than to satisfy any logical demands on the system. He has nothing to do at the beginning, save to endow "one or a few primordial forms" with the lowest degree of elementary life, leaving the rest of the work to natural selection and the ordeal of battle; and He has nothing to do ever since (on the earth at least) but to sit passively by and watch laws which execute themselves, without need of any interference on His part. He is a monarch that "reigns but does not govern," like the sovereigns under our parliamentary *régime*, and accordingly, in the evolutionary monism of Haeckel, the passive personal supernatural Creator is dethroned, and the real ruling and efficient agency, Matter, eternal and governed by its own laws, is placed on the vacant throne. There is no need to suppose creative agency either at the beginning or since, because "physico-chemical laws," which now regulate the behaviour of matter and all the processes of life, were quite competent to introduce life at first (pp. 44, 45).

The reader will remember that the Sermon speaks of the system in general, and as it is in the minds of the great majority of its followers, many of whom have taken up with its results without troubling themselves as to the question, how these results have been reached. The Sermon does not enter on the question, how much of real truth there may be in the system, a question which could not be treated on such an occasion. The true part of the system is sure to survive the illogical fantasies of some of its advocates, and to be harmonized, by Catholic and Christian "evolutionists," with all the other truths with which those advocates endeavour to make it irreconcileable.

With regard, in particular, to the points mentioned in this note, there is no apparently necessary contradiction between the doctrine of Creation by God, in the Christian sense, and the doctrine of Evolution, when that doctrine is divested of the trappings, so to say, by which it has been overlaid.*

* See Harper, *Metaphysics of the School*, vol. ii. App. A.

SERMON V.

THE DECAY OF CHARITY.

Quia abundavit iniquitas, refrigescet caritas multorum.

Because iniquity hath abounded, the charity of many shall grow cold

(Words taken from the 12th verse of the 24th chapter of St. Matthew's Gospel.)

I.

IN the last sermon, dear brethren in our Lord, I spoke to you about a characteristic of the last days, as they are foreshadowed to us in our Lord's great prophecy, which will distinguish the generation on which the Day of Judgment will actually come as a snare, or as a thief in the night. That characteristic was the hardness and indifference to the many wonderful signs which are to go before the second Advent, which will prevent the men of that generation from recognizing those signs as what they are meant in the good Providence of God to be. But that hardness and that indifference will be produced in the hearts of those men by the dominion of a false creed, a creed which will make it impossible for them to understand that the Son of God is coming to judge the world which He has made, and which He has redeemed, and to pass sentence on the souls of all men, a sentence founded on their deserts, good or evil, which will settle, once for all, their lot throughout all eternity. In their case, then, the fact of their dulness and blindness will be the result of their incredulity, or rather, of their firm faith in a delusion and a lie. But now, in the text which I have chosen to-day, we have another characteristic of the latter times, of which I cannot but think it must have been most painful to our Lord to speak. He speaks very sparingly of it, and seems to pass it over as a thing of which He is glad to speak sparingly. He gives, as it were, a reason and an excuse for it: "Because iniquity hath abounded, the charity of many shall grow cold."

Now this, my brethren, is a feature of the last days which does not belong to the world outside the Church. Let worldlings invent creeds for themselves if they so choose, and so steel their hearts against that last appeal, which God, in His mercy, will make to them before He finally closes, by an act of His power, the history of the world. The incredulity of worldlings is bad enough, but charity is the characteristic of the Christian Kingdom and of the Catholic Church. No need to say that the charity of the world is cold, or grows cold—the world outside the Church knows not the glow and brightness of that heavenly flame. It is the fire which our Lord came to set upon the earth, and He was straitened until it was kindled. It is this fire which it is the work of the Holy Ghost to kindle and to keep alive, Who came down on the Apostles on the Day of Pentecost in the shape of tongues of fire. It is the life and light of the

Catholic Church, because in the Church the love of God is shed abroad in our hearts by the Holy Ghost, Who is given to us. What is it, then, for our Lord to say that the charity of many shall grow cold? What is it but to say that the hearts of many of His own redeemed, of large numbers of His own children and friends, are to be overpowered by the lawlessness and iniquity all around them, and that the light and fire of the Holy Ghost are to be at least partially quenched in the very Kingdom of God itself? Oh, my brethren, here is something, then, far worse than the miserable proud incredulity of the world. Here is an evil feature which must belong to ourselves. Here is a plague which will make havoc of the very Church of God. Here is a triumph of evil which will almost reach to the banishment, from the hearts which He has made, of the Eternal Spirit of God. Surely no greater pain to our Lord's Sacred Heart can be imagined, no nearer approach to the victory of His enemies. We still have His promise, that the gates of Hell shall not prevail against the Church, and His words cannot pass away. But He does not promise that the Church shall not be in sore affliction and trial in those last times. And certainly, of all afflictions and of all trials that can befall her, there can be none more grievous than even a partial extinction of the charity of her children.

My brethren, I am speaking of these features of the last days mainly for the practical purpose of pointing out to you that we can find so many things, in our own time and among the men of our own generation, which correspond to the predictions of the end of the world, that it is true to say that the features of our own time have only to be deepened and intensified, in order to produce that state of things on which the last fearful Judgment will fall. I have shown you already, that this is true with regard to what is called the rising creed of science outside the Christian pale, and now I have to point out to you the features in the present condition of the Christian community which may be said to correspond to these mournful words of our Lord about the cooling of Christian charity. And here, at the very outset of our consideration of this matter, I am met by an objection which many will make, and with which it is necessary for us to deal.

For you will say to me, perhaps, that we live in a time rather of revival than of declension, that we live in a time of great Christian activity, if of much occasional loss and affliction; that if we look back a hundred years, we shall see Europe and the Church on the verge of that disastrous overthrowing and upheaval which we call the Great Revolution, and that, in our own days, if the evil fruits of that period have spread on every side, at least the Church has been purified and invigorated by her sufferings, she has begun to reconquer something of what she has lost, she has taken possession of countries where before she was almost unknown, she has spread the network of her hierarchical organization over parts of the globe where before she was unable to plant it, and she has also gathered her Bishops in Council, and she has raised her voice in the definition of dogma, and in all her outward decadence she has shown renewed signs of her eternal youth and her indefectible majesty. And surely it would ill become us in this country, it may be said, where we have entered so largely into the labours of our forefathers, to cast the reproach of coldness and tepidity on the Church of this time. All this is true, and yet I think it is true also, that to the eye of faith the time already wears the marks of that special lawlessness and coldness of which our Lord spoke when He said, "Because iniquity hath abounded, the charity of many shall grow cold."

II.

In the first place, dear brethren, let us remember that the words which we are considering came forth from the Sacred Heart of our Lord Himself, and therefore they bear that meaning which belongs to them in His own Divine thoughts. We must measure the charity of which He speaks, not by our own cold standard, but by the standard of the Sacred Heart. Again, we may be quite certain, my brethren, that whenever the day comes for the prophecy to be fulfilled, the fulfilment thereof will not be recognized as such by the men to whom it applies. A generation that has lost its fervour will not think that it has lost it. On the other hand, a generation that is all on fire with Divine love will be much more likely to accuse itself, even bitterly, for not having enough of it, than think that it is liable to no complaint in this regard. If the Christians of our day think that they have all the fervour of charity which they ought to have, that might be considered a certain proof that they are lamentably deficient in fervour and charity. Let us not content ourselves, therefore, with measuring ourselves, if so it must be that we are to measure ourselves at all, by the state of the Church in any particular century that has passed over her head since she came forth from the Cenacle at Jerusalem. If what St. John calls the last time had begun when he wrote his Epistles, because there were already many who had become Antichrists, on account of heresies and schisms, it may be that the last time began also even before the Apostles passed away, in respect of the decay of charity.

Now, in these sad words our Lord gives us the cause of this decay, the abounding of iniquity or lawlessness, and this cause certainly cannot be supposed to be limited to the last time. Lawlessness means independence of restraints, even of restraints enacted by God and enforced by the discipline of the societies of which He is the Author—the natural society of the State, and the supernatural society of the Church. And, if we are to recognize this abounding and multiplication of iniquity in every age in which individual pride and passion revolt against constituted authority, of whichever order, certainly we cannot well find an epoch in the Christian centuries in which there has not been enough of this to make that age an age of lawlessness, and certainly we cannot deny that our own time is as lawless as any. It may be that we are obliged to face the sad conclusion that, while there never has been, nor ever will be, a time when there shall not be charity enough in the heart of the Catholic Church to secure her life and existence, according to the promises of our Lord, so also there never has been, and there never may be, a time in which it might not be said that the charity of the many has grown cold. But what would make a time like ours in some especial manner more like to the last time of all than other ages have been, would be this—if it were in our own time as to charity, as we saw last Sunday it already was as to faith. I mean, if it could be truly said that the decay of charity had gone so far among Christians that its further decay was almost inevitable, unless God chooses to interpose by an act of His power to renovate and re-invigorate the world. That was the conclusion to which we came last Sunday as to what is called the creed of science—that it is not only a miserable and a foolish falsehood, but also a hopeless falsehood. It was a falsehood which was likely to gather strength as time goes on, and to blind men more and more fatally. What answers to this in regard to charity would be, if some "operation of iniquity," as St. Paul says, were to be established as a recognized principle in the Christian world, which might make men not only fail in charity one to another, but even give up the attempt of regaining the love and union which they have lost. And now let us ask ourselves, are there any features in our time with regard to charity, which make us fear that our Lord's intention with regard to the life and operation of charity in the Church has been finally and almost irrevocably defeated?

And now let us endeavour to enter into that Sacred Heart, from the abundance of which these words of our Blessed Lord proceeded, and let us endeavour to understand the part which He had allotted to charity in the carrying out of that great design which brought Him from the bosom of His Eternal Father to take on Him a human nature and to die upon the Cross. For so it must certainly be, if we can come to understand, even imperfectly, what our Lord looks for, as it were, in the working of charity in the hearts of His children, we shall be able to understand also what is the loss and what is the danger when charity grows cold, and how mournful must have been the prospect of this cooling to the Sacred Heart.

I have already alluded to the saying of our Lord, "I am come to send fire upon earth, and what do I wish for but that it be kindled?"* and I suppose among the many meanings which these words may convey, there is none more true or more profitable to us than that which understands them of charity. It is as if our Lord had implied that His own personal work, which depended on Himself, and on no one else, was not all to which He looked forward, but that there was a still further work which in part depended on others, and that without this other work His own might not be fully fruitful, and for this work He looked to charity. His own work, my brethren, was perfect and complete in all the perfection and all the completeness which belongs to the work of God. On the Cross He fully atoned

* St. Luke xii. 49.

for sin, He fully reconciled man to God, He purchased the eternal glories of Heaven for all believers, and partly after He rose again, and partly before, He created and organized the Church, a perfect system fraught with graces of every kind—sacraments conveying the fruits of the Precious Blood to the souls of men in every possible occasion and necessity, the Word of God, the gifts and presence of the Holy Ghost. And you will remember that in our Lord's conversations with the Apostles about what was to be after He left them Himself, He spoke mainly and above all things of the Presence of the Eternal Spirit of God, as the great source of all the strength and light and joy which they were then to receive.

My brethren, no invention of the wisdom and charity of God can be compared in beauty and wisdom to the work of our Lord in creating the Catholic Church. And yet it is not too much to say, that this is not enough for the perfect conquest of the world to God, not because God has not the power to conquer the world by means of the Church, but because in His Providence He requires that the armoury, so to speak, of the Church shall be wielded by men like ourselves. Here then is the great and endless difficulty. It is as when St. Paul says to the Corinthians, "You are not straitened in us," it is not in us Apostles that the cause of your weakness lies, "you are straitened in your own hearts."* For the complete conquest of the world to God, we may venture to say, three things are required in the counsels of God:

* 2 Cor. vi. 12.

First, the work of the Eternal Son Incarnate, redeeming mankind on the Cross, and setting to them by His life on earth a perfect pattern and lesson how to please His Father, and how to gain Heaven. Secondly, the work of the Holy Ghost, applying in the Catholic Church, and through her system, the merits of the actions and sufferings of the Eternal Son made Man. And in the third place, one thing more is required—the work of men like ourselves in the Catholic Church, generation after generation, the work of men on fire with the flame of charity, and doing, on account of their burning love, that part of the great enterprise which belongs to them.

We know that the work of the Eternal Son is already done. He has gone to Heaven to prepare a place for those who love Him, He sits on the right hand of the Father in His Human Nature, all things are made subject under His feet, and from thence He rules the Church and the world according to His will. The work of the Holy Ghost is always going on, and this work, like the work of the Eternal Son, can never be defeated. But the work of men like ourselves, may prosper and advance and succeed, or may fail and wane and falter and linger. When it prospers and advances and succeeds, it is because the charity of God is spread abroad in our hearts by the Holy Ghost, Who is given to us,—and when it fails and wanes and falters and lingers, it is for the cause our Lord gives—because iniquity has abounded, the charity of the many is grown cold.

And now, my brethren, let us remember this: the work of the Church on earth is not like the triumphant parade of a conquering army through a country which welcomes its conquerors as its deliverers, which opposes no obstacle to their progress, which opens the gates of its cities to pour forth glad and rejoicing crowds to invite them to all the best that they have to bestow. It is a march over the country of an enemy bristling with fortresses, already occupied by hostile armies, all the resources of which are shut against the new-comers, all the natural features of mountain, or forest, or river, or swamp, made use of to impede their advance, with foes and snares and unseen dangers lurking in every brake and corner of the way. It ought not to be so, but so it is. The natural man turns in rebellion and suspicion and hatred from the messenger of the Gospel, much as a strong sick maniac, who is ready to tear to pieces the physician who brings him health and food. The Apostles, and all who come after them, are sent as sheep into the midst of wolves. Their one weapon, and their one protection, is their charity. Charity is like the discipline which keeps the army together, it is like the skill of the leader who guides it aright, it is like the courage and prowess of the soldiers, it is the life and light and strength of all.

Now I suppose, in order not to be too long on this point, I may fairly sum up the work and the effect which our Lord expects from this Divine virtue under three heads, though under each many others might have to be ranged, in order to give a full account of its function, so to speak, in the system of our Lord. I will make these three heads, then, and in these we may class the various effects of charity in our Lord's intention. First, He expects from it the most perfect unity and concord and mutual love between the various members of His Body, the various regiments, if one may say so, of His great army, and the unity of an army implies discipline, subordination, obedience, self-effacement, self-sacrifice. In the second place, our Lord looks to charity as the great source and stimulant of courage, of heroic devotion, that sacrifice and entire self-immolation, which is the heroism and valour of the Christian host. He looks to it for the sufficient principle which is to prompt men to throw all aside in order to give themselves to the Apostolic life, like St. Patrick, or St. Augustine of England, or St. Francis Xavier,—and not one or two, here and there, but a great army of ambassadors of peace and victims of love, whatever may be the particular field to which their devotion may be directed, whether they are to serve Him as rulers, or as preachers, or as ascetics, or as penitents, or as hermits, or as devoted to works of charity in the relief, for the love of Him, of the thousand and thousand forms of human misery. In the third place, our Lord looks to charity as the great furnace in the hearts of His people in which the flame of prayer burns day and night, prayer the unceasing pre-occupation of the citizens of Heaven, prayer the most powerful of all the weapons for the advancement of the love and faith of God on earth. These three things, at least, our Lord must have looked for in order that the work of His army, so to call it, may be done. Charity is to unite the

Church on earth with the Church in Heaven and with the suffering Church below. It is to bind in one heart and one mind all the various grades and orders in the Church on earth together, rulers to their flocks, the flocks to their rulers, and make all nations one great family of brethren under one Head and one Shepherd. And the members of the great host are, one by one, to be animated by this Divine fire to undertake heroic works for the glory of God and the common good. And all the while the bright flame of prayer is to be burning in each several heart and in the hearts of all, bringing down on all their enterprises, and on their whole warfare, blessings from above, and arming the poor weak human nature to which this great work is committed, with the might of the strength of the power of God, as St. Paul says. I might add other features to the picture, but these will suffice.

III.

Such, then, we may suppose may have been, in the desires and intentions of the Sacred Heart of our Lord in founding the Church, and in committing to her the continuation and accomplishment of the work, for the glory of the Father and for the good of souls which He had Himself begun. He had before Him, as no one else could have, both the power of the grace which He was to leave behind Him, to be applied to this great work, the multitudes of human souls to whom that grace was to be applied, the space of time in which the work must be done, and the whole history of the world during the succeeding ages as it was to be unfolded, in what He calls in one of His last discourses, "the times of the Gentiles," that is, the period which in the Providence of His Father was to be allotted to the Gentile nations, in their order and turn, for their acceptance or rejection of the Gospel. He saw all the opportunities which the Church was to have, and how, when they had once been offered, they would never recur. And now let us ask ourselves, what has been the result, what the correspondence on the part of men to this great design of the Sacred Heart of our Lord? And, of course, I am speaking mainly of the working of the great principle of charity to which our Lord looks for the accomplishment in the souls of men of the work which He expects from His Church.

And, in the first place, let us not doubt that the whole history of the Catholic Church in the world has been the history of successive triumphs of this principle of charity. Let us not doubt that, within her blessed pale, this principle has ever been, and ever will be, active, fruitful, prolific, glorifying God by a continual harvest of noble sacrifices and of successful labours. The work of charity is the great evidence that the Church is the Church, and that God is in her. This we cannot but acknowledge, with intense thankfulness to God, and yet, my brethren, it must be remembered that Christians are men, and not angels, and that from the very beginning it has been the great effort of the rulers of the Church and of her Saints to preserve and to increase the charity of the faithful, that even in the times of the Apostles, even in the first days of the Church in Jerusalem, there were murmurings and complaints in the Corinthian Church. St. Paul had sharply to rebuke the tendency to division, which showed itself in the formation of cliques and personal followings around the teachers of the Gospel, and in manifestations of selfishness and hardness even in the very "lovefeasts" themselves, and again, ere he died the same Apostle had sorrowfully to complain that the general interests of the Church were postponed to private ends: "All seek the things that are their own, not the things that are Jesus Christ's."* Alas! the whole subsequent history of the Church is but a comment on that early history which is set before us in the Acts and the Epistles of the Apostles, and never has there been a time and a place where or when the earnest pleadings of St. Paul for the following after charity have not been needed. And the effects of that chilling down of charity which can be found in a Christian community when the evil does not spread so far and so deep as to cause open breaches among the faithful and open rebellion against the rulers of the Church, are very terrible indeed in the sight of God and of His Saints—such as the languishing of works of zeal, the loss of the spirit of prayer, the feebleness and inefficiency of missionary efforts, the dimming, in the eyes of the world outside, of the brightness of that witness to the Divinity of the Spouse of Christ, before which the devils tremble and their weapons fall from the hands of her earthly enemies.

* Philipp. ii. 21.

This is enough to say about the falling off, in the case of a great many, from the perfection of charity in the Church. But there is far more to be said about this decay of which our Lord speaks, when we turn to the thought of that larger Kingdom of His on which it is impossible that His Sacred Heart should not have thought with yearnings unutterable. You remember, my brethren, how St. Paul, in one of his arguments with those Jewish Christians who were too exclusive in their sympathies, breaks out into the question, "Is God the God of the Jews only? Is He not also the God of the Gentiles?"* And may we not say to ourselves, "Is God the God, is our Lord the Redeemer, of Catholics alone? Is He not the Redeemer of the heretics and the schismatics also?" The Catholic Church, if we speak only of the visible unity of the communities which are within the pale of the obedience of the Successor of St. Peter, is but a part of that far larger body which goes in the world by the name of Christian, the members of which, at least in the greater number of cases, are baptized rightly in the name of the Father, and of the Son, and of the Holy Ghost. In consequence of their Baptism they have a right, of which no one but themselves can deprive them, to the privileges of the children of God in His Kingdom on earth, and to the inheritance of the brethren of our Lord in the Kingdom of God in Heaven. Our Lord's prevision of the children whom God hath given Him † must include them. And yet, my brethren, consider

* Rom. iii. 29.   † Isaias viii. 18; Heb. i. 3.

how it is in matter of fact. Look over the far East, and consider how many countries there are there which are alien from the Catholic unity! Look at the new Continent of America, the latest gift of God to the world already made Christian, and think how many millions it contains who are called Christians, who yet know nothing of Catholic unity, except to revile it, and whose religion is not only imperfect and defective according to the Catholic standard, but is also in many points erroneous as well as deficient in the essential doctrines of the faith. And then look, again, to the northern parts even of Europe, and remember how centuries have passed since these also were torn from the bosom of the Church and have never yet been won back to it. And if you look to the South, also, the picture is much the same—it is a picture of separation, division, revolt, ending in permanent alienations and bitter hostility, and, as a consequence of this, miserable declension and unfruitfulness.

Now, my brethren, I am not going to apportion the blame of the state of separation, in which so many self-styled Christians are content to live and to die, as if it were no crime, or sin, or loss, to be separated from the great body of the Church of Christ. I am only concerned with the fact as far as it illustrates the sad words of our Lord in the text before us. Surely it is not too much to say of the state of things which we see before us, that the charity of the many has gone cold. It has grown cold, not simply because there is separation, but because separation has become a normal state of things in which people acquiesce, and of which they think as if it were no harm. People who recite daily or frequently the ancient Creed, in which the notes of the Church are contained as making her One, Holy, Catholic, and Apostolic, talk unconcernedly of the " broken unity of the Catholic Church," as if their very words did not condemn them as putting a new interpretation on the holy words which they utter, and which they profess to believe to be as true as those in which they declare that God is one in Three Persons, the Father, the Son, and the Holy Ghost.

My brethren, consider these truths—we believe that God has planted the See of St. Peter, to be indeed to all the Churches the centre of the true faith, the beacon by which the pure doctrine may be known, the security and the test of orthodoxy. But God has made the See of St. Peter not only the centre of the orthodox faith and Catholic truth, but also, and no less than that, the centre of unity and of charity, as well as of faith and of government. Is not this, as we teach, what our Lord meant when He said to St. Peter thrice over, " Lovest thou Me?" and not till He had the reply and the profession of the Apostle did He give him the promised keys, and make him in His own place the Shepherd of the sheep and of the lambs? Yes, this is the office of the See of that Chief of the Apostles, to be the security of the mutual charity by which Christians are to be bound together before the world and before God, as well as the security of their maintenance of the one faith in all its purity. And with this thought in our minds, let us recall the history of that See in its treatment by the other communities of which Christendom is made up. How early was it that Rome began to be the object of rivalry, of jealousy, of hate? And at this moment, were the East free from the yoke of the misbeliever, to which it has been subjected in the just judgment of God, would it, do you think, run like a long separated and bereaved child to the arms of its mother? Have not the Easterns been known to hug the yoke of the Turk, as a protection against Rome? No; if the East were set free to-morrow, it would require almost a new Pentecost to kindle in those separated brethren of ours the spirit of unity and charity.

But why need we speak of the East, when we have instances of the same truth in our own days and in our own land? Even when there is, in some separated community, a revival of the true Catholic intincts which are so natural in the baptized and cannot altogether be stifled—a yearning for the ancient faith, for Catholic practices and privileges, for long-forgotten sacraments, for rites and prayers which have been cast aside, for greater honour to the sanctuary of God, for the Adorable Sacrifice of the Altar, for the worship of our Lord in the Blessed Sacrament, for the veneration of the saints, for prayers for the departed, and many other portions of the Catholic system, which either have been proscribed by the dominant heresy, or which have withered away, unproscribed, in the Arctic atmosphere of schism—alas! my brethren, is it not true to say, that the love of unity wakes up last of all, and although, as we know with thankfulness, hundreds of souls are thus, by the mercy of God, brought home to the Church, yet that the very leaders themselves of these movements are often the loudest in reviling her, and the most unscrupulous in calumniating her? Are not these the men who go beyond the wildest of ultra-Protestants in their language against her, the men who seem to rival in their malignity the very Pharisees who said that our Lord was in league with Beelzebub, when they tell some poor soul, who is struggling out of their hands into the light, and whom they can stop in no other way, that to submit to Catholic Unity is to commit the unpardonable sin against the Holy Ghost! They may do or believe almost anything, but they must not join the unity of the Church. These leaders will teach, in the face of day, truths on the denial of which their communion was built, and for refusing to deny which hundreds of Catholics have suffered in life and limb. They will preach our doctrines, they will imitate our worship, they will wear the vestments and adopt the religious institutions of Catholicism, as far as it is permitted them so to do. But they have no thought more foreign to their minds, no desire less congenial to their hearts, than the thought of returning to charity, the thought of placing themselves once more in the obedience of the Church, the desire once more to find themselves happy and rejoicing children of him whom our Lord has appointed to be the Chief Shepherd of the Fold. Alas! such movements are among the choicest and rarest gifts that God can bestow on a nation and a generation outside His Church, and on their issue may probably depend the whole fortune of the country in which they appear, and through that, of millions of souls. He who furthers them and interprets them rightly, who follows the "kindly light" to the haven whither it is meant to lead him—what more is required than this faithfulness to number him even among the Saints of God, as well as among the jewels of the Church on earth? But oh! for those who prefer to be leaders of parties, to give their names to sections of divisions of schismatical bodies, rather than to lose themselves in the happy multitudes of the children of the Church! what more than this single perversity is requisite to place their names in the role of the heresiarchs, with Arius and Nestorius and Luther and Calvin and other enemies of the truth and of Jesus Christ? Surely here is enough to make us sadly convinced that the days of charity are gone by, that the zeal of Catholics may still strive hard to win back the wanderers to the fold, and to restore the separated nations to unity, but their efforts will have but scant success, on account of the absence among those for whom they labour of this heavenly fire which our Lord came to kindle upon the earth.

IV.

I pass by the other fruits of charity of which I have made mention, for something in so great a subject must be left to your own meditations. But consider what has been suggested already, my brethren, about the manner in which providential opportunities are presented by God to the Church, which if not seized at the time it is never again within her power to seize. Unless I read history amiss, the life of the Church upon earth has been a series of such opportunities, of which I do not say she has not availed herself, but of which she has been prevented, by this very want of charity of which I speak, from availing herself, at least to an extent which has been sufficient to mar the perfection of her work in the world. Our Lord placed His Church in the old Roman Empire, and with her face, as we may say, to the east, and the north, and the west, and the south, as when it was said to Abraham, that all the land in which he was, in every direction, was to be his. In those early ages the treasures which lay concealed in the far West beyond the Atlantic, and in the far East, beyond the limits to which Alexander had penetrated, and to the south beyond the valley of the Nile, and to the north beyond the forests of Germany, were in great measure unthought of. Our Lord knew when the north was, in the just providence of God, to send down its hordes on the civilized portion of Europe, but He provided for their conversion and gradual assimilation to the nations already Christian by the charity of the conquered West. He knew too when the false prophet was to arise and subdue so fair a portion of the ancestral lands of humanity to his detestable sway, and to meet this contingency there was the Eastern Christendom, which might have coped with him and defied him, but for the spirit of schism and rivalry already rife in its chief sees. The victory fell, in consequence, to falsehood and not to truth. From that moment the realms of Islam have been a circle of fire round the Christian countries; barring their access to the south, barring their access to the east, and, indeed, leaving them but scanty breathing time to think of their own safety. The struggle of Christendom against the infidel power lasted for ages, and if that power was not allowed to overwhelm Europe, and to stamp out what still remained of the visible Kingdom of Jesus Christ, it can hardly be said that even this result was owing to the unity and mutual charity of the Christian nations.

It is a miserable history, my brethren, and I will say now of it no more than is necessary for our immediate subject, which is this—that, when we are asking ourselves about the fulfilment or the failure of the designs of the Sacred Heart of our Lord for the benefit of the world, we must consider, not only whether the hostile powers in the world have been able to destroy His Kingdom, but whether they have been able to hinder its progress and its development during the centuries in which that progress and that development were, in the counsels of God and in the order of His providence, still within the range of possibility—whether, while Christian Europe was as yet one in the faith and in the obedience of the Church, they so hemmed her in, and gave her so much anxiety for her own safety, that she had no power and no opportunity of spreading the truth and the knowledge of our Lord to the furthest ends of the earth. It was not in the counsels of God that the infidel power should become the arbiter of the world, in the sense in which that power belongs to the possessor of an universal monarchy. Something like that may be for a short time at the end of the history of the world. The power of which we are speaking was so internally corrupt and morally degraded that it was sure in the process of time to become even physically effete. But, if I may so say, it throttled the Church of God just during the time when God was preparing for her new kingdoms and new continents, and was about to open to her what may most truly be called new worlds. But the revelation, so to say, of the Western hemisphere, and the opening of the far East to the commerce and the arms of Europe came upon her when the great schism of the North was about to break out, and the Christendom to which these marvellous gifts were made was already divided religiously as well as politically.

It was an opportunity unparalleled in the history of the world, and you know, my brethren, what came of it. The Catholic nations of Portugal and Spain were the first to reach the new fields, opened, alas! not less to the avarice and greed of their children than to their evangelical zeal and enterprise. The Gospel was first disgraced before the eyes of the New World by the lives of those who professed to be guided by its teaching, and, in a short time, the Protestant nations of England and Holland met the Catholic powers on those distant shores and beat them back. It would not be true to say that the far East and the new Continent of America owed nothing, and owe nothing, to the Catholic nations who first discovered them. But even where they had an undivided and unquestioned Empire, the story is one which no Christian can read without shame. And from that time to this, the propagation of the Gospel among the heathen has been paralyzed by the divisions of Christendom, and the poor savages all over the world can laugh at the missionaries who contradict one the other. Now there are no more worlds to discover, no part of the globe which is inhabited by man has been left unveiled and unvisited, except perhaps it be that in the interior of Africa there are countless tribes and populous nations, whose fate as to the reception of the Gospel it is only too easy to predict. There too the ventures of commerce will outstrip the ventures of the apostles of the truth, there too the lives of so-called Christians will turn the hearts of the heathen against all that bears the name of our Lord, there too the rival creeds will be presented side by side, and the truths that the Catholic may preach will be obscured by the calumnies of the Protestant.

Again and again we have to remember, in dealing with facts such as these, that the arm of the Lord is not shortened, and that He can at any time, if it so pleases Him, regenerate the world, and add undreamt of glories to the Church. But these are solemn truths in themselves, and surely they furnish a most instructive commentary on the words of our Lord in the passage of which we are speaking. They may help us to see that the living and all-pervading charity which is the fruit of true unity, is no ornament or accident of the Church and of the Kingdom of our Lord, but its very essence and lifeblood. They make us intensely grateful for the gift which we have in

I

the Church of this true charity and unity, and they prompt us to pray ever more earnestly for the increase of this precious gift, in the sense in which it admits of increase and further perfection, in the sense in which the Church speaks when she puts daily into the mouths of her priests at the Holy Sacrifice the prayer, that according to His will God will vouchsafe to " pacificate and unite His Church "—*eamque secundum voluntatem tuam pacificare et coadunare digneris*. They let us see not only the hatefulness, but also the mischievousness, of the great sin, which inflicted so deadly a wound on the Kingdom of our Lord in the sixteenth century, the sin of schism—malignant enough in its outrage on our Lord's Heart, not less malignant in the desolation it brings on His Kingdom.

These truths suggest also an answer to the question that is in our minds all along with regard to the days in which we live. They are days of cultivation, and refinement, and of a kind of benevolence and softness, days in which men extend their tenderness to animals, invent a thousand remedies or preventives for bodily pain, and turn away with the tenderness of girls from the sight of blood. But for the Divine charity, the work of the Holy Ghost in the hearts of the faithful, the charity of the Beloved Disciple, who speaks so strongly of the enormity of the sin of division, for this the days in which we live have no name but that of bigotry and intolerance. As far as the eye of man can see, schism has set up its throne all over the Christian world, and it is no longer even thought of as the throne of an usurper. To thousands of Christians the Unity of the Church of God remains in the Creed, but it remains nowhere else, and they deny it in their lives while they profess it with their lips. The last days may not be yet. But if the decay of charity is their mark and their characteristic, the last days can hardly surpass, in this detestable note, the days in which we live.

SERMON VI.

THE NATIONAL SPIRIT.

Consurget enim gens in gentem, et regnum in regnum.
Nation shall rise against nation, and kingdom against kingdom.
(Words taken from the 7th verse of the 24th chapter of St. Matthew's Gospel.)

I.

THESE words of our Lord may have sounded more strange and alarming in the ears of those who first heard them, than in our own. We are already accustomed to this feature of the latter days which our Lord here speaks of, but it was not so with the men of the generation in which He came on earth. It has always been considered as a special action of Providence in those days, that the whole world was at peace. For a short time the old prophecy had come true which the Psalmist had spoken, that God had "done wonders upon earth, making wars to cease even to the end of the earth."* The temple of Janus, as men said, was closed. But not only was the temple closed, signifying thereby that the great Roman Empire was not at that time disturbed by any external foe. The mere existence of that great Empire was a security for the peace of all

* Psalm xlv. 9, 10.

the various nations and tribes of which it was made up. It was in the midst of the great Pax Romana, as it was called, that the Church of Jesus Christ was first set up to lead the nations, and to weld them together by a more secure, a more abiding, a more happy tie. God made use of the peace of the Empire to facilitate the progress and advance the establishment of the Church. Peace not only enabled the Apostles to pass without hindrance from one part of the Empire to another, it not only secured them all the individual liberty and protection which belonged, as of right, to the subjects of that Empire as long as they obeyed its laws. It did far more, because it enabled them to address themselves to populations far better prepared to listen to them than if they had been full of the excitements and passions of political conflicts, or of the jealousies, hatreds, and furies of national strife, and suffering under the dangers and desolations of war. Peace has always been more or less necessary for the advance of the Church, for the spread of her system of charity from land to land, as well for the active life of that system in the government of her hierarchy, the legislation of her councils, the exercise over all the world of the authority of her central throne.

It is most remarkable, dear brethren, that the Church of God was first founded in the midst of a people of the most intense nationality— and, as if in this also there had been a design of Providence to remove a great possible impediment to her progress, the nation which had given birth to the Church, drove her from its doors, and forced her, or would have forced her, if that had not been her wish, to repudiate and go counter to the nationality of her first teachers and founders. Thus the peace of the nations under the sway of Rome was the rule of the world when our Lord spoke these words. And it was so, in consequence of a distinct Divine provision for the facilitating the work of His Church. It was a hard stern yoke to the rebellious, a gentle yoke to the submissive, and no one without the gift of prophetic vision could have foretold this change which was to come, a change so momentous and so fraught with danger and alarm that it was worth the while of our Blessed Lord to point it out as one of the features of the dreadful days which were at hand. "Nation shall rise against nation, and kingdom against kingdom." That is, to use the language of our own day, there shall then be a great development of national life, national unity, national vigour—and not only this, but this development shall unlock, not merely the patriotic instincts of nations, but their combative instincts also. It is not only that nations shall be great, but that they shall be continually at issue with one another, there shall be wars and rumours of wars, nation rising against and assailing nation, one kingdom making war on another, and this is to be as much a sign of terror as the pestilences and famines and earthquakes which are to accompany it.

Now I say, my brethren, that it is surely remarkable that we should find among the features of the last time as revealed to us beforehand by our Lord, a thing with which we are so familiar that we consider it to belong to the normal condition of society in the modern world. The very fact that the words of our Lord proclaim nothing that surprises us may be considered as a proof that, in this respect at least, our days are not different from those of the generation on which the Judgment is to come. We are so accustomed to the sight of nation rising against nation, and kingdom against kingdom, that we wonder what there can be in this to make our Lord fix on it as a mark of the approach of the last time: what He calls the "beginning of travails"—of those terrible birth-pangs out of which the new creation, the new Heaven and earth, are to come forth after the purification of all things. If, therefore, all that it concerned us to notice as to these words of our Lord were to point out the resemblance of our days to the last days in this respect, I might stop at once here, and we should have added one more proof to our argument that the signs of the Judgment Day might come immediately on us, without any want of fulfilment in the predictions which relate to the moral, social, and religious condition of the world in that last period. And this is all the more true, because we look on the spirit which will produce the conflicts of nations of which we hear in these words of our Lord, as on a thing good in itself, and we regard the state of mutual hatred and division which is thus engendered as an accident which must necessarily follow from the development of national unity and national life—an accident in itself, perhaps, deplorable, but still not without its good results in the exertions to which it leads, in the bracing and stimulating effect of such energies as are called forth by a state of warfare. Thus we are both content with the things in themselves of which our Lord speaks, and we should consider it a loss to be deprived altogether of the principle from which these phenomena proceed. The reign of universal charity has no charms for us, and we prefer the vigorous national life which we enjoy, even with all its cruel side of bloodthirstiness and malignant hatred, to the shallow sentimental cosmopolitanism which, except the principle of charity, is its only possible substitute.

II.

This being the case, my brethren, there is all the more reason for our dwelling a little on this prediction of our Lord, much as it may astonish us to hear the national spirit, with which we are all so familiar, classed among the features of the last times, along with the establishment of a false creed as to God, and the universe, and the human soul, or even with the decay of charity, with which decay, in truth, this instinct, or feeling, or passion, or principle of nationalism has a great deal to do. And perhaps it is well for us to dwell on it all the more here because it might almost be said that there are many Christian and Catholic Churches in the world, in which it would hardly be safe, even for a Christian preacher, to speak the whole truth about the spirit of nationalism. For it has come to this in the times in which we live, that on the one hand, the Christian bond between nations is altogether ignored, and on the other, the Christian principles, which ought to regulate their mutual dealings, whether of friendship or of controversy, are ignored also. It is no longer a misery that one Christian nation, as such, should quarrel with another, and also we hear no longer of Christian principles as swaying the councils of Christian nations, we no longer hear of justice, and respect for right, and mutual charity, as regulating the intercourse of the masses of Christians one with another. The charity of Jesus Christ would be laughed at, if it were invoked as a principle of public action.

What we hear of is national policy, national aggrandizement, the paramount duty of the strong to secure the power which they have received or acquired, it matters not by what means, and the corresponding necessity for the weak to submit and make way for the strong, especially when the strong write on their banners the motto of nationality. Religion, truthfulness, faithfulness to engagements, a regard for the just rights of others—these are well enough, we are told, for the guidance of individuals in their dealings with other men, but when they come to be applied to the direction of nations and of empires, they are the mere expressions of sentiment and cant. And the popular writers of the day treat those who speak of nations as having any Christian duties at all, whether as to the advance of the Kingdom of Christ, or as to the observance of His Law among themselves, with a mixture of hatred and contempt quite unexampled. The spiritual world, the invisible world, there is the dominion of God, they seem to say, but why are we to have His laws interfering in the domain of men, the world in which we live? We are Catholics and Christians in our private capacities, but as members of human polities we are Englishmen, Irishmen, Frenchmen, and the rest. Our first duties are to our nation, and to our country, and if the Church and our religion come across the interests of these, the Church and our religion must be swept away. Language of this kind is not, perhaps, always used with perfect plainness and openness, but it is sometimes used, and the principle which it expresses influences large numbers of souls who would be shocked and afraid to adopt all its consequences. And, in the same way, men who are Christians and Catholics themselves, and who would be the first to repudiate the almost atheistic language of those to whom the profession of public morality is the same thing as cant and sentiment, are yet most fatally influenced by the same spirit of nationalism in another way. They use their personal weight, and such means of influencing others as they possess, not merely to set up the national spirit as an idol, but also to intensify and hound on to action the national hatreds and feelings of vengeance, which, the history of the world being what it is, are the natural and necessary growth of the conflicts and rivalries of which the world is full.

Influences of this kind, my brethren, cannot prevail in the hearts of large masses of men without writing their effects in the history of the world, and what they so write is the record of a perpetual struggle between half a score of giants, a struggle which can have no issue until one devours the remainder, and in the meanwhile, we have the fulfilment of the prediction of our Lord in the text, "Nation rising against nation, and kingdom against kingdom." For there are only two ways conceivable by which we can hope to see prevented a state of endless conflict among powers more or less equal. The requirements of justice and right must either be enforced, against the law of might, by some iron external bond holding peoples together without mutual destruction, or by some strong internal principle, such as that of religion. The first does not exist, and the second, the principle brought into the world by our Lord, and intended by Him to be the fundamental principle of the community of Christian nations, as well of each polity in its separate life, that is just the principle which provokes the hatred of the public writers of whom I speak, who cannot help knowing that it has once ruled the world, and fearing that perhaps it may yet claim to rule the world again. These men know that the old spirit of Christendom, in the best sense of the name, is dead among modern nations, but they cannot help knowing also the intrinsic vitality and power of anything that comes from the Sacred Heart of our Lord, and they tremble lest the dead should once again live in modern Europe, and that a new period of domination of the Gospel of Christ may perchance set in.

This being the case, my brethren, as to the manner in which the world is now inclined to look on the only principle which can practically restrain that appetite for mutual destruction, which sometimes seems to characterize the nations of the earth almost as much as it characterizes the beasts of the field and the forest, and, on the other hand, it being also the case that the nations of the modern world are far more powerful, far more military, far better armed and equipped for this deadly purpose than their ancestors, it does not seem rash to predict that we may at any time find ourselves in an era of internecine warfare, of which the history of our race has scarcely any precedent. We are richer, more populous, better equipped, more aggressive than our forefathers, and a single campaign of two great modern armies can accomplish an amount of destruction of life and property as great as that which resulted, in former times, from long protracted warfare. Thus both the motives and the instruments of destruction have been reinforced, and the restraining power of the public conscience has been as notably enfeebled in us. Thus there is abundant reason for the fulfilment of our Lord's words, nations are more able and more likely than ever to rise against one another, and there is less hope of restraining them.

III.

But there ought not to be any exaggerations in treating of a subject of this kind, in this place, and perhaps we shall see that here also we have another instance of the truth that the greatest miseries in human affairs ordinarily come, not from causes and motives absolutely bad, but from the exaggeration of partial goods and the exclusive urging of subordinate rights. So we must lay as the foundation of all our considerations on this subject, the truth that the national feeling in itself is a good feeling, it is founded on the ordinance of God, and it has produced, and may still produce, both in the hearts of single persons and in the hearts of great masses of mankind, many noble and glorious deeds, much self-devotion and self-sacrifice, virtues on the exercise of which God reckons, if we may say so, in His government of the human race. God, as you have so often been told, is the author and the supporter and maintainer of human society—of the natural society of men, as well as of the supernatural society into which they are gathered in His Church. But, while He has made the Church one and indivisible, though she is meant to contain in her unity the children of all the nations and tribes and languages upon earth, He has not made the human society, outwardly, one and indivisible, as it might be if all the world were one great union or republic, or an empire under one head and with one form of government.

St. Paul, to whom we have so constantly to refer on this subject, and who is so fond of dwelling on the Providence of God in His dealings with society, tells us in his speech at Athens that God Who made heaven and earth, and all things, has made of one all nations to dwell on the face of the earth, determining their "appointed times and the limits of their habitation."* And we can imagine, dear brethren, many beautiful and beneficent designs of Almighty God in this arrangement, both for the

* Acts xvii. 26.

good of men and for His own greater glory. His Kingdom is always a Kingdom of variety, a Kingdom in which there is no dead uniformity or unbroken equality in external gifts, no endless repetition of the same types and forms of characters, as when a brickmaker makes millions on millions of bricks or tiles all of the same size and shape. That lifeless, blank uniformity is the characteristic of the works of man, not of God. As He has made the visible world so multifarious in its variety, so that in this one little globe on which we live there are so many thousands of types and species of life and organization, or climate, or configuration, or production, blended together to make up the whole of our petty universe, so He has made mankind, as St. Paul says, of one stock, and yet He has divided them into great natural portions, more like than unlike one to another, and yet separate in their places of abode, their forms of social life, their polities, their nationalities.

And it is one of the most precious results of this distribution of various gifts and products on the part of God, that the various regions of the earth, so to say, need one another, and contribute to the wellbeing one of another, and this serves to create fresh ties of brotherhood, and fresh occasions of mutual assistance among men of different climates. So too, in the moral and intellectual order, the several nations and empires have their Providential purposes and offices. Egypt, and India, and Greece, and Rome, and Italy, and France, and Spain, and England, and Germany, to speak of no others, have each contributed in their turn to the education, the development, the civilization, the welfare of the race. So too in the Catholic Church, as we may well say, the various races and nations and classes of mind and genius have their office, and great glory to God and good to man result from their original diversities, that the great wonder of the Day of Pentecost, ever lasting on in the Church, might be possible, and that she might have the glory of bringing them all into subjection to her unity, blended in one harmonious world-wide community and empire, of which the Gospel of Jesus Christ was to be the law and the bond of peace!

Those pregnant words of the Apostle to which I just now referred, involve a whole range of truths on which the true theory, so to say, of nationalities might be raised—the unity of the race, the Divine origin of society, and of separate and distinct societies, their mutual duties and rights, the appointed place which they are to fill in the great plan of God for the history of the world, their allotted dwellings and the times, as he says, of their habitation. The government of God over the various nations which He has set on the face of the earth, makes up the Christian philosophy of history, and the principles of this history are sketched for us by the hand of inspiration in the successive books of the Old Testament. These principles, rightly understood, reveal to us many things concerning God of which we might otherwise have been ignorant, just as the Apostle tells us that the Church, in her course through the world, reveals to the heavenly dwellers around the throne of God secrets of His wisdom which they might not otherwise know. And if this is so, then it follows, without further need of proof, that the citizens of each state have duties to the whole community, which in a certain sense and for them inherits the rights and authority which God has conferred on human society at the beginning. This truth is the foundation of all civil authority. Thus it is that the Apostle lays down so strongly the doctrine that "(the powers) that are are ordained of God; therefore, he that resisteth the power resisteth the ordinance of God."* It is this truth, again, that places our obedience to the laws under which we live under the sanction of conscience, as St. Paul says in another place. And, finally, it is this truth that limits and defines the duties which we owe to our country, and to the Government under which God has placed us, and as it points to the wickedness of rebellion, so also does it secure the due subordination of allegiance. Thus, if this truth were rightly understood, there could not be among Christians that exaggeration of the rights of patriotism of which we have to speak. For this truth implies the higher unity of the human race, and the fellowship of nations, as founded on that higher unity. It involves mutual duties on the part of one community of men to all the rest, and, above all, it implies the absolute supremacy of the law of God over the human law of our country, and, in consequence, the subordination of the natural human society to the super-

* Romans xiii. 2.

natural empire of the Catholic Church, in all points and on all subjects as to which there can possibly be between them either contact or collision. And thus it is that the very same great doctrine, of the Divine origin and rights of society and of country, which puts our allegiance to these on the one true and solid foundation, also secures, or ought to secure, us against the abuse and exaggeration of these claims of country and patriotism which, when exaggerated, lead to conduct positively bad and wicked. It requires no more than this truth to make us see that Christian countries have their duties one to another, that nationalism in regard of the Catholic Church is a monstrosity and a heresy, and that to set our country before the Church or before the moral law is a sin against God.

My brethren, the Christian philosopher might have much to say to you about the designs of Providence in this particular ordinance of its goodness, but on these points it is not our business to dwell this morning. It is enough for us to know that this condition of our existence here is as much ordained by God as any other of the natural conditions of our existence, and that, in consequence of its Divine origin, it brings with it a whole cluster of duties and affections which it would be unnatural and wrong of us to disregard. It is the very essence of the mischief of an exaggerated and unbalanced spirit of nationalism, that it abuses things which are in themselves sacred. I have said that the nation to which we belong immediately represents to us the human society, with all its rights and claims, which

J

God has established on earth, and on which indeed, in a very true sense, He has engrafted and built the supernatural society of the Church. To say this, is to say quite enough to justify the natural and instinctive love which we all bear to the nation and country to which we belong. For how can we ever exhaust in our gratitude and devotion, the true claims on both involved in that great gift and blessing of society in the natural order? But, inasmuch as this love and duty are founded on the arrangements of Divine Providence, it follows certainly that our duty and our devotion to our nation cannot be directed and ruled by anything but by the law of God, and that they must therefore be subordinated to the great law of justice, truth, faithfulness, charity, regard for the rights of others, and the like, which God has written in the hearts of all His children. It follows, also, that we have duties to human society, not simply as represented to us by a single national unity, large or small, to which we may happen to belong, but that we also have duties to the whole of human society as such, to the universal race of man, and that nations are bound by duty one to another, and this even apart from that new law of brotherhood by which all men are united together in Jesus Christ. And how is it possible to measure the amount and intensity of the happiness which might be spread all over the face of the earth, if this great ordinance of God were honoured as it ought to be honoured?

Thus our national duty and patriotism can never override the law of God, which enacts that obedience to rulers on which St. Paul most strongly insists, any more than this can override the law and the duty which are upon us as members of the Church. And, again, it is clear that we do not fulfil the duties which are incumbent upon us, in consequence of this arrangement of Providence, if our affections and interests and benevolence and beneficence know no wider range than that of the single human society to which we belong as members of this or of that particular nation. Just as our first natural affections are given to the members of our own family, and yet we are bound, even by the natural law, to feel and act in a kindly and brotherly way to the members of other families outside our own, so are we bound not to let our own affections stop short with the seas or mountains or rivers, or the still slighter boundaries, which separate us from other nations. We are bound, even by natural charity, to remember that we are not created Englishmen or Frenchmen or Irishmen, but men, and that when God decreed that we should belong to our own national unity, He also decreed that others of our brethren should form other national unities, and that all these several unities should be like the brothers in a family, or like the various families in a city, bound together by mutual ties, over and above those by which the members of each family are linked to one another.

IV.

This is enough to say now, my brethren, in order to pay that tribute of honour to the national spirit, to loyalty, to love of country, which they deserve. Nor have there ever been more true patriots, or men who have done more, or suffered more, for these, than the true Catholic heroes who have still set the law of God and the rights of the Church far above the claims and interests which are, after all, interests and claims but of this world. Alas! how easy it is to invert the relative position and dignity of the natural and the supernatural, how easy it is to make country and loyalty the pretext for rebellion against God! These subordinate claims can never be kept in their proper place except by the true Christian spirit and the true Catholic doctrine. And as these last die away in their influence on the powerful nations which they have mainly served to create and foster, the old natural Pagan spirit, and the old heathen views on these subjects, must assuredly revive, and then the world cannot be far from that state of things of which the words in the text are the mournful prophecy. Substitute for Christian patriotism what goes by that name in the Pagan system of society, and you turn the antechamber of Paradise into the resemblance of Hell. With the Christian, patriotism is the law of charity applied to national relationships, with the Pagan it is the law of selfishness written in larger letters.

Let us spend a moment on this contrast. The Christian loves his country for the sake of God's ordinance, and for the many benefits which he receives from its laws and its protection. He loves it for the sake of conscience, and therefore not more than his conscience. He knows that he must obey God rather than man. He knows that he will lose his soul if he makes his patriotism an excuse for hatred against his fellow-men, for violence, for revengefulness, and other bad passions. He knows that he is a citizen of a higher and nobler unity, the Kingdom of God in this world and in the next. He is a Christian first, and after that, and in harmony with the duties and the charity which that name implies, he is an Englishman or an Irishman or a Frenchman. The Pagan knew none of these qualifications to his love for his country. His country or his city was to him a divinity, it was the highest unity and polity that he knew. Its interests overrode his conscience, its commands justified sin. He read his own duty in that bad sense of which our Lord complains in the Sermon on the Mount, "thou shalt love thy neighbour and hate thine enemy," and all outside his city walls were enemies to him. His country could do no wrong, commit no injustice—its gods were his, its religion his, it was a crime to set anything in the world higher than what its service required. This is the explanation of the conduct of the Pagan persecutors of the Church in the early centuries, many of whom were virtuous men according to the heathen standard; the proconsuls and prætors who ordered the torture or the execution of the Christian martyrs, did so because they saw in them enemies of the divinity of the Empire. And when in this country of ours, three centuries ago, Elizabeth and her Ministers persuaded themselves that it was high treason to offer Mass or to remain firm in allegiance to the Holy See, it was on the same principle of the supremacy of the country over every other right, or law, or person, or institution, to which allegiance might be due by the law of God or of man.

My brethren, it is hardly worth while to ask whether the nationalism of the days in which we live is a Pagan nationalism or a Christian nationalism. Nationalism is in itself a partial principle, a principle of unity up to a certain point, but also it is a principle of separation from all that is outside that unity. It is also a principle which belongs entirely to this present stage in the condition of mankind, and in this sense it is of the earth, earthy. It needs, therefore, to be accompanied by, and even subordinated to, other and higher principles, the principle of the law of God, the authority of conscience, the brotherhood of men, the confraternity of nations, and, above all, since our Lord came, the principle that we are all citizens of a larger and more universal unity than any national unity, the Catholic Church, in which there is neither Greek nor Jew, barbarian, Scythian, bond nor free. Thus, in the older dispensation of the government of the world by God before the coming of Christ, it was the rule of His Providence, not indeed to extinguish or suppress national unities, but still to subordinate them in great measure to a succession of great Empires, which rose one after the other, and which are described at great length in the prophecies of Daniel, who lived under the earlier of them. Such was the Providence of God in the old world, before the Christian times, and it is foretold by the same Prophet that the Roman Empire was to be succeeded by another Kingdom which should not be taken away. That is, the

Kingdom of the Catholic Church was to absorb the subject races of all the former great Empires, and to mould them into one great people, thus preserving their national unities and at the same time keeping them in due subordination, and brotherhood, and peace.

This is the work committed to the holy Catholic Church and it has been with this as with all the other great powers and offices committed to her. That is, she has shown that she is able to do the work for the benefit of the world which has been committed to her, as a witness to all nations, and then the revolt has come, and she has not been permitted to accomplish it. And surely it is easy to understand how this must be so, if we consider the other features of the last days of which I have already spoken. Nationalism is a good and a healthy principle, as long as it is not paramount and alone, as it was in the ancient pagan times, and it cannot be paramount and alone as long as the religion of Christ retains its hold on peoples and nations. But let any false infidel creed, such as that of which I spoke in a former sermon, rule the world, and all the religious and moral checks upon this undue magnification and deification of nationalism are taken away. Again, the peace and concord of Christian states, even in the temporal order, and the due subordination of all principles of secondary rank, such as this, are secure, as long as the charity of Christians all through the world remains fervent and glowing. But let schism rule, let charity grow cold, in the hearts of the many, and then the gentle constraining influence of the Catholic Church is gone, and men are left to those natural and partial principles, of which nationalism is the most potent. So that when a false religion, or atheism, dominates the world, and the charity even of multitudes of Christians is chilled, then is the time for the undue and violent reign of this principle of nationalism of which our Lord speaks. Then nation shall rise against nation, and kingdom against kingdom, because men will recognize no higher principle than that of a material, temporal, and visible unity, and of all such principles national patriotism is the noblest and the most powerful.

And, again, why need I add, that this is what we see before our eyes. We see the civilized world, which boasts itself of its enlightenment and refinement, made up of a set of gigantic nationalities, some already formed, some in process of formation. We have ourselves seen the formation of the Italian Unity, carried out under circumstances of violence, injustice, mendacity, treachery of the blackest kind, with the additional feature of persecution of the Church in her Head. We have seen the formation of German Unity. We are witnessing the formation of other unities also. Even Catholic peoples are taught to set their political independence above every other right, to seek the accomplishment of their nationality by outrages on law, by assassination, by attacks on the fundamental principles of society, by leaguing themselves with those secret conspiracies against governments which are proscribed by the Catholic Church. And we see the nations armed to the teeth, their peace establishments, as they are called, surpassing in numbers even the almost fabulous hosts which Xerxes led to the conquest of Greece. We see all civilized countries groaning under the burthen of their own armies, which call the peasant from the field, the artisan from the loom, the child from the parent, the husband from the wife, the Levite from the seminary, even the priest from the altar—and all this is made necessary by the ambition, the distrust, the mutual hatred of Christian nations! What more is wanted to fulfil our Lord's prediction, but that some "scourge of God," in one of the Cabinets of Europe, should give the signal for general conflict, and hasten on the final catastrophe of the world by letting loose the plague of war?

V.

Sad as this picture is in itself, my brethren, it is still sadder when we consider it as a contrast to that on which our Lord's Sacred Heart may have dwelt, as made possible by what He had suffered and won for us, and by what He was to leave behind Him in His Church when He rose to Heaven, to prepare for us there that one happy country of which all of us are made citizens by Him. You have already had set before you the contrast that must be allowed to exist between the glories of the spiritual kingdom of our Lord in this world, as He designed them, the universal peaceful reign of the Catholic Church over the whole earth, and that stunted, shattered, partial, though still heavenly and Divine dominion which she has been allowed to establish for the benefit of mankind. And I do not know whether there is a greater and a sadder difference between the spiritual victories of grace and charity in the hearts of men, as they ought to have been, and as they are, than there is between the state of the community, if community it can be called, of Christian nations as it ought to have been or as it might have been, and as it is. Faith is all but gone, and charity is dying away, and the consequence is seen in the world as well as in the Church. It requires a stout heart indeed to hope against so much discouragement. But in regard to our subject to-day, at least our duties are clear, and I suppose no thoughtful person will deny that our dangers are very great. Our dangers are great, because our country and nation have always great and pressing claims on our devotion, claims which are always tending to become more and more exclusive, as the union between the members of the greater and nobler country to which we belong, the Catholic Church, the Kingdom of Jesus Christ, becomes feebler and less recognized. Our dangers are great, because in many cases, to speak of Catholic peoples in general, their country has been oppressed and trodden under foot, and often mainly on account of its religion, and then the tempter comes and suggests thoughts of hatred against the descendants of those who have injured their ancestors, or of the achievement of liberty by unlawful means, ending in the nurturing in their souls of the most detestable and unChristian spirit that can harbour in a mortal's heart, the spirit of revenge at the cost of crime. And again our dangers are great, even if we are not among what are called the oppressed nationalities, because every generation, in the history of modern Europe, has bequeathed to those who come after it the traditions of former struggles, or struggles in its own day, and thus there are many deadly hatreds now burning in souls which think that they are the children of God, hatreds which have absolutely no ground in nature except these traditions. Strange indeed are the doctrines behind which Christian men are fain to shelter, as if it mattered in the sight of God whether we hate our brother in Jesus Christ on account of his nationality or on account of anything else, as if the sentence which will condemn the unforgiving and the revengeful to eternal death, would take any account of the grounds on which this wicked passion was founded!

Are we not justified in thinking that it was with some special design of His ineffable wisdom and compassion, that, when our Lord had to draw the picture of charity in the parable of the man who fell among thieves, He made the person who practised to him that charity which it was His own object to recommend, one of a nation hostile to and hated by the Jews. And when He bade His questioner "go and do likewise," He surely meant to teach us that national differences and the traditions of old wrongs, were things as difficult, and yet as necessary for us to overcome, as other selfish motives, such as those which steeled against the poor sufferer the hearts of the Priest and the Levite of whom He spoke. The positive side of patriotism is good in itself as far as it goes, but it is, as I have said, partial and petty and unenlightened, for it may be as strong in the heart of the Eskimo or of the inhabitant of the poorest and barrenest island in the Pacific, as it is in the heart of the Englishman or the Frenchman. What can our country give us which is not given us in a far higher and nobler measure by our true country, our true mother, the Catholic Church? Is it a glorious ancestry, or a history starred by heroic deeds and examples of virtue, public and private? Is it liberty, or great privileges, or dignity, or influence, or power, or peace in our possessions, or security against loss and injury and injustice, or a share in the greatness and the goodness of the truly great and the truly good? Is it happiness and nobility here, and the prospect of far greater honours and blessings hereafter? All these things the Catholic Church confers on all her children, and she makes them children of the Father of our Lord, and fellow-citizens with the Angels and Saints, besides linking them in an indissoluble unity with all that is noble and great and virtuous and spiritual in the world. A grander thing this, my brethren, even than that which was imagined as the privilege of the Roman citizen of old, that he might go over the whole world and find his rights respected wherever the sun shone! How foolish to cast away the rights of the heavenly country, which are dependent on the exercise of charity, for the sake of supposed claims of an idol of Paganism which we call our country, or rather, not for devotion to that idol, but for the sake of hatred of everything else which is not it! Alas! my brethren, the words of our Lord are but too prophetic of the effects which this love of country are to have on the world into which He sent His Church to mould all nations into one great polity. He does not foresee how nation will help nation, and kingdom assist and benefit kingdom. That is the intention of God in making these lesser unities, unities which are to last for a time and then to pass away for eternity. But instead of this our Lord looks on, and He sees them rising against and striving to exterminate one the other. Their patriotism is a cloud with a slender lining of silver light, the rest of which is dark and black, with thunder or hail or storm in its bosom, ready to be shed forth on the plains below. The positive good of it is not very great, and it lasts but for a moment. But what a misery, then, that it should have so large a negative side—that for one ounce of charity, so to speak, that it engenders, it should have the power of giving birth to thousands of malice and of hate! that it should spoil the fairest promise of the heritage of the Church, by making the rule of her universal charity and the onward progress of her empire impossible, on account of the jealousies and animosities of which it is the parent—that it should be able to pour the poison of mutual hatred even into the hearts of the children of God and the brethren of our Lord Jesus Christ!

SERMON VII.*

THE ABOMINATION OF DESOLATION.

Cum ergo videritis abominationem desolationis . . . stantem in loco sancto.

You shall see the abomination of desolation . . . standing in the holy place.

(Words taken from the 15th verse of the 24th chapter of St. Matthew's Gospel.)

I.

THESE words are taken, as you know, dear brethren in Jesus Christ, from the last prophecy of our Lord delivered to His Apostles, two days before the Passion, as He sat on the Mount of Olives, gazing upon the magnificent Temple in which He had taught for the last time. And you know that that great prophecy contains two distinct parts, in answer to the twofold question which had been addressed to Him, referring in the first place to the approaching destruction of Jerusalem as a punishment for the crimes of the nation which was about to put Him to death, and in the second place to that still more dreadful judgment of God which is to fall on the whole world immediately before the coming of our Lord in power at His second Advent. Now these words of the text, and the first part of the

* Preached on the last Sunday after Pentecost, November 23, 1874.

Gospel which I have read to you, refer primarily and directly to that first question as to the destruction of Jerusalem, and so they have had their fulfilment in what took place at that time. The latter part of the Gospel of to-day refers to the second question, to the signs which our Lord gives as those which shall go before His last great manifestation as the Judge of all the earth. And you know that there is a principle in God's government of the world which brings as it were both the parts of this prophecy into one, which causes the words which apply to the first event to have a true meaning with regard to the second event, and makes the prophetic signs of His last Advent apply in a certain measure to the great chastisement of the Jewish nation. The principle is this, that God in human history, both in what He does and in what He permits, acts in a manner which repeats itself, and on this account the earlier of these great catastrophes is a sort of prophecy and anticipation of the latter, in that there are features in the one which belong also to the other, and thus the words which predict the one may serve as predictions and descriptions of the other. This is remarkable all through this prophecy of our Lord, though of course it is possible and necessary to separate off what belongs to the destruction of Jerusalem from that which belongs to the destruction of the world. There are certain things peculiar to each as well as certain things common to both, and certain things which are more perfectly fulfilled in one and yet have their less perfect fulfilment in the other.

Now, this saying of our Lord's in the text about the abomination of desolation is one of these last. If it were entirely past and gone, I do not know that the Church would select it for us on this Sunday, when she wishes particularly to turn our thoughts to the future, and to the holy season of Advent, which is now at hand, one of the occupations and duties of which is to prepare ourselves for the second coming of our Lord. Therefore, though the abomination of desolation of which our Lord speaks may have been seen at the time of the siege of Jerusalem, I shall consider it this morning as something to which we may turn our thoughts and look forward as what may come upon us at the end of the world; and not only that, but as something which may be fulfilled even now in our own days, though our own days be not the last. I say that there may be a fulfilment of this saying of our Lord's now as well as at the end of time, for this reason. Not only is it true that these great judgments of God, and these great developments of evil which God has permitted and will permit in His wisdom and in His justice, resemble one the other in so many of their main features, that the prediction of the one is so often the prediction of the other, but it is also true that the reason which underlies this fact is the reason for other repetitions and anticipations also, which may occur during the whole interval of time which makes up the life of the Church and human history. The reason why these two great events resemble each other is, that, in the main, there are always the same elements working for the benefit or the detriment of human society and the Church. Man is always like himself, Satan is always the same, and God is the same in His justice and providence, by which He permits certain rebellions against Himself and His ordinances, and then chastises men, as our Lady says, "in the imagination of their hearts," punishing them in those very things in which they have risen in rebellion against Him. And though He allows Satan more at one time and less at another, and interferes according to His own inscrutable counsels, as He wills, with special manifestations of His mercy and goodness, in answer to the wants and sufferings of His servants and the prayers of His Church in Heaven and on earth, still there is a sameness and a repetition in the great features of human history which give to a prophecy such as this a manifold interpretation. The Scriptural authority for this is well known to you, for it has to be constantly repeated in these discourses. When St. John says, that though Antichrist is to come, as the Christians to whom he writes have heard, yet even then in his time there were many Antichrists,[*] and if that were true then, it has been true ever since. Thus there are continual fulfilments, century after century, of the chief features of our Lord's great prophecy, false Christs and false prophets, kingdom rising against kingdom, days of woe and tribulation, and thus, to come again to our text, though the abomination of desolation spoken of by Daniel, stood in the holy place at the time of Titus, and though there is to be a final corres-

---

[*] St. John ii. 18.

ponding manifestation of the power of evil and dominion of profanity in the latter days, still we may also have in our own time evils and dangers and embodiments of abomination against which we have to warn ourselves and to contend, which correspond to this and other features of the dark picture which our Lord has drawn of what was to be in the final desolation of Jerusalem, and of what is to be again more fully and more dreadfully at the end of time.

II.

And now, dear brethren, what is this abomination of desolation standing in the holy place, which our Lord gives as a sign of the approaching destruction of Jerusalem, and which shall be again at the end? There seems little reason for doubt that the words, both here and in Daniel, refer to the ensigns and eagles of the armies of the Roman Empire, the standards with images of the Emperors which were treated with idolatrous homage in the camps, and which, shortly before the final overthrow of Jerusalem and of the Jewish polity, were to be seen ostentatiously displayed around the Holy City as if in defiance of the religious feelings of the Jews. In our Lord's own time, and during the period in which the Jewish nation dwelt in peace under the dominion of Rome, the conquerors, as was their wont, so far respected the religion of their subjects, that they never displayed their standards in Jerusalem or in the Temple, and also refrained themselves from entering except into that part of the building which was open to all Gentiles.* For, in general, the rule of Rome was wise and moderate as well as firm, and it was a part of that policy which won for her the empire of the world to indulge and conciliate her subjects as far as it was compatible with the well-being of her government so to do. But when the time came for a war of extermination to be declared, when the Romans had determined to keep no terms with the Jews, but to trample down the whole place and nation, they no longer used any moderation or reserve, and they outraged the feelings of those whom they were determined to exterminate by the display of their standards on the hills all around the city, and at last in the Temple itself, just as Baltassar the Babylonian King insulted God by drinking with his wives and concubines out of the sacred vessels which had been brought from the Temple of Jerusalem. This was the profanation which our Lord speaks of as the abomination of desolation, and in the latter days we are taught to expect something similar, for we are told by St. Paul that the Antichrist, the great enemy of God, and the rival, if we may so speak, of our Lord Jesus Christ, "will lift himself above all that is called God and worshipped, and will seat himself in the Temple of God, in the holy place, showing himself as if he were God." † That will be here-

---

* See Corn. à Lapide and Grotius *in loc.* Grotius give the passages from Tacitus and Josephus which justify the interpretation. Pontius Pilate began his government of Judæa by entering Jerusalem with standards flying, but he was prevailed upon to withdraw them (Merivale, *Romans under the Empire*, c. xlvi.).

† 2 Thess. ii. 4.

after, dear brethren in Jesus Christ; we know not how soon or at how long a distance of time. What is most important to us is to see what may be those workings of the antichristian spirit in our own time which may issue in something which we are bound to resist and to detest, as we should the abomination of desolation itself if it were to come about in our own day.

And now perhaps, dear brethren, you will say we are far enough indeed from Roman ensigns, images of the imperial state rulers, honoured with idolatrous worship, and far enough also from such a portent and monster as an impious child of Adam, so inflated by earthly success and power as to set himself up as an object of worship in the Temple of God. Yes, by the mercy of God, such things appear to us impossible, and yet, when they come, my dear brethren, they will impose themselves upon men who will probably look back on us, the men of this generation and century, as unenlightened and uncivilized, much as we look back on those who have gone before us two or three centuries ago, and wonder why they did not deliver themselves from the superstitions of which we are rid. But there is something in our own time which we are not far from, which is going on almost before our own eyes, and the influence of which has lately been felt in a strange and sudden attack made on our own peaceful lives as subjects of the English crown. The Roman ensigns were not adored for their own sakes, but as the symbols and representatives of the imperial secular power, proclaiming itself as the master of the world, the God of physical force, and when Antichrist is enthroned as God amid the applause of the world, receiving the homage of the statesmen and parliaments and newspaper writers of his time, it will be as the embodiment and type of the natural forces of humanity and of the secular power in which they are summed up. He will be hailed as the man of the time, the genius of the age, the deliverer of his fellows from the bondage of those old superstitions about the law of conscience, and God, and future retribution, and an eternity of woe for the wicked. And, in particular, he will be the great triumphant statesman and prince who has at last beaten down the spiritual power of the Church, which for so many centuries has been disputing the rights of kings and peoples, and dividing or diverting the allegiance of the subjects of earthly states. As the Roman eagles flaunted themselves on the sacred soil of Judæa, and at last made their way into the Temple itself, so Antichrist will be the man who shall fulfil the dream of modern politicians, and erect the undisputed empire of the State in his own person on the ruins and in the very place of the spiritual dominion of our Lord Jesus Christ. Hence we can see how that in our time, or in any time, it may be or it may have been that fulfilments of these words of our Lord about the abomination of desolation should take place. Whenever political power and the secular State invades the sanctuary, whenever the State takes upon it to claim obedience in matters of faith and religion, to lay down laws as to sacred things or sacred persons in relation to sacred and spiritual functions, then we have some kind of repetition of the abomination of desolation, some kind of anticipation of the dreadful reign of Antichrist, whom our Lord shall destroy with the brightness of His coming.

III.

My dear brethren in Jesus Christ, you will not expect from me here and now an account of what are so well known to you as the two powers which God has set up upon the earth, the two societies of which He is equally the author—the temporal human society and the supernatural Divine Kingdom of our Lord Jesus Christ. You have often been told that God is the author of the temporal and civil order, as He is the author of the spiritual order, that He has given to each its laws, its rights, its sanctions, and that He has set them side by side, or the one growing out of the other, the one with the end of securing the happiness and well-being of His children in this world, the other with the end of ruling them as heirs of Heaven, and training them for the future enjoyment of the rights of their heavenly country which is above. It is enough to say, as both come from Him, they cannot be, in His designs, intended to be in conflict or contradiction to each other, any more than faith and reason, than human science and revelation which comes from Him. No, He means them to have each its own sphere and its own rights, and that the spheres and rights of each should be harmonious. What it is necessary for us to think of to-day is this, that in the history of the Church and of man, we find that there are three possible relations which these two powers may bear to one another. There is what we call the Christian system of Church and State, and again, what may be called the un-Christian or non-Christian system, and in the third place, there is the anti-Christian system. In the Christian system, the two powers are in perfect harmony, in the non-Christian system they are entirely separate, and, as it were, have no dealings with each other; in the anti-Christian system, the State dominates the Church and tyrannically invades the spiritual sphere. A very few words will be enough to explain how this is.

The Christian system of Church and State once prevailed in Europe, though never quite perfectly. In that system the two powers worked harmoniously together; the laws of God, as it is said, were the laws of the land, all the members of the State were children of the Church, and, as such, obedient to the Church in the spiritual order. Now, there is a large branch, if I may so speak, of the work and commission intrusted to the Church which may be called her prophetical office, because it is strictly analogous to the office which God in the Old Testament committed to His prophets, and if the Church did not discharge it, she would fail to carry out her duty, which is to inherit the work of Him Who said, when He stood as an accused prisoner before the Roman representative of the civil power, "For this was I born, and for this I came into the world, that I should give testimony to the truth."* God expressed the duties of this office when He said to Jeremias of old, " Behold I have given My words in thy mouth : lo, I have set thee this day over the nations and over kingdoms, to root up, and to pull down, and to waste and to destroy, and to build, and to plant."† It is an office therefore of warning and rebuke and reproof ; but also of instruction, guidance, direction, edification. And this office, dear brethren in Jesus Christ, the Church has always fulfilled, and must always fulfil, if she is not to be unfaithful to God. She must lift up her voice, and denounce sin and offences against God, and cruelty and tyranny towards men, she must set her mark upon what is dangerous to society, and denounce the machinations of the enemies of the human race and their tools and instruments. As it was Nathan's office to say to David, " Thou art the man !" after his adultery, or that of St. John to warn the lustful Herod that it was not lawful for him to take his brother's wife ; so it is the office which the Church has always fulfilled and must always fulfil, to rebuke the lusts, whether of princes or of peoples, to defend the otherwise defenceless, to vindicate the insulted law of right, and to bear testimony to the truth, in whatever order and sphere, religious, moral, social, intellectual, when the eternal interests of souls are at stake, whether men are inclined to listen to her or not. But in the Christian system men and their rulers are ready to listen, and to acknowledge the blessing of the guidance with which God has thus provided them. Nor can it be otherwise, for

---

* St. John xviii. 37.   † Jeremias i. 9, 10.

unless men are prepared to deny the mission of the Church and to declare that she is an impostor, they must of necessity acknowledge that Christian states and laws, as well as men individually, must be under the influence of the truths which the Christian revelation teaches, and must defer to the declarations of the appointed organ of those truths.* Nor can any Christian refuse to listen to that voice, unless he maintain that there is no Divine witness to truth in the world except that of the individual conscience.

What I call the un-Christian or the non-Christian system of Church and State is that in which the two powers are absolutely independent, and without any mutual ties or concordant action. Such a state of things necessarily prevails in countries in which the Government and the mass of the population are not Christians, or where they are divided into a number of denominations, and where the State, though heathen, does not persecute or fetter the Church. We have such a system at work in a great country across the Atlantic, the United States of America, which, as a body politic, have no religion at all, but tolerate all. The mass of the population is, however, Christian, of various denominations, and it is perhaps to this that we owe it that the system works so

* "Supposto il fatto della rivelazione conosciuta e accettata, questa relazione del ordine, questa influenza del Gerarcha nella etnarchia Cristiana nasce della natura stessa dell' uomo. Onde, chi vuol che la Chiesa non abbia influenza, non ha altro partito da prendere, che negarle la sua divinità e persuadere le genti della impostura; ma dopo aver detto che divino è il Cristianesimo, divina la Chiesa, soggiugner poi ch' ella non dee guidarsi da se nell' esterno, nè influir sulla condotta delle genti Cristiane, egli è un cozzare contro la natura delle cose" (Taparelli, *Dritto Naturale*, § 1446).

harmlessly as to the Church. I believe that there is one grievance under which Catholics there labour, which may perhaps be some day imposed upon us— that they have to contribute taxes to a system of public education of which they cannot in conscience avail themselves for their children, on account of its irreligious character; but except in that particular, the Catholics in the United States are at least free and unmolested, the State utterly ignoring the Church. And then, in the third place, we have the anti-Christian system, in which, as I say, the State invades the domain of the Church, sets what bounds it likes to the exercise of spiritual power, and consequently puts itself, in great measure, in the place of that power. This system has been introduced of late years into more than one country in Europe and in South America. The State denies to the Church her natural right, for instance, to hold property for the support of her institutions; it seizes that property, and applies it to its own purposes. The State makes war on the practice of the Evangelical counsels in imitation of our Lord; it proscribes religious orders, and sets the brand of exile on their members. The State tears the priest from the sanctuary, and forces him to bear arms in wars, just or unjust, as it lays hands on the student in the seminary and educates him as a soldier, though God calls him to the altar. The State takes the child from the parent and from the pastor, and educates him in its own schools in a mixed religion of its own; it even enters once more into the seminary, prescribes what the future priest shall learn, what books he shall study, and makes itself the final judge as to his fitness to enter upon the sacred ministry, and then it supervises his doctrine and his preaching, and takes into its own hands the control of his relations to his bishop, or the conditions of his communications with the Chief Pastor of all the faithful. And so I might go on, dear brethren, to other encroachments and usurpations and forms of tyranny which are no imaginations, but which have been actually in operation, or are at this moment paralyzing the free action of the spiritual power in some parts of Europe. I might speak of usurpations as to marriage, or as to the teaching of doctrines of faith, or as to the reception of the decisions of the Church. But surely these are enough to describe the system which is the anti-Christian system of relations between Church and State, and which is the result of the working of the same domineering and impious spirit which carried the Roman ensigns into the holy place, and which shall have the fullest manifestation which God will ever permit, when Antichrist shall seat himself in the Temple of God, showing himself as if he were God.

So, then, dear brethren in Jesus Christ, if this be the spirit of the anti-Christian system, the abomination of desolation of which our Lord and the prophets speak, I need not point out to you how rampant and dominant it shows itself in some European countries at the present moment, so that we have in this, our own day, not far to seek for the partial fulfilment of this great prophecy. As it has been before, so it is now. The Church is a body of which, as St. Paul says, when one member suffers anything all the members suffer with it, and if one member glory all the members rejoice with it.* Three centuries ago, persecution was raging in this our land, and it had the same cry and the same motto which are now used by the persecutors of our time, for the charge made against the Catholics of England and Ireland was that they could not be at once loyal to their Church and loyal to their civil allegiance. Then, as now, the tyrant and the aggressor used the hollow hypocrisy which belongs to his character, and declared that it was only in self-defence that he had recourse to the prison, the rack, and the gibbet. Then our brethren on the Continent of Europe cheered and supported by their prayers and alms and sympathies the hearts which were so severely tried here, tried by calumny first, and then by that most detestable of all the forms of persecution, the grossest injustice and the extremity of violence under the name of law.† Our Catholic forefathers suffered, and we have entered into the fruits of their sufferings, and now in our turn we are called upon to aid as best we may, by sympathy and prayer, our brethren in the faith in Germany, Italy, and Switzerland, who are suffering the same persecution, often under the same calumnious cry of disloyalty to the State. ‡

---

* 1 Cor. xii. 26.

† Cf. St. John xix. 11. "Jesus answered, Thou shouldst not have any power against Me unless it were given thee from above. *Therefore*, he that hath delivered Me to thee hath the greater sin."

‡ This Sermon was preached, as the date given above implies, mmediately after the appearance of Mr. Gladstone's pamphlet, the aim of which was to prove that Catholics in this country could not be loyal to the Vatican Council and, at the same time, faithful to their

IV.

[But you will ask, is this cry raised nowhere but abroad? Have we not heard it ourselves in our own country in the last fortnight, and does it not threaten us already with at least the danger of the same treatment, under which our forefathers suffered and our brethren are now suffering? Has it not gone through the length and breadth of the land, nay, wherever our language is spoken, has not a powerful voice been raised denouncing us to our fellow-countrymen, as men whose religion, if they are true to it, must make them again traitors, at least of doubtful allegiance, as men, therefore, who ought to be suspected and watched, if they are not once again to be proscribed and persecuted? Well, we may at least say that as a fact our fellow-countrymen know us, and whatever may have been said against us, they are not ready to believe that we must either be bad Catholics or bad neighbours and bad subjects. Those who rule us, and the mass of the people whom they represent, have no present idea, whatever attempts

civil allegiance. Although that pamphlet was printed in hundreds of thousands of copies, and scattered, it may almost be said, over the face of the whole civilized world, it would be difficult, at the present moment, to say what tangible effect it has produced, except in a considerable amount of petty social persecution and vexation which Catholics have had to bear in consequence. The latter portion of this Sermon might therefore have been omitted in this volume, but from the fact that Mr. Gladstone's publication may be considered as the symptom of a delusion which may very well possess the minds of even the most distinguished public men of Europe outside the Catholic Church. Such a delusion may easily be revived at any moment, and may also pass, in course of time, from the minds of the leaders of modern States into those of the great mass of their population.

may be made to poison their minds, of any measures against us that would deprive us of our liberty, or fetter the free exercise of our religion. They are content to believe that our loyalty to our faith does not prevent us from being, rather helps as nothing else helps to make us, loyal Englishmen. And so, in our own case at least, there is no present danger of the State encroaching upon our spiritual freedom.

Thus much we may thankfully say. But on the other hand, it must be said with equal truth that what has lately been done against us before the face of our countrymen cannot be altogether exempted from the blame of being in the true spirit of the anti-Christian system. For, in the first place, it is but an echo, though a powerful echo, of what has been said in other countries, and, in those countries, not only said, but carried out in act : and it must at least have this bad result, that it will strengthen the hands of the German persecutors of the Church by the apparent support of English sympathy and English opinion. In the second place, in the country in which we live, legislation follows the lead of opinion, and when a man labours with all his might to make our fellow-countrymen, at the cost of great and grievous, I do not say conscious, misrepresentation, hold opinions concerning our religion which stamp it as dangerous and mark it as deserving of persecution, he has laid the logical and natural foundation for that persecution at a future time. And lastly, we must judge of the tendency of a measure or a cry or a movement by considering what would be its results if it ever were successful, and we can do no truer justice to its author than by making him already responsible for such results. But the result of the attack which has been made upon us in the form of an invitation, if successful, would be this, that in England and Ireland, and, indeed, all over the world, Catholics would do that which a few here and there, who bear the name of Catholic among us, have been found willing to do—that is, they would repudiate the teaching of the Church and set utterly at nought that prophetical office of hers of which I have spoken, her own children would all rise up against her, and she would be denied her right to speak and to be obeyed by them in her warnings and directions, and the end would be that the civil power would be universally acknowledged as having the right to lay down and define the limits within which the spiritual power is to work. And, whenever the supremacy of the State is acknowledged, there is no longer any safeguard for faith or religion, and the logical issue of such a condition of the world would be the State enthroned in the sanctuary, the civil ruler drawing to himself the homage and obedience which is due to the Spouse of Jesus Christ.]

Much need then have we, dear brethren in Jesus Christ, to give ourselves to prayer in that spirit which is suggested to us by St. Paul in the Epistle which I have read to you, first, that "we may be filled with the knowledge of God's will in all wisdom and spiritual understanding"—that, as the controversy rages all around us, and none of us but is called to give an account of himself and of his faith, we may be able to answer our assailants in meekness and firmness and lucid intelligence of the truth which we have to maintain—secondly, that "we may walk worthy of God in all things pleasing, being fruitful in every good work, and increasing in the knowledge of God"—that our life and example, our harmony and charity, our obedience and devotion, may move in some manner, at least, the hearts which are now so strongly stirred against us—then that "we may be strengthened with all might, according to the power of His glory, in all patience and long-suffering with joy"—that as it is inevitable that the movement which has been begun against us with so powerful a hand must necessarily bring many occasions of trial to us, high and low, the naturally strong and the naturally weak, to many a lonely convert, many a poor servant, to the children in workhouse schools and orphanages, as well as to the priest or the layman who moves in society, we may have the mighty strength of God given to us all to suffer, if we have to suffer, with joy and gentleness and patience, glad, if so it is, to have our share of the Cross which is so heavy upon our brethren—and then, once more, that we may be filled with due gratitude to God the Father, "Who has made us worthy to be partakers of the lot of the saints in light"—partakers of their lot of suffering, now and here, and hereafter and in Heaven of the joy and the glory which they have gained by their sufferings—because "He hath delivered us from the power of darkness and translated us into the Kingdom of the Son of His love"—because we are citizens of a country which is a true country, an Empire which lasts for ever, a home and a city which are above. Yes, it is a great thing to be children of a mighty nation, a glorious race, subjects of a kingdom which rules in both hemispheres and is famous in the history of the world; but what is all that, with its benefits which pass away and its glories which come to dust, and its prosperity which shall vanish away like a dream; what is it all to the honour and the blessedness of being the humblest citizen of the city which hath foundations, whose maker and builder is God; what is it all to the one only benefit which lasts for ever and for ever, of having "redemption through the blood of Jesus Christ, the remission of our sins"?*

* Coloss. . 9—14 (the Epistle for the day).

SERMON VIII.

THE DAYS OF NOE.

Et sicut factum est in diebus Noe, ita erit et in diebus Filii hominis.

As it came to pass in the days of Noe, so shall it be also in the days of the Son of Man.

(Words taken from the 26th verse of the 17th chapter of St. Luke's Gospel.)

I.

I HAVE been trying to point out to you, dear brethren in our Lord, the resemblance which exists, as to many remarkable features in both, between the days in which we live, and the days which, if our Lord be not a false prophet, will be at the end of the world immediately before His coming to judge the whole human race. You have seen, in the first place, that we live in the presence of a false popular creed, the influence of which is spreading every day, and is likely to spread further and further. This false creed, with those over whom it prevails, will certainly account for the strange feature of the last days which our Lord mentions, the indifference of the men of that time to the signs of His coming. It will account for that indifference, because it will destroy in their minds all the principles, doctrines, and feelings which could make them otherwise than indifferent. Such a creed, whether it survive to the last days or not, is at least like that false belief which will then prevail. In the second place, you have seen that the present condition of the Christian populations throughout the world, taken as a whole, abundantly justifies the application to our own times of those mournful words of our Lord, in which He predicted that in the latter days there would be a great decay among the many of true Catholic and Christian charity. We tested this by the opinions and doctrines prevalent over large portions of the Christian world, whereby the necessity of Christian unity is denied, and in consequence of which a very large number of so-called Christian communities are paralyzed by that disease which is the special antagonist and death of charity—that is, the sin of schism. Again, we saw last Sunday that our Lord describes the political state of our own times in the very same words in which He described that of the last age of the world, when He said there were to be wars and rumours of wars, nation rising against nation, and kingdom against kingdom. And, if any one of these features of the last days which are to be found in our own time strikes us as pointing to the conclusion that we may at any moment have the reign of the last persecution, the reign of Antichrist, and the final judgment upon us, surely the combination of these several features together points with still greater force to the same conclusion. There still remain more features than one of resemblance between our own age and the last to which your attention must be drawn. I shall speak of one of these to-day, and draw from its consideration one or two practical reflections.

The first of these features of the last days of which I have to speak, is one of which we certainly have a very strong and remarkable anticipation in our own time. I mean the absorbing and engrossing manner in which material pleasures and enjoyments hold the souls of the mass of mankind in captivity, dulling them and blinding them, as our Lord says of the men of His own generation, making their hearts gross and heavy, so that they have not the power, it may almost be said, to perceive the truths which God sets before them in His Church. In the passage from which the text is taken, our Lord selects two times from the whole of human history, and He says that it shall be in the latter days as it was in those times. Those were times of great catastrophes, of great punishments of God on the sinfulness of man, when the chastisement took men by surprise, because they were so engrossed in the enjoyments of life. It may be that the chief point, so to say, of the comparison in our Lord's words lies in the suddenness of the chastisement, but still it cannot be without a meaning that He should have chosen those two periods for the purpose of His warnings to us. For the suddenness of the chastisement which will fall on the last generation of mankind will not consist in the absence of warnings beforehand, but in the dulness and blindness of men to warnings, however startling. Such dulness and such blindness, as we know well from Scripture, are the inevitable results of engrossments in temporal and material goods, and when this engrossment is possible, then are its fruits possible, as we see in those of times which our Lord speaks. They were times of enormous degradation and licentiousness, but that degradation and that licentiousness were brought on by the fearful engrossment of those who were the subjects of God's chastisements in the pleasures of the senses and the enjoyments of this world. The first of these two periods is the period before the universal Deluge, and the second is the time of Lot, when God destroyed the Cities of the Plain on account of their loathsome and unnatural sensuality. If these times have in common the feature of the entire unexpectedness of the calamity which then fell on men, they have also that other feature in common, of the excessive sensual enjoyment of those who perished in those great catastrophes.

With regard to the antediluvian world, there is this feature besides, that God undoubtedly warned the race of mankind that His judgments were about to come on them. It appears from the Scripture account that the ark took a hundred years to build, and that during that time Noe was a preacher of repentance. We know but little indeed of those marvellous days, when human life, as the Scripture tells us, was so long, but, if that were so, it would be quite enough to account for the forgetfulness of the things of God and of the soul, and for the extreme profligacy of which we also read of the antediluvians. Alas! so it is. If life in our days could be prolonged for twice or thrice its ordinary span, it would more probably be for the greater misery than for the greater happiness of mankind. And when we are told, as we are sometimes told in Scripture, that God has shortened the days of the ordinary human lifetime, it is certain that He has done so in pity rather than in anger. Then also, the antediluvians seem to have dwelt in the very fairest regions of the earth, they seem to have been more full of natural knowledge and of acquired skill in the use of the resources of enjoyment and physical wellbeing than those who came after them, and it is very likely indeed that their numbers were not such as to cause that struggle for existence which is now the lot of the populations of so many countries of the world, in which the great enjoyment of the good things of the earth is not yet the free inheritance of the many. At all events, they were so fearfully and outrageously corrupt, morally and socially, that the sacred writer tells us that their wickedness was so great, that it made God repent in His heart that He had created them. Such was the population of the earth, or of those parts of it then inhabited by man, on whom the great destruction of the Flood came like a thief in the night.

As to the other period and generation of which our Lord speaks, and to which, in its heedlessness and unwatchfulness, He compares the men of the last days, why need I speak? Sodom and Gomorrha, the Cities of the Plain—their very name is synonymous with everything that is most foul and licentious, even to the degradation of our human nature. The land in which they dwelt was one of unexampled beauty and fertility. We are told in the book of Genesis, that "the country about Jordan was watered throughout, before the Lord destroyed Sodom and Gomorrha, as the paradise of the Lord, and like Egypt as when one comes to Segur."* And as the Flood had been brought on by lust, so also was it with the destruction of these fair cities and their wicked inhabitants. Here, then, we find also these two features, immense material enjoyment and the most intense moral degradation. We are not told that the people of these cities were directly warned of the chastisement which they were bringing on themselves, but, at all events, they had had for some time resident among them a chosen servant of God, Lot, the sister's son of Abraham, of whom St. Peter speaks as if he had been a witness to virtue and morality, "oppressed by the injustice and lewd conversation of the wicked, for in sight and hearing he was just, dwelling among them, who day by day vexed the just soul with ungodly works."† So that if they had not a direct warning, they had the witness of a holy life among them to reproach them for their profound foulness of lust. And we may fairly suppose that if they were not warned by any more direct signs or predictions of their coming destruction, it was because they were so deeply engrossed in their sensuality as not to be capable of conversion, or of arousing, by any such means, as it is indeed the characteristic of men who are given to those enormous sins of lust, to be incapable of compunction, and beyond the reach of the most startling warnings of Providence.

* Gen. xiii. 10. † 2 St. Peter ii. 7, 8.

II.

Now I have already said that the direct point of the comparison between the days of which we are speaking, and the days at the end of the world, which is drawn by our Lord, lies in the unexpectedness of the destruction which fell upon them, and which will fall on the men of the last days. But our Lord's description points also to the resemblance in moral and social matters which shall be found between these periods. For He describes them in His own merciful way, as eating and drinking, and marrying and giving in marriage, that is, as being occupied in the ordinary enjoyments and rejoicings of this world, without a fear of the coming judgment. And we know from experience that, when men do these things which our Lord names without any thoughts of God, and of His laws, they indulge in every sensual pleasure and lust without remorse or fear. And what is required to make any period of the world's history like, in this respect, to the two periods here named by our Lord, is not so much necessarily that it shall be a period of loathsome sensuality, as that it should be a period in which the common good things and enjoyments of life are so engrossing to the majority of the population, as to make them entirely heedless of Divine warnings and utterly unprepared for a doom which is hanging over them.

And now, my brethren, let us look around us, and we shall certainly find features in our own times, which may at least prepare us for the state of things of which our Lord speaks. I am not about to say whether or no the men of our time are equal to the antediluvians and to the men of Sodom and Gomorrha in the extent of their unbridled licentiousness. That may or may not be the case, though if it were true that we at all approached to the excesses of those days, it would be one of the most disgraceful charges that could be fixed upon us. For we live in the light of the pure doctrine of our Lord; we live when the work of the Church has been upon the world for centuries; we live with the example and character of Jesus and Mary before us, reflected to us from the lives of thousands and thousands of saints, men and women like ourselves. What is quite certain is, that we are far more luxurious than our forefathers, and that the possibility of an almost boundless luxury is far more nearly within the reach of the generality of men, than ever before since the introduction of the religion of our Lord into the world. This is, in great measure, due to the advance of our knowledge of the physical world and of the treasures which it concealed from those who went before us. If we ask ourselves in what chiefly has the progress of physical knowledge marked itself on the history of the human race, we are obliged to answer, in two things chiefly—in the multiplication of the powers of men to destroy one another, and in the multiplication and generalization of the means of enjoyment. These are the chief uses which we make of the revelation of the resources with which God has provided the world in which we live. We apply our knowledge to the comforts and pleasures of life. The treasures of the earth's surface, the stores of metals and minerals, and the other gifts of nature to the several climates and countries of the globe, are at our command to a degree hitherto unknown. Earth and air and water contribute now to our enjoyments far more than ever before. Consider in a great city like this, how every portion of the world sends its contribution to furnish our tables or to adorn our dwellings—fruits, dainties, rarities, what can we not have, almost for the asking? The old satirists of Rome are full of the way in which the tables of the great gluttons of those times were supplied from every country known to the masters of the world, but we have a far greater command than they of the resources on which their luxury fattened. And, my brethren, I do not think that any Roman or Egyptian glutton in palace or villa the most luxurious of those days, gave himself more entirely to his enjoyment of what he had, in the spirit of those words quoted by St. Paul, "Let us eat and drink, for to-morrow we die," than do men and women in the midst of Christian England or Catholic France or civilized America. And if a creed such as that of which I have had to speak takes possession of men who can command so many of the gifts of nature of which their ancestors were ignorant, what can we possibly expect but that they will give themselves body and soul to sensual enjoyments, it may perhaps be with less of brutality and grossness as to outward appearance than those old giants of sensuality, but still with the same entire absence of all check and control except that of what is possible to them and what is not? And in our case there is this difference between the sensualists of the day and that of the old Roman Empire, that in those days the extravagance of indulgence was confined to the few, while the tendency of modern times is to open the door of physical enjoyments far wider than it has ever before been opened, and whole classes can now indulge themselves where before only a few here and there could do so. The decay of religion and the growth of the creed which tells men they have no God and no responsibility, go hand in hand with the growth of the facilities of gross enjoyment for the great mass of mankind in many countries of the world.

And here also, my brethren, we have an evil or a feature which is not likely in the course of time, taking into consideration the natural and probable course of events, to grow less prominent, but rather more so. The popularization of physical enjoyments and luxuries by means of the progress of the age is a thing of which we are more likely to see rapid strides in advance than any retrogression. The advance has a natural cause which cannot be changed or checked, and which has its root in the increased knowledge of mankind of the gifts of nature and the powers of nature, all of which can be made to become the vassals of man in the enjoyment of his brief span of life. And all this is simultaneous with the rise in so many countries of vast and crowded cities such as our ancestors never dreamed of, cities at once the centres of commerce and so of luxury, and also, alas! the seats of the deepest moral corruption. We shudder at the thought of what that corruption was which brought on the Cities of the Plain the vengeance of God, but comparing the probable population of those cities with what we know of the hundreds of thousands that are to be found either in or around a few great centres of modern life, such as London, or Paris, or New York, it is hard to think that in any of those great cities there is, day by day, and night by night, much less of foul offence to the Divine Majesty in the violation of the moral law which He has written in the heart of every child of Adam, than what would equal the accumulation of sin which brought on the Deluge, or devoted the Cities of the Plain to the fire which came down from Heaven.

Now it is well for a moment to have dwelt on such a feature as this of the last days, and of our own days as well as of those. It is well, because here is a point as to which we may all contribute to the balance on the side of good or on the side of evil. The men and women from whom we inherit the faith and religion of our Lord were men and women in few things more superior to those who have come after them than in the severity, the simplicity, the manliness and virtuous dignity, of their lives. They rose early and ate and drank simply and sparingly, and were not afraid of heat or cold, they could brave the weather and live in the open air, and their houses and their chambers knew nothing of the thousand so-called necessities of the men and women of our time. Their amusements were manly and vigorous, their table was plain, their dress inexpensive, they could dance without danger to modesty, they conversed together without the chance of shameful anecdotes or inuendoes. When they were children they obeyed their parents, and did not expect to be petted and indulged in every whim and fancy, and when they became parents they watched over the purity and the piety of their children. I need not draw the other side of the picture, for it is but too plain how we have degenerated from them. But I say, here is a matter not for the priest alone, or the religious alone, it is a matter for laymen and gentlemen and fathers and mothers of families, as they value their own souls, and the souls of their children, and as they will give an account of their responsibilities to the great Judge at the end of their time. Then they will be asked what they have done towards staying the plague of luxury and licence of manners, or whether they have been on the side of the increase of that licence and of the gradual declension of virtue and morality in a land which still calls itself Christian. It matters comparatively nothing how far the world may at this moment be from the final victory of licence and this immorality. What does matter to us, now and here, is this—that we should stand up in our generation for ancient purity, for frugality, and temperance, and virtue, for the holy discipline of the Christian home, for the manly severity of life, which made those who are gone before us able to resist as they did the tyranny of the State and the civil and social proscription under which they suffered, in order to hand on to us the treasures and traditions of old Catholic manners. If we throw these to the winds for the sake of the pleasures and effeminacies of modern life, how far more guilty shall we be, how far more severely punished, than those around us, who have lived like animals in the use of all that is pleasant to the senses, believing all the time that they were no better than animals and no more bound than they to deny themselves any satisfaction—ignorant of God, ignorant of Jesus Christ, without the faith and the hope which might have been enough to give them courage to despise the things which are seen for the sake of the things which are not seen, to forego the momentary enjoyments of earth for the sake of Heaven and of eternity!

SERMON IX.

THE LOOSING OF SATAN.

Fiunt novissima hominis illius pejora prioribus.
The last state of that man becomes worse than the first.
(Words taken from the 26th verse of the 11th chapter of St. Luke's Gospel.)

I.

I HAVE had to speak to you, my brethren in our Lord, of a series of subjects which naturally hang together in our consideration of the last days of the world, and especially of those elements at work in human society which are more or less always to be found there, and which therefore are to be found in our own day, as well as they will be found in those last times. And, of course, the object which we have in view is to trace out the evil principles against which we are always bound to be fighting, even though we do not know that our own days are absolutely the last, and even though we know also that in those days these evil principles will for a time be allowed by God, partially, at least, to win a victory over those who struggle against them. Now, as far as we have gone, we have seen how the features of the latter days will be such as might be expected in the conflict which is always going on between good and evil in the world of men, and how the state of the world at the end, such as it is described to us in prophecy, will be the natural outcome of the decay of the power of the good influences in society, and of the consequent increase of the contrary influences, availing themselves also of the occasional opportunities which cannot but present themselves, as the drama, so to say, of human history gradually unfolds itself and hastens towards its appointed close.

Before parting finally from this subject, I must once more recapitulate what has been said, for the purpose of briefly speaking of one feature in the picture, and also of drawing your attention to the connection which may be observed between its various features as already delineated. In the first place, then, observe how the evils of which we have been speaking seem to require one the other, by a sort of miserable necessity, which has about it the air of a judicial provision of God. The first feature that we had to notice was the decay of faith, according to the sad words of our Lord about the state of things which He will find when He comes again. Now this feature has its natural counterpart in the next. Answering to the decay of faith is the rise of false beliefs concerning those great truths and interests of mankind on which faith speaks with an unerring voice about God, and the soul, and the moral law and future judgment and eternity—false beliefs which will rest themselves for their pretended foundation on the discoveries and revelations of science, on the increase of knowledge of the history of the past of our globe, and the like. To the decay of faith will succeed the decay of charity in the great mass of men who call themselves Christians, and on the decay of charity, the supernatural tie between man and man, and race and race, and kingdom and kingdom, and nation and nation, will of course follow the undue preponderance and exaggeration of the natural ties which gather men together in polities and unities merely temporary and limited, the immense domination of what is called nationality, with all the hatreds and ambitions and discords and aggressions which it is capable of engendering, and with the appliance, to the furthering of the purposes of these hatreds and discords and ambitions, of all the marvellous array of physical powers and forces which are the fruits to us of human progress. Here again, there is a kind of natural judicial sequence which is too obvious to require any lengthened explanation.

Observe also, next, how the decay of charity must naturally lead to the encroachment of the civil power in the world on the spiritual power, the rights and laws of the Church of God. Is there anything in what we are told of the last days which may be considered as a consequence or result of this civil encroachment on sacred rights, as the delusion of a false belief is the consequence of decay in allegiance to the revealed truth of the Church, and as the exaggeration of the spirit of nationality is a result of the enfeeblement of the supernatural bond by which God intended to unite all nations in one great brotherhood? The natural punishment of civil governments, when they invade the dominion of the Church, is that they become themselves the objects of subterranean plottings and conspiracies, or, again, of a widespread spirit of disloyalty and disobedience, so that, where dynasties are not overthrown by revolutions, at least the whole social order is imperilled, and the authority of law is disregarded. It would take me far into the regions of contemporary and recent history to illustrate this subject as it deserves, for it may be truly said of the governments of Europe since the great upheaval of the Reformation, that not one of them is free from the guilt of having usurped the rights of the Church of God, and also that not one of them has escaped the due punishment of that usurpation, in revolution, in regicide, in the banishment of royal families or in the degradation of the royal authority, while it is also true to say that society itself is already in great danger in many kingdoms of what used to be called Christendom. These are plagues which work themselves out in history, and if the last days are to be days of signal lawlessness, according to the words of our Lord, it is not easy to see how much farther lawlessness can be carried, without an absolute dissolution of society, than we have ourselves seen it carried. But this is enough to have said, for the sake of not leaving altogether untouched this other feature of the prophecies, which is certainly not likely to become less prominent on the face of human society as the years roll on. This then is another point which belongs to the picture we are sketching, and simultaneously with this we find that in the last days there is reason for expecting that men will be far more masters of the resources of the world, of the fruits and products of the various climates and regions of the earth, and the like, and will be able to use all these resources for the purposes of enjoyment and pleasure in a way and to an extent which will make an immense and nearly universal sensuality and moral corruption inevitable. Such are some, at least, of the features of the last times of traces of which our own days are certainly not devoid, and when we find them, as we do find them, not singly prominent, one more and one less, in a time like our own, but also prominent altogether simultaneously and collectively, we have certainly reason for arming ourselves for the last struggle for the truth and the law of God.

II.

Now to-day I shall pass on to another and a different feature in the last times, as they are represented to us in the Sacred Scriptures interpreted to us by the Fathers of the Church. All the elements of which I have hitherto spoken are, as we may say, the human side of those evil times which will come upon the world before its renovation by the second advent of our Lord. I do not mean to say that all these human elements are not used and set in motion by the spiritual enemies of our race, for they always, it may be said, prefer to make man fight against himself, to assail the honour of God by the very gifts and benefits which He has bestowed on His creatures, and to turn in this manner His own goodness against himself. But we must never forget, though it is quite certain that the men of the last time will forget, that the warfare which we have to wage here and now for the salvation of our souls, and in order to escape the eternal doom of him whom the Judge will condemn, is not a simply human warfare. That is, it is not waged either by human forces alone, or against human principles and power of evil alone. We are aided in our warfare by God, by His Mother, the blessed saints and angels, and by the spiritual powers at the disposal of the Church, and on the other hand, we are fighting against foes of far greater power than ourselves, foes of the same nature and order with the blessed citizens of Heaven who assist us, the deadly enemies of God and of man, Satan and the fallen angels. Our battle, as St. Paul says, "is not against flesh and blood, but against principalities and powers, against the rulers of the world of this darkness, against the spirits of wickedness in the high places."* Now with regard to this conflict, there are a few certain truths of which it is well to remind ourselves now that we are speaking of the latter days, and of these I shall now speak.

In the first place, it is the doctrine of Scripture, that Satan and his evil angels, who are indefinitely more powerful as well as more subtle than man against whom they are contending, are only allowed to tempt us and assail us, not to the utmost of their power, but just as much and no more as God permits. If God did not hold them in, they would devour us and destroy us in a moment. In the second place, it is the universal belief of the Church that the power of the evil angels against man is at some times allowed to proceed to greater lengths than at others. For

* Ephes. vi. 12.

instance, Satan was immensely powerful in the world before the coming of our Lord, and after that coming his power in the world has been immensely diminished. This is what, as many of the Fathers tell us, our Lord meant when He described the conflict between Himself and Satan under the image of a strong armed man who kept his hall and goods in peace, until a stronger than he came upon him, and first bound him, and then despoiled him of his goods and distributed them*—that is, the image means that Satan was in full force and dominion, in peaceable possession, so to say, of the world until our Lord came, and that then, our Lord subdued him and chained him up, and took possession, through the Church, of that human world upon which Satan had exercised such a tyranny. This is what took place, first, in the lifetime of our Lord, especially at the Temptation and at the Passion, when Satan was first weakened and put to flight and then finally conquered by our Lord. And later on, as the Christian Church spread throughout the world, the same process of the weakening and dispossession of Satan went on, and at the present moment he is stronger and far more able to seduce men in regions outside the Church than within her pale.

But our Lord went on to tell the Jews another parable, as it were, how the devil once cast out comes back again with seven other devils worse than himself, and how that which was expressed by that image was to come to pass in that very generation.† And certainly the whole history of the Jewish commonwealth between the date of our Lord's death

---

* St. Luke. xi. 21.   † *Ib.* 24.

and the destruction of Jerusalem is more like the history of a nation possessed by evil spirits than any other. Now the Fathers tell us that in the latter days something of the same sort is to take place. There is a part of the Apocalyptic vision which they interpret in this way, namely, that Satan has been bound up and chained by our Lord, and not allowed to seduce the nations as before, during a certain time, which is the time of the reign of the Church on earth, and that then Satan is to be loosed for a short time, the time of the last great seduction, apostacy, and persecution, and that during that time he is to have leave to put forth his full power against the Church. Thus what their teaching leads us to as a conclusion concerning the last days is this—that in those days Satan will be more mischievous and powerful than he has hitherto been allowed in the presence of our Lord or the Church. "After that," says St. John, "he must be loosed for a little time."*

Thus we are to expect that, in the later days of the world's history, Satan will be allowed greater freedom than before, partly, we may suppose, to test to the uttermost the spiritual powers of the Church and her children, that the glory of our Lord may be greater in their final victory, partly because of the exceeding wickedness of that apostate world which shall deserve as its immediate chastisement to be handed over to all the seductions of the powers of evil. This is implied in the great prophecy of St. Paul as to the partial success of Antichrist.

* Apoc. xx. 3.

His coming, says the Apostle, is "according to the working of Satan in all power and signs and lying wonders, and in all the seduction of iniquity to those who are lost, because they received not the love of the truth that they might be saved. Therefore God shall send upon them the operation of error, to believe lying, that all may be judged who have not believed the truth but have consented unto iniquity."* The two great features of this prophecy are, first, the truth that Antichrist is to be supported and recommended to mankind by all the power of the devil, "in all power, and signs, and lying wonders," and secondly, that this permission of God to Satan is judicial. Because men have not loved the truth, they shall be allowed to believe lies, and because they have consented to iniquity and have not believed the truth, they shall be judged.

III.

Now, my dear brethren, what may be the particular and special inventions of Satan for the seduction, of men which he will be allowed to palm off on the men of the last days, we do not know. But we may be sure of certain things concerning him which it may be well to consider in reference to this point. I speak to those who believe in Satan. For certainly, it is possible to imagine persons persuading themselves, as is commonly said, that there is no God, no devil, no spiritual world, nothing beyond what we see and feel and touch. That is a very childish, unreasonable, degrading belief. But it is intelligible.

* 2 Thess. ii. 9—11.

And it is far more intelligible than the belief of those persons who believe that there is a devil, but who practically believe also that he lets us alone and is no longer active in the seduction of mankind. It is more reasonable to believe that there is no evil one at all, than to believe that, being what he is, he may be considered as asleep or as dead as far as concerns all attempts to impose on and to ruin mankind. In the next place, I say this—that there are many phenomena in the present state of the world which are more or less seen in our generation, and which are most reasonably to be explained on the supposition that Satan has been allowed a greater freedom and a more open power of action than he has been allowed in earlier ages of the Christian Church. There are some who would place among these phenomena what I have just been speaking of, namely the extraordinary fanaticism of the conspirators against social order, when those conspirators are allowed by the state of public affairs to come, as it were, to the surface and have their way for a short time in some diseased polity or country. And surely we cannot call this conclusion unreasonable, when we remember the perfectly fiendish hatred against religion, against God, and everything dedicated to His service, which characterized the short reign of the secret societies in a country not far from our own shores, in the interval which followed on the late great humiliation of that noble country at the hands of the Germans. The furies that were then let loose were surely more than human, and no one can tell how soon they may be let loose once more — no one can tell how soon the instinct of the Church in denouncing these societies may be again fearfully justified, by the discovery of their true character in some still greater convulsion.

But to-day I am going to dwell on another and a very different manifestation of the power of Satan to delude mankind. I find this sufficiently illustrated in a false belief, which numbers among those of our own race adherents enough to furnish the whole male population of many an European country. It is said that there are now in the world, and, I grieve to say, chiefly in the Anglo-Saxon world, in the English-speaking races of Europe and America, as many as ten or eleven millions of persons who believe in what goes by the name of Spiritualism. I give that as an instance, for there are several phases of the same kind of belief, and not all would class themselves under that single name. For the purposes of our argument, it is only necessary that there should be a number of forms of delusion prevalent in the world, of which the simplest account is that they are invented, supported, and propagated by the agency of evil spirits. The characteristic of all these sects, for that is the proper name to give them, and the whole system of what they practise, comes from a false creed, which like others, has in it some one or two elements of truth. The characteristic of them all is this—that certain persons are said to have communication with the unseen world, and especially with the souls of the departed, by means of which they are able to find out what is going on at a distance, and to produce certain marvellous effects which have a miraculous appearance, and of which no one is able to give a natural explanation.

For surely it is reasonable to say that this delusion of Spiritualism is far too widespread, and is practised by a far too large multitude of persons, for us to be satisfied with the hypothesis that it is a mere conjuring trick, an affair of sleight of hand. It is a different thing to say that there is not such an element here and there, but the thing itself, when we look the phenomena in the face, is far too well attested to be set aside on that plea. As to the phenomena in general, and without speaking of particular instances, I do not think that any natural explanation ever has been given of them, or ever will be, and I think, moreover, that Christians have no right to, and cannot without danger, pass the whole system over as a mere human trick. I think this for this plain reason—that the evidence for the Christian religion, the evidence on which it first made the conquest of the minds of men, and by virtue of which it still retains its hold, rests logically in great part at least, on human testimony. It is true, that the testimony on which the Christian faith rests is of the highest kind, and such as cannot be found in favour of the wonders which are alleged to have taken place under the system of which I speak. The system moreover, itself, the *séances* which take place, the effect produced, the messages communicated and the like, are mixed up with a triviality, a frivolity, an emptiness, a childishness, which are enough to render the system contemptible, even if its moral and religious aspects did not, at best, make it far worse than contemptible. But still, it is never safe or right for Christians to refuse all authority to a large mass of independent human testimony. And this is especially the case, when there is a simple rational explanation of the whole phenomena, an explanation recommended by the very strongest internal evidence. What I mean is this. There is nothing in the phenomena of Spiritualism which cannot be far more rationally accounted for by the agency of souls under the influence of evil spirits, or of evil spirits representing souls, than by any other hypothesis. This is the most rational explanation to those who believe in such agencies, whereas no other explanation fits into the facts with even reasonable success.

I add that this conclusion is recommended to us by the strongest internal evidence, and what I mean is this. Put aside all questions whatsoever as to the particular phenomena of which we hear so much. Let us grant that there is a great deal of delusion, let us grant that there is a great deal of imposition, and attribute as much as you like to unknown natural causes. Say that the effects are trivial and foolish, or say, what is not less true, that they are constantly mixed up with moral turpitude, and that at all events they are known to debauch and demoralize the whole mind and heart of many who patronize this system. One thing you cannot account for naturally, and that one thing is the most important of all. The religious effect of the system is universally that which I am going to say. The agents who speak to us through the poor human instruments of which we hear so much differ in details and smaller matters, they will agree in this. They do not, I believe, openly deny God. We have even been told by those who have dealt in the system, and who gave it up on becoming Catholics, that these spirits have been known to profess even to love Jesus Christ and to recommend in many particulars the Catholic religion. But in one thing they are unanimous, and their creed falls in with that of the false science of which I spoke at the beginning. There is no eternal punishment, no ultimate difference between good and bad. Our Lord's words, "he that believeth and is baptized, shall be saved, he that believeth not shall be condemned;" His words about the worm that dieth not and the fire that is not quenched—these are not true. Men are not to be judged for what they have done in the flesh, or if they are, the sentences are all favourable, whether for the wickedest sinner or the greatest saint.

Now I say, account for the phenomena of Spiritualism as you like, but give some account of this universal testimony of the adepts of the sect if you can, which does not point to its Satanic origin. By their fruits we know them. If I find the father of lies in the doctrine, it is not amiss to find him in the evidences of the doctrine. What religion can the mind of man imagine more delightful and more convenient to Satan and his fellows than this! Now this is the growth of the last half century or less. It is true the thing itself, in some shape or other, has always existed. But it has never existed in proportions so full blown as now, and it has never had so many adherents, or so organized a system as now.

Dealings with the evil one there have been almost from the beginning of man's history, but dealings on such a scale, and which have been defended by so many persons of high education and fortune, there have never been. Now there are a score of phases of this system, because that particular development which sprung up in our own memory in America has had many sister developments, especially in un-Christian countries. Who can say it is unreasonable for the eye of Christian faith to see in it a beginning of that operation of Satan of which St. Paul speaks, a feature in this nineteenth century in which we live which has only to be intensified, enlarged, developed, in order to bring on the very state of things of which the Apostle speaks in his account of the days of Antichrist? Add this one more element of evil to the others of which I have had to speak, and why should we be surprised if we were to see at once the last great signs in Heaven and on earth, which are to herald in the great day of the judgment of the world!

And observe, dear brethren in our Lord, one strange and significant element in the welcome which this false system has received at the hands of the world. It might have been thought beforehand that a system such as this, which, with all its childishness and turpitude, does still retain the one Christian truth of the existence of the soul independently of the body, and of the spiritual life, the future state, would have found on that account its bitterest opponents among the adepts of the false science of which I spoke to you in another of these Lectures. Brethren, do not these two systems contradict one the other, almost as forcibly as each of them contradicts the religion of Jesus Christ? Is not Satan divided against Satan, in propagating at the same time these two irreconcilable creeds? No, my brethren, as all the sects in the world find a common ground in their hostility against the Catholic Church, for the sake of which they are content to sink their differences in order to act together against the common enemy, so do we find the very generation which is so fond of that creed of false science of which we have spoken, welcoming at the same time the revelations of Spiritualism. Nay, it would not be too much to say that these revelations have had a kind of attraction for some minds even among men prominent in the development of modern thought, whether in the direction of positive materialism or in that, at least, of the negation of Christianity, as if in order that the words of the Apostle, citing the words of his Master Jesus Christ, may be true in them, that those who are incredulous to the faith, are, by a certain punishment, credulous of its negation, and those who receive not the love of the truth that they may be saved, shall be handed over to the working of falsehood, and believe a lie!

IV.

And now, dear brethren, what are we to gather from all these considerations for ourselves, on whom, as the Apostle says, the ending of the world has come, or may come, and who live in days which are already marked by the features which are to distinguish the close of this world? Many things, indeed, we are to gather, but they cannot be summed up better than in the words of our Lord and His Apostles. "Seeing, then," says St. Peter, "that all these things are to be dissolved what manner of people ought you to be in holy conversation and godliness?"* "Take heed to yourselves," says our Lord, "lest perhaps your hearts be overcharged with surfeiting and drunkenness and the cares of this world, and that day come upon you suddenly, for as a snare shall it come upon all that sit on the face of the whole earth. Watch ye therefore, praying at all times, that you may be accounted worthy to escape all these things that are to come, and to stand before the Son of Man."† Those are great words, "to stand before the Son of Man." We have been thinking all these Sundays what sort of men those are to be who are to be the victims of all these evil elements of which we have been speaking, but we are bound also to consider what sort of men those will have to be who are to bear the name of Jesus Christ in those days and to suffer in His cause. No common men, my brethren, no men of careless, indolent lives, no men of imperfect faith, faint hearts, and small courage, no men who have already half capitulated to the world by seeking for its favours in their daily life, though they preserve their faith, no men who are not conquerors first of themselves and the lower parts of their nature, before they are called on to brave all the powers of Antichrist and of Hell let loose on the world! There is surely great reason for us to anticipate that that will be no persecution such as we have read of in the early

---

* 1 St. Peter iii. 11.   † St. Luke xxi. 36.

ages, nor such as our forefathers had in the days of the penal laws. All the powers and resources and inventions of modern civilization will be at the command of the persecutors, and the exquisite discoveries of science will add the most refined torments for those who persevere to the most captivating seductions for those who fall. Every seduction to make us yield, every most dreadful penalty if we stand fast! You know what the Israelites were told when they went to war, that a proclamation was made that men who had built new houses or planted new vineyards, or betrothed men, should go away from the battle, and then it was to be said, "What man is there that is fearful and fainthearted? Let him go and return to his house, lest he make the hearts of his brethren to fear."* No chance, my brethren, in those days, for the fearful or fainthearted, all will have to be men: and if there are to be men then, we must be men now. For every generation of Christians is more or less what its parents and its educators make it, and, if you persuade yourselves that these things are not yet, at least have mercy on the souls of those who are to come after you, and on whom those evil days may fall if they do not come on you. You have read how, in that glorious Church of Japan which was all but drowned in blood in the course of a few years, the children were educated by their parents to desire martyrdom, to practise martyrdom, to rehearse martyrdom, and by that means prepared for the glorious witness to God which so many of them rendered. My brethren,

* Deut. xx. 8.

learn a lesson from your slaughtered brethren two centuries ago, and if you cannot think of so distant a country as Japan, think of what was required in the way of manliness in England and Ireland to preserve the precious deposit of the faith for us. Be men yourselves and make your children men, men brought up to toil, to suffer, to pray, to bear witness to the faith. Resist all those evil influences we have been considering, and you will certainly train up your children to resist them. Misery of misery, anguish of anguish, to the parents by whose fault those who are to fall away in the days of Antichrist do so fall away! "They shall die in their sin, but their blood I will require at your hands." Joy of joy, triumph of triumph, crown of crown, to those parents by whose example and instruction it comes about that their children are vigilant, watchful, ready, enduring, persevering, able to escape all these things that are coming on the world, and to stand before the Son of Man!

SERMON X.

THE MAN OF SIN.

Veni in nomine Patris Mei, et non accipitis Me; si alius venerit in nomine suo, illum accipietis.

I am come in the name of My Father, and you receive Me not; if another shall come in his own name, him you will receive.

(Words taken from the 43rd verse of the 5th chapter of St. John's Gospel.)

I.

IN these words, addressed by our Blessed Lord to the Jews of Jerusalem, we are taught by some of the Fathers that He meant to foretell the future reception of Antichrist by that people which had rejected Himself. The other who is to come, not in the name of the Father, not in the name of any God but himself—"in his own name"—is the great enemy, the Man of Sin, the child of perdition, of whom St. Paul speaks in his Epistles. It is thought by Catholic and ancient writers that he will be Jewish by origin; at all events it seems probable that he will connect himself with the Jews and be received by them for a time before their final conversion, that he will build his false religion in some measure on Judaism, and that he will for a short time reign at Jerusalem, and make himself an object of worship at the Temple.

However this may be—for here we are touching on some details of the prophecies as to which we have no absolutely certain information to guide us—we cannot but recognize in this sad prediction of our Lord an allusion to a general law which constantly operates in the providential course of human events. Our Lord is characterized in the Gospels as coming to His own, and not being received by them. You know how often He speaks of Himself and His Father as inviting, calling, beseeching people to come to the banquet or the kingdom which is prepared for them. Men reject God, and turn away from His offers and invitation with disdain. "I pray thee hold me excused," is their most courteous reply; at other times they turn upon His servants and messengers, beat them, handle them roughly, and slay them. And then comes in this law of retribution which is so observable in the providential government of the world. Those who refuse God are not able to refuse His and their own enemy. If they reject God's light service and loving invitation, they bring upon themselves the yoke of a hard master, and the burthen of a hungry slavery instead. The prodigal son had to become a servant and a swineherd in a far country, because he could not bear his happy dependence on his father in his own home. St. Paul tells us that the heathen were punished for their ingratitude to God by being allowed to fall into idolatry and degrade their moral nature in the hideous and nameless filthiness of paganism. We see the same law obtaining in the case of nations or persons, who emancipate themselves from the control of conscience to become the slaves of sin, who cast off the happy constraints of the Catholic faith to fall into endless delusions and fantastical forms of heretical error, or who cast aside the bond of Catholic unity because they think the rule of Christ's Vicar too severe, only to find themselves bound hand and foot, gagged, in chains and in darkness, the prisoners of the civil power, whose aid they have invoked to free them from Rome. But of all instances of the working of this law, none will be more striking and more wonderful than that of which our Saviour here speaks; when those who have rejected Him, the blessed, the merciful, the gentle and humble, the very incarnation of the sweetness and tenderness of God's ineffable love, shall give themselves up body and soul into the power of the Antichrist, to be the willing slaves and eager worshippers of one who will be the most detestably diabolical of all those servants of Satan that have ever been let loose on the world to punish it for its neglect of God.

The prophecies in Holy Scripture which, with more or less of certainty, may be referred to the subject of the great enemy of God, the Man of Sin, are very numerous, and are widely scattered over the several parts of the sacred volume. We may say that his figure is to be found at the source of the sacred stream of Divine prediction, where the enmities placed by God between the woman and her seed on the one hand, and the serpent and his seed on the other, are spoken of, and where it is said of the serpent, *Tu insidiaberis calcaneo ejus*—"Thou shalt lie in wait against her heel."* I say, if we compare this prophecy

* Gen. iii. 15.

with part of the Apocalyptic vision of St. John, we seem to see in it a distinct forecasting of the future Antichrist.* Then again, we may observe that in a passage in which the Prophet Ezechiel seems to speak of Antichrist, he uses words which appear to show that this same Antichrist was a familiar subject to the Prophets before him. "Thou then art he," he says, "of whom I have spoken in the days of old by My servants the Prophets of Israel, who prophesied in the days of those times that I would bring thee upon them."† Then again, we find him filling a large space in the prophecies of Daniel,‡ he is to be found in our Lord's words concerning the latter days, he is conspicuous in the passage of St. Paul which I quoted to you last Sunday, and we seem to feel his presence when St. Peter, St. Jude, and St. John, in their Epistles,§ dwell on the evil times that were to come at the end of the world. Lastly, as so much of Daniel's prophecy relates to him, so also do large portions of the Apocalypse of the Beloved Disciple,‖ who uses, concerning him and the events connected with him, language and imagery borrowed from the Prophets of the Old Testament, whose predictions he thus tacitly applies and fills up. Here then, my brethren, I have at once said enough to excuse myself from going in detail through the whole of this chain of prophecies, and, if the short time at our disposal did not preclude me from attempting it, I should still

---

* Apoc. xii.
† Ezech. xxxviii. 17.   ‡ Dan. vii. 8, 20; xi. xii.
§ 2 St. Peter, Epist. iii.; St. Jude, 4—18; St. John, 1 Epist. ii.
‖ Apoc. xiii.

shrink from the task, because these predictions are in many parts, as we might naturally expect them to be, difficult and of doubtful interpretation. The great enemy of God of whom we are speaking is to have, and has already had, many types, many anticipations, many forerunners in history, just as the last great persecution of the Church has had so many preludes and foreshadowings. Many of these forerunners of Antichrist, many of these anticipations of his time and of his work in history, have been themselves the subjects of prophecy, and thus we may frequently be mistaking for predictions of him passages which refer more immediately to them. It is enough for us then, if we can put forward such general outlines of his history, and such prominent features of his character, as seem to stand out unmistakeably from the sacred pages in which Daniel, St. John, and St. Paul appear evidently to speak of Antichrist, and thus to give ourselves clear and distinct ideas of the great evil which in course of time is to come upon the world.

II.

In the first place, then, my brethren, it is hardly needful to say that Antichrist is to be one particular person, a child born of a woman. I say it is hardly needful to point out how utterly foolish, as well as how untrue, must such an interpretation be as that which would explain the prophecies concerning him as if they related to a power, a principle, a system, and, above all, to a chain and succession of persons reaching from the earliest ages of the Church to the latest, such as is that once common Protestant figment, that Antichrist in prophecy was a personification of the power of the Holy See, and of the Pontiffs who have succeeded St. Peter. Antichrist could not come at the end of the world, and have a particular history, as we shall see, and a short and strongly-marked career, if he were merely the symbol of a line which began with Christianity itself and has endured ever since. Again, we are taught by Christian writers to put aside another wild notion, that Satan, or one of his evil angels, is to become actually incarnate, in imitation of the Incarnation of our Blessed Lord, and that thus the great enemy of the faith will be a demon in human form or nature. Satan is allowed much, but he will never be allowed so closely to imitate the blessed mystery of our Redemption, the greatest work of God, the union of two natures in one Person. No, Antichrist will be a man like other men, a child like other children; he will be borne in the womb, and suckled at the breasts of a woman, a daughter of Eve, and, moreover, he will have all the blessings granted to him, and all the prospects offered to him, which are the common heritage of the children of our race. A Guardian Angel will watch over him from the first, Saints will pray for him, he will have the door of the Church open to him as to others, the fatherly care of God will not neglect him in the ordinary course of providence, the tender and winning grace which is sufficient to enable him to do right and practise virtue, to imitate Christ and save his soul, will not be denied to him. But we are told by the

Fathers that he will at an early age fall under the corrupting power of the devil, and we see too much of the intense activity of the emissaries and tools of the evil one to pollute and pervert Christian children even in their tenderest years, we are too much occupied in daily conflict, even in Christian countries, to maintain for the Church and for the parent the right of the Christian education of the offspring, to see anything incredible in what we are taught will be the future of that unhappy child who is to grow into the enemy of God. He is to begin in obscurity, and to rise from a contemptible rank; but in a short time he will obtain a kingly station, and find himself in the possession of immense wealth and influence. God will have given him wonderful natural abilities, and his character will impose on and fascinate all who come within his reach. After a rapid series of victories of unexampled brilliancy, Antichrist will be for the time the master of the world.

The character of this miserable man is drawn out for us from the Scriptures by the Fathers and Christian writers,* and there is but little in it that has not been frequently foreshadowed by those who have been his types and precursors. Pride, cruelty, ambition, artifice, are among its leading features; and to these we may safely add, as a matter of course, extreme voluptuousness and licentiousness of manners.† What is more peculiar to him is that he

---

* The reader will find the authorities here referred to in Suarez, *De Incarnatione,* p. 2, disp. 54, and in Roberti's *Lezioni Sacre sopra la Fine del Mondo,* l. 4 and 5.

† Dan. xi. 37.

will be the author of a religion of his own. A great part of this will consist in the denial of the truth, and in insolence against God; but he will not only formally teach impiety and infidelity, and "speak great words against the High One," and deny "the God of his fathers,"* but he will specifically teach that he himself, and not our Lord Jesus Christ, is the true Messias, and he will set himself forth in the restored Temple of Jerusalem as the object of worship, as the only true God.† Here there are some lines in the prophetic description which seem to us as yet obscure and confused, because our eyes are not yet keen enough to see the harmony of statements, different though not conflicting—for we hear something of his making a god of his own to be worshipped,‡ and something also of a kind of restoration of paganism,§ of which he will be the author. It is certain, however, that he will have the command of all the power of Satan for the purpose of working false and illusive miracles in confirmation of his teaching, among which will be that he will call down fire from heaven, and have the power to make an image of his false god to speak.‖

Once more. Antichrist will be a great persecutor of the Church; a persecutor in cruelty, and in refinement of malice, and, as it would seem, in success, surpassing all those who have hitherto played that fatal part in the history of the Church. He will "make war with the Saints and overcome"¶—not indeed the Church, which is immortal and inde-

---

* Dan. vii. 8, 25; xi. 36, 37. † 2 Thess. ii. 4. ‡ Dan. xi. 38.
§ Apoc. xiii. 3, 14, 15. ‖ Apoc. xiii. 13, 15. ¶ Apoc. xiii. 7.

fectible, but large numbers of her weaker children. He is to reign in his seductions "over every tribe, and people, and tongue, and nation."* We are specially told that he will do what has already been done by former persecutors, and notably in the countries in which we live—he will proscribe and forbid the celebration of the Adorable Sacrifice of the Mass, the great act of worship of the Church.† Moreover, he will impose by law the worship of his own false religion; and in this, again, he has been anticipated by his forerunners. "Whosoever will not adore the image of the beast shall be slain." ‡ Again, we find foretold of him a species of cunning legal persecution, by no means incredible when we remember what the devices are which have at various times been adopted by the enemies of our holy religion, and what is the inquisitive nature of modern legislation. It appears that he will in some way exact an impious homage to himself, as a condition to be complied with by every one who would mix in the ordinary business of life, in traffic, commerce, and the like, so that no one can buy or sell except they have his mark on their right hand or on their forehead.§ All this points to a skilful warfare against souls, combined with, and a refinement upon, the old brutal cruelty of heathen or Protestant persecutors—a warfare which no doubt will be represented as a necessary condition for the security of government, as a just right of the State. Lastly, we are told that God will send special messengers and ministers of His Word, beside the

* Apoc. xiii. 7.
† Dan. xii. 11.　‡ Apoc. xiii. 15.　§ Apoc. xiii. 16, 17.

ordinary Hierarchy and ministers of the Church, to oppose this great enemy of the truth. You may remember how it stands recorded in different parts of the Scripture that two great servants of God have as yet not paid the common debt of mortality, but are preserved in some wonderful way, as has always been thought among Christians, to re-appear at the end of the world, and then to die for the truth. From the Patriarchs before the Flood Enoch was taken, and from the Prophets in the days of the Jewish dispensation Elias was taken ; and these two, as the tradition of the Church tells us, are to come and preach and work miracles, and, as it would seem, to convert at least a great part of the Jewish nation to God before the last day.* They are to oppose Antichrist, and at last are to be slain by him ; and then, in the moment of his triumph, at the height of his power, when all the earth seems silent before him, the enemy of God will be destroyed by the coming of our Lord Jesus Christ, as St. Paul tells the Thessalonians—" Whom the Lord Jesus shall kill with the spirit of His mouth and shall destroy with the brightness of His coming." †

III.

And now, my brethren, I suppose, when we look forward to these coming events in the history of the human race, our first view of them represents them to us as something perfectly novel and unheard of before, and we are inclined to suppose that all the

* Apoc. xi. 3—7.   † 2 Thess. ii. 8.

conditions of society and the whole character of the world's history must be radically changed before such things can take place. What! is a man to make himself worshipped in the temple of God? Is heathenism again to rise? Is the human race, after all its moral and material achievements, to grovel once more in idolatry, falsehood, and superstition? Now, I do not deny that there are many features in the character and in the proceedings of this great enemy of Jesus Christ which will be unexampled, at least in greatness and intensity, in all that may have gone before. We are told that Satan will then be "let loose;"* he has always by nature an immense power to hurt and to deceive the world, but he is permitted by God to exercise this power just as far as God sees fit, and there is a greater or less degree in this permission at various times. At the end of the world, when he makes what will be his last effort, God will permit him a greater amount of power, for the punishment of mankind who have treated the Gospel so ungratefully. This is true. In the latter days the power of evil will be in this sense increased, and the malice of the evil one will be intensified, because, as St. John says, he knows that "he hath but a short time." †

And yet we may go a great deal too far in allowing that there will be an altogether new state of things in the days of Antichrist. It is a pernicious delusion as to the ancient history of man, as it is recorded in Scripture, to suppose that the persons and the events, the principles and the motives, which

* Apoc. xx. 7.   † Apoc. xii. 12.

come into prominence in the sacred pages, were entirely different from those with which we are familiar. I say it is a mischievous delusion, because it leads us to feel as if we had nothing practically to do with the sacred history, and thus we are prevented from realising that the same things may happen in our day as happened then, that God is just as active in the guidance of human affairs, and in the notice which He takes of human crimes, as He was of old. And so I say, rather, that the days of Antichrist are to be the natural issue and outcome and fruit and development of the days in which we live, and that the elements and principles which are to be at work then in their greatest force are at this moment working around us. As to Antichrist himself, he will be a man of his own day, the legitimate child and offspring of the generation to which he belongs, gathering up in his own person and character its chief features and essential notes. To us, as he is described in the pages of Scripture, he is the enemy of God, the Man of Sin, the child of perdition, the persecutor of the Saints, the worker of lying wonders, the slave of Satan, the author and propagator of a false religion, the tyrannical proscriber of every worship but his own. To us he is, as he will be in reality, a man of blood, a soul stained with the deepest sin, given up to corruption, fearfully degraded, full of falsehood, vanity, impurity, cruelty, a soul in which evil has been carried to its higher pitch, as little mixed as it is possible to be in this world with the faintest shade of good; excluding, as far as may be, not only virtue and moral excellence, but even anything that can attract sympathy or admiration.

But Antichrist will not wear this aspect to the men of his day. Nay, I may venture to say still more—that, were he to come now, he would not look like this. No, my brethren, the world and the Church are always at war, and on each side there are heroes, great men, men who express the ideas and attract the sympathy and devotion of the side which they represent. At the head of the heroes of the Church is the lovely and noble beauty of Jesus Christ, the Incarnate Son of God; at the head of the world's heroes, their fitting and proper leader, the natural object of their devotion, will be the enemy of Jesus, the Antichrist. Evil and sin in this world do that much of homage to conscience and to virtue, that they never proclaim themselves to be what they are, and always present themselves, as it were, under the colours of their adversaries. Every giant of wickedness here calls himself the advocate of right and justice, every monstrous deed of public and worldwide wrong is done under the name of some watchword of goodness or of truth. It is liberty, or freedom, or enlightenment, or progress, or fraternity, that is inscribed on every banner that marshals behind it the hosts of evil. Words like these will be in the mouths of those who form the herd of the flatterers of Antichrist, who are the executors of his behests and the preachers of his doctrine. Men will talk then, as they talk now, of a great deliverance from the bondage under which religion has so long kept down the intellect and restrained the free exercise of the instincts of human nature. We shall hear of the emancipation of thought, the banishment of superstition, the breaking to pieces of the old fetters, the removal of old lines of distinction, the exploding of old fables about God, and judgment, and eternal punishment; about a nature infected with sin, and under sentence of degradation, a nature in need, forsooth, of a saviour and a deliverer, in need, forsooth, of grace from God to enable it to do right, a nature whose nobility lay in its being subdued, and whose highest perfection consisted in self-sacrifice and mortification! Humanity, it will be said then, has been groaning for centuries under a despotism which has withered its brightest flowers and poisoned its most enchanting pleasures by the old foolish chimeras of sin and responsibility and judgment hereafter; and the man who has revealed the glorious truth of the independence of nature will be hailed as the greatest of benefactors, and take his place, as it will be said, at the very summit of the historical grandeurs and glories of our race.

These things his admirers will say of Antichrist, as men like them may have said the same things of other conspicuous instruments of Satan and enemies of the truth, as it is in Jesus Christ, in ages before him. But the great fascination by which he will win the homage and submission of the men of his day, will be not only that he will give them an easy creed and persuade them that conscience is a bugbear and that the indulgence of their lowest passions is a right or a duty, but also the great and rapid and unexampled success which will mark his course. It will be permitted him to rise suddenly, and to be almost in a moment the victorious master of the world; and his brilliant abilities and irresistible march to the highest power will so dazzle the eyes of men that they will forget to examine the legitimacy of his claims or the soundness of his policy, the truth of his creed or the honesty and purity of his life. You know how often we hear it said that "nothing succeeds like success," how ready the men of this world are to idolize prosperous adventurers, men who have made their own way, men who have left their mark on their age, even for evil, men who have gained the object of their ambition even at the cost of honour and truthfulness. You know what a fascination genius of the lowest kind, and success by the most unprincipled means, exercise over the bulk of men, and how often we are startled by some instance which reveals to us how little their standard is in accordance with the character of our Lord, nay, how eagerly they will hail direct antagonism to Him. You may have read, my brethren, in the history of the last century, how that miserable man whose name has become famous as the patriarch and apostle of modern unbelief, the man who began, or at all events carried to its height, that system of calumniating and scoffing and sneering at Christianity which has so many followers still—though his contemporaries knew him, as we also know him from his biographies, to have been eaten up by meanness, petty spite, vanity, jealousy, avarice, insatiable pride, ostentation, and love of applause, so that his character appears to us to have nothing in it that any one could heartily admire or love in any way—yet how, at the very close of his long drawn-out life, when the hand of death was already creeping upon him, he had himself transported once more to Paris, and how he there became the object of universal homage and, it may almost be said, of worship. Worship, for no other reason so much as that he had been a brilliant forerunner of Antichrist in his doctrine, in laughing at religion and encouraging men in infidelity! And then all ranks of that gay and thoughtless society, dancing, as it were, at that moment, its last fling over the half-wakened fires of the volcano beneath its feet, which was so soon to burst forth and engulph the revellers in destruction—all ranks, I grieve to say, from the partner of the throne of the successor of St. Louis down to the lowest hangers-on of the light literature and the theatres of the time—came or sent in succession to the ante-chamber of that dying sinner as if to burn incense before him.* Ah! my brethren, have there not been triumphs in our day, and not far from us, which might remind us well enough of that last miserable triumph of Voltaire? triumphs, in which men of blood and crime and the most barefaced villainy, men who have hardly condescended to veil their rapine and violence under the cloak of some colourable pretext, have been made the heroes of a cultivated and refined society that calls itself Christian, while their chief claim on the homage of their worshippers has really been this—that they have been great enemies and injurers of the Church

* See Maynard's *Voltaire, sa Vie ses Œuvres*, t. ii. p. 590. Voltaire died in 1778.

and of the Holy See? What wonder then if we are led to think that Antichrist will be the idol of his day, when to the charm of being a great denier and assailant of the checks and restraints which God has placed upon the unbridled indulgence of natural appetites, he will add the fascination of success such as the world has never before seen, and when he will enforce his claims by the aid of lying wonders, and when—to add that last sad element of all—the men of his time, because they have resisted and hated the truth, will be handed over by the just judgment of God to a spirit of blindness and delusion, so as to believe a lie!

IV.

Yes, my brethren, the world is always ready for its Antichrist. Its principles, and motives, and manners of judging, its aims and desires and longings, are all such as will find themselves satisfied, encouraged, answered to, in him. On the other hand, there is this consolation for the children of the Church, for those who form their thoughts and minds, who regulate their judgments and their lives, on the pattern of Jesus Christ and of His Saints, that they have in their own hearts and consciences a light and an unction of the Holy Ghost which will enable them to withstand all the wiles and seductions of the evil one, to see through all his false wonders and lying miracles, and to baffle his power, if it be so, even by death. Only, my brethren, let us not deceive ourselves by thinking that all this that we have been speaking of is a thing of the future, a matter of merely historical interest and excitement to ourselves. No, my brethren, whether the latter days fall now, or centuries hence, Antichrist, as we have already seen, is in the world at present. We recognize the workings of Divine Providence in the events of our time, and we should think ourselves faithless if we did not see the finger of God both in what befalls the Church, and in what befalls ourselves. But we must recognize also the working of the enemies of God. There is another hand continually active all around us; and it behoves us very much not to mistake it or to ignore it. We need that holy simplicity of the Saints, which always saw Satan behind the forms of his instruments, and called by their right name the machinations of the evil one. In the days of St. Catharine of Siena, there was a war against the Church at the head of which were many of the Church's own princes, and she, humble, meek, and charitable as she was, did not speak of these tools of evil as a party, or as representing an idea, or as advocating a policy or a mistaken principle, but in the plainest language she called them *devils*.* Well, my brethren, the hand that is to guide Antichrist is always plotting against the Church and against society. Satan is always, generation after generation, preparing men to be his instruments in the final conflict, he is always undermining our holy faith, always blinding and misleading the world, ever and anon setting forth his chosen instruments and servants in the work of impiety, and teaching them to clothe and bear themselves in such

* *Dimoni incarnati.* S. Catar. Epist. xviii. t. 1; edit. Burclamacchi. Lucca, 1772.

guise as to attract the attention, the interest, the influence, the popularity, which will at last centre around Antichrist himself.

Let us then, dear brethren in Jesus Christ, take care, in the first place, never to bow down or do homage to the world's idols—to intellect, to power, to success, to wealth, to the achievements of dishonest policy, to the prosperous lying, the unblushing wickedness, the boastful injustice of our time. Let us stand on the old paths, and give honour where alone honour is due, to humility, and purity, and meekness, and self-sacrifice, and charity, and zeal for the glory of God. Let us shrine in our heart of hearts, as the measure of all good, the object and centre of all love, Jesus Christ our Lord, Who has come to us in the name of His Father. And in the second place, let us be like men, looking forwards rather than backwards, men waiting for, and looking out for their Lord—not so much counting up what those before us have done and suffered for the cause of God, as if, forsooth, the days of persecution and conflict were gone, never to return; as if henceforth we were to lead quiet and unruffled lives, enjoying our truce with the world, making the most of our position in society, eating, and drinking, and marrying, and giving in marriage, as in the days of Noe—like men who have hung up their fathers' armour in their halls, and sit round the fire telling tales of their prowess, and yet know not and think not themselves how to lift a hand in the fight in which their fathers bled. No, my brethren; the Church of God is now preparing herself for her last persecution, and she is preparing herself by nothing so much as by waging vigorous warfare now in our own days against the evil influences of the world, and in repelling its assaults upon her outworks, such as marriage and education, as well as upon her doctrines and upon her unity. The last persecution may come in your days, or in the days of your children, or in the days of your children's children ; but your children, and your children's children will be what you are, what your example and your teaching make them. If you are soldiers, watchful, self-denying, eager to beat back and advance upon the enemies of your souls and of the Church—then, my brethren, you will have done a twofold good. You will have served the Church and God in your own day, and so have weakened the power of evil in all days, and you will have left behind you and handed on to your little ones the traditions of faithfulness, warfare, toil, and sacrifice for God. If you are soft, self-indulgent, worldly, indolent, careless of the dangers, and at peace with the evils, of our time, then, though Antichrist come not yet, you will have done a twofold evil which will descend in misery upon those who come after you. You will have weakened the cause of God in your own day, and so you will have made the future triumph of evil more easy and more complete ; and you will have bequeathed to your children the traditions and the training which will but ill fit them to withstand in their own generation the wiles, the seductions, and the cruelties of the great enemy of Jesus Christ.

SERMON XI.

THE CHURCH IN THE LAST DAYS.

Ubicumque fuerit corpus, illic congregabuntur et aquilæ.

Wherever the body shall be, there the eagles also shall be gathered together.

(Words taken from the 28th verse of the 24th chapter of St. Matthew's Gospel.)

I.

THIS is one of those enigmatic sayings of our Blessed Lord, taken from natural and well-known facts, which strike upon the mind and memory, even when we do not at once perceive their meaning. Perhaps our Lord did not wish to make it clear to all, as He here gives us, in a few words, almost a complete parable, and His parables, as we know, were meant primarily for those only who are admitted to the knowledge of the mysteries of His Kingdom. I shall not attempt to-day to draw out all the meanings which have been attached to these words by the commentators of the Church. But they will furnish us with the occasion of dwelling on certain truths concerning the last days, which ought not to be left out of consideration, when that great subject is treated at any length.

We have been endeavouring to consider one by one, my brethren in our Lord, a series of these features of the last time which are more or less constant and permanent in the world, because they are the natural results of elements and principles which are almost always at work among men. We have considered the mischief that will be produced, that has been already produced, in our time and in times earlier than our own, by the decay of faith and the increase of false creeds and false doctrines, by the waning and growing cold of Christian charity, by the immense development of the national spirit, by the encroachments of the civil power on the rights of the Church, and by the corresponding undermining of the civil power by the spirit of lawlessness—a certain effect of civil encroachments in the spiritual sphere—by the increase of luxury, the engrossment of mankind in the enjoyment of temporal and sensual pleasures, and by the immense corruption and blindness and hardness of heart which must naturally ensue from these causes. Lastly, we have considered that in the latter days, as has been the case, at least partially, in our own, the spiritual enemies of God and man will be allowed a large measure of licence, for the delusion and perversion of mankind. All these are great elements and powers of evil. Any one of them by itself is a great danger, and when they all combine in any larger extent of development and influence than before, in any one generation, there is at least reason for thinking that that generation is not unlike that on which the end of the world will come. And finally we have considered how the prophecies tell us that all the evil principles and elements in society are to be summed up, and, as it were, personified in the appearance of one great champion, the hero of his day as men will account him, the Archenemy of God, as the Church will know him to be, who is already named in the New Testament as the Antichrist, the opponent and rival of our Blessed Lord.

Now it is certainly natural for us to ask, what, in the face of all this collection and combination of the powers and influences of evil in the world, will have become of the Church of God? We know, from the words of our Lord, that the gates of Hell are not to prevail against her. We know far more than that, for we know that she is furnished and equipped with Divine power, and that she has, within the range of her resources, even more than is required for the perfect "healing of the nations," if the nations of the world would be healed. How is it then to be with her in the midst of all these tempests and woes, these birth pangs of the new creation? What will be her lot and her conduct, what will be the strength of her children, how will they bear themselves in these last struggles, and how especially will it be with the provisions which she supplies for the weak, and the timid, and the helpless, on whom yet, if we are to judge from the history of her first conflicts in the world, the battle will fall as well as on the strong and well-trained soldiers of Jesus Christ?

II.

For an answer to these natural questionings, we may go back once more to the great prophecy of the last days in which the words of the text are contained. We have had to refer to it over and over again, and this is not wonderful, for the words of our

Lord on any great subject of Christian thought must be the great storehouse of our information on that subject. Our Lord is speaking to His Apostles on Mount Olivet, at a very short interval of time before His Passion. The key-note of His whole discourse is given in the words with which it opens in the account of it which is recorded for us by St. Matthew: "Take heed that no man seduce you."* The prophecy relates to two question which had been asked, one as to the destruction of Jerusalem, the other as to the end of the world, and, as you know, these two events are in our Lord's mind as the answers. I need not go through that Divine discourse. You will remember how earnestly He speaks of the danger of seduction. Many are to come in His Name, teachers of heresies, authors of schisms, declaring that they come from Him, and speak His truth, and they are to seduce many. There are to be wars and rumours of wars, the latter perhaps not less disquieting than the former. There are to be national strifes, there are to be earthquakes and famines and pestilence. They are themselves to be persecuted—even hated of all nations, for the sake of His Name. There are to be scandals, and false brethren, betraying one another, hating one another. Iniquity is to abound, and charity is to grow cold. The Gospel is to be preached in all the world, and then the end will come. Then, after a passage about the sign of the destruction of Jerusalem, our Lord returns to the general picture. The Apostles, or Christians through them, are warned not to believe people who say to

* St. Matt. xxiv. 4.

them, "Lo, here is Christ; lo, there." The false Christs and prophets shall even show great signs and wonders. "If they shall say to you, Behold, He is in the desert, go ye not out; behold, He is in the closets, believe it not." And then He gives two ways in which the presence of the Son of Man is to be known. "For as lightning cometh out of the east, and appeareth even unto the west, so shall also the coming," or the Presence, "of the Son of Man be." That is the first way in which men may know where our Lord is to be found: His Presence will be as manifest and as unmistakeable as the sheet of lightning, which darts in one single moment from one end of heaven to the other. Who can doubt where the lightning is? There is no part of the heavens in which it is not. It is not here or there, it is everywhere. And then our Lord gives a second sign of His Presence, which is altogether different from the former. "Wheresoever the Body is, there also will the eagles be gathered together." Thus our Lord in this place does what He was so often wont to do in the Parables, in which He set forth the secrets of His Kingdom. He uses one image to express one part of a truth, and then an entirely different image to express another part of the same truth. First, He implies that His Presence in the Church will be unmistakeable, because it is everywhere at once, and then He uses as the image of the faculty of discerning His Presence, the marvellous instinct which brings together the eagles over their prey. For travellers tell us that the camel or other animal that may die of exhaustion in the midst of the desert, may fall to the ground on some spot from which, if you look all round the horizon, east and west and north and south, you will not see a single bird of prey in sight, or any rock or eyrie where its nest may be. And yet, before the poor quarry breathes its last breath, the eagles will be there from every point of the compass, ready to fasten on their helpless prey.

> Need to tell the famished eagles where the reeking carcase lies !
> It can draw them to itself from every corner of the skies.

They come, guided by instinct or nature, which God has given them. And so it will be, and so it is with our Lord. Those that are His know Him, and can find Him out in His Church. Their instincts are more keen and more certain than those of the eagles. There have been saints on earth who would enter a large church, and make their way without guide or note or mark to the altar where the Blessed Sacrament is kept. These are special and personal gifts, the occasional reward of immense devotion and intense purity of soul, just as other saints have had the gift of discovering the foulness of sin in the souls of those who came to them by their air or their look. But there is also a general power of perception as to our Lord's presence in the Church, in confirmation of and as a supplement to, her great external notes and marks, which are evident to all alike, and this instinctive knowledge of Him will be a further safeguard to those who love Him in the dark days which shall go before His second Advent.

Thus we have our Blessed Lord telling us, in the passage of which we are speaking, that there are two very different ways by which His presence may be known. I say His presence, because, even if we are to limit the direct meaning of the words before us to that which shall be at the time of His second coming, for which limitation there seems no certain reason in the context, still it would remain true that what is said by Him of that second coming, cannot but be true in its measure of His continual presence in the Catholic Church. The one of these methods of His presence or coming is manifest and unmistakeable to all, the other is for the few or at least not for all. The one is for His friends and for His enemies alike, the other is only for His friends. That is, the one is like the shining of the lightning from one end of the heavens to the other, the other is like the secret attraction by which the eagles are drawn unerringly to their prey. And we find our Lord using this last image, that of which the words of the text speak, in another place, where He does not use the first. He is speaking of the last days, and saying how from the same field and the same bed, one shall be taken and another left. That is, side by side with those who belong to our Lord, and are to be caught up to meet Him in the air, there will be those who do not belong to Him, and who will be left for destruction, "I say to you, in that night there shall be two men in one bed, the one shall be taken and the other shall be left. Two women shall be grinding together, the one shall be taken and the other shall be left. Two men shall be in the field, the one shall be taken and the other shall be left." And the Evangelist goes on, they "answering say to Him, Where, Lord? Who said to them,

Wheresoever the body shall be, thither will the eagles also be gathered together." * Here there is question of some secret attraction or discernment, which is not common to all, like that indication of the presence of our Lord, which can be compared to the lightning, seen from one end of the sky to the other—all men see the lightning, the eagles alone can discern the body on which they are to be fed.

III.

So it is, at all events, my brethren, with the knowledge of our Lord in His holy Catholic Church. Ever since the time when she became the great feature in the world that she now is, ever since she came forth from the catacombs into which the fury of the persecution had driven her, she has been cognisable by the whole world by means of what we call her visible Notes. These Notes, from the earliest times, have been enshrined in the Catholic Creeds, and never has there been but one body on earth to which they would truly and plainly apply. She is herself her own great witness, and her history, and her powers, and her institutions, and her adaptation to the needs of mankind, show her to be as Divine as she claims to be. They show her to be this in two ways —first, positively, by the manner in which she has proved that she can cure all the ills of society, and has created a happiness and a beauty and a dignity in human life which did not exist before, whenever she is allowed her way and not hindered from the exercise of her beneficent influences, and she has

* St. Luke xvii. 34—37.

shown the same negatively also—by a proof which is unfortunately going on in its exhibition in the days in which we live, and which will probably continue to be more sadly exemplified as the years roll on—by the manner in which paganism, and barbarism, and materialism, and cruelty, and lust, and ambition, become magnified as the great dominant influences in the world, by the denial of the supremacy of conscience, of the spirituality of the soul, and other such fundamental truths, which becomes rife and wide spread the moment her salutary rule is thrown off and her teaching disregarded. But these ways of knowing the Church are open to all, the last as well as the first, and there are now many intellectual men who are not Christians, who will not shrink from the candid acknowledgment that there is no alternative between the full Catholic creed and the denial of all theism itself.

Now, my brethren, it is surely true to say that evidences of this kind, although they are most powerful and most convincing, and although they are the appointed proofs, in many respects, of the Divine mission of the Catholic Church, are still in the main external. They are evidences such as can be grasped by those outside the Church herself, as indeed we see it constantly to be the case, as I have just now said, that they are acknowledged to be most cogent even by those who are not converted by them. It is not to depreciate these proofs of the Church to say there are evidences of another kind which address themselves more to those who are inside the pale of Catholicism than to those who are outside. Such are the proofs on which devotion feeds, after conversion has taken place, which are the delight and the support of those who do not need external evidence. It is very natural that we should find the Apostles speaking of the existence of such evidences to their converts, because in the beginnings of the Church, although there were not wanting the proofs of her divinity, such as were afforded by miracles, by the fulfilment of prophecy, and the like, still the evidences of the great Notes of the Church, by which we now prove her to be what she asserts herself to be, could not, in the nature of things, be existing or be recognized in their fulness. Surely, if we believe the Holy Spirit of God to be shed abroad in our hearts, it is natural to suppose also that He will make His presence felt in some secret but most convincing way. You remember what the men of that Samaritan city said to the woman who had first informed them about our Lord and His conversation with her—"We now believe, not for thy saying, for we ourselves have heard Him and know that this is indeed the Saviour of the world." * How can any one live, in the constant use of the holy sacraments, a life of prayer and intercourse with our Lord, how can any one watch over the movements and breathings of his own conscience, and know what it is to have holy inspirations, and to walk in the continual presence of God, and not at the same time have an experimental knowledge of the actual truth of the claims of his religion and of the Church in which these blessings fall to his lot?

* St. John iv. 42.

Faithfulness to grace, purity of intention, continual self-discipline and diligence in the practice of the Christian virtues—I do not say that the light and the peace and the joy which these things generate are infallible guides, without the external witness of the Church, much less against that witness, but when they coincide with the external evidence by which we know where the Catholic Church is, it is not possible but that they must add a security and a certainty to the soul, just as an impure or careless life tends, in great measure, to impair even the vividness of faith. See how confidently St. John appeals to this kind of evidence in his Epistle to his own spiritual children, among whom there had been some seducers attempting their perversion. "These things," he says, "have I written to you concerning them that seduce you. And as for you, let the unction which you have received of Him, abide in you. And you have no need that any man teach you, but as His unction teacheth you of all things, and is truth and no lie, and as it hath taught you, abide in Him."*

This is the language of one who can trust those to whom he is speaking, because he can reckon on the work of the Holy Spirit of God in their souls. And it seems to me to be confirmed by the language of our Lord Himself in the passage from which the text is taken, where He tells us that there shall arise false Christs and false prophets and show great signs and wonders, "insomuch as to deceive (if possible) even the elect." "If possible," He says,

* 1 St. John ii. 26, 27.

and by that He implies that it is not possible for the elect to be deceived. The false signs and wonders will all be external evidences, by means of which the teachers of falsehood will be allowed, in that dark day, to parody the external evidences of the Catholic Church by what seem to be similar prodigies worked in favour of their own errors. But the elect of God, the faithful and true followers of the Church, will be guarded against the snare by a twofold shield, besides the evidence of the great worldwide notes. In the first place they will have the shield of prophecy. For all these seductions are foretold by our Lord, and so they cannot harm those who know them beforehand and are prepared to expect them, and this, besides the notes of the Church, will be, so to say, the external shield of the elect. And in the second place they will be protected by that interior unction of which St. John speaks, by the light and fire and fragrance and instinct of the Holy Ghost in their hearts, whereby they will be so united to our Lord as to be able to find Him out and cling to Him, even when the world is overclouded with the darkness of evil, and to endure all the contradictions of the last persecution, as St. Paul says of Moses, "seeing Him that is invisible." *

IV.

My brethren, you may know that men have often been led astray by putting too much faith in their own interior feelings or convictions, and in what they deemed Divine inspirations guiding their indi-

* Heb. xi. 27.

vidual conscience. For it is not the will of God that we should be guided in matters which belong to the teaching of the Church by anything but that Divine teaching. And so, if there were to be nothing but this interior unction at the last period of the world to secure the saints against deception, if they were taught to look to that exclusively, they would not be armed against the dangers of that time as God means them to be armed. This is a certain truth. But it is not the less true, it may be, that we need the twofold guidance of which our Lord here speaks, and that even the lightning declaring to us the presence of our Lord in His Church might not be enough, because it might indeed show us where He is, but it might not give us the force and the courage to seek Him, in the face of all the manifold difficulties which will then beset His elect. In those days men will want love as well as knowledge, they will want that desire and longing for our Lord which He describes under this image of the hunger of the eagles hastening to their prey, as well as the light which shows them where He ought to be sought. How common is it even in the days in which we live, to find men who tell us that if anything in the way of religion is true, it is the Catholic Church, but who have not the strength to make themselves her children against the cravings of their passions, or the influences of worldly interest! As far as we can guess, the number of such men is on the increase, as it cannot but be on the increase, as the hollowness of all the rival claims of the sects and establishments founded on national feeling or on policy, becomes more and more evident to thinking men, and as the pretended national churches are gradually deprived of the support of the State and of their ancient endowments, which have ever been their strongest sources of influence. What is this but to say, that more and more we have need of the overmastering hunger of the eagles, as well as of the shining of the lightning from east to west? The external evidences of the Catholic Church do not address themselves with any cogency to men who do not feel the need of any religion, and it is this state of mind and heart that will characterize the last period of the life of the human race. It is quite conceivable that then the Catholic Church may represent to the world the one solitary remaining religion, that she may be the only considerable body which even calls itself by the name of Jesus Christ, and that her difficulties in that time will not be in her struggle with a swarm of sects, but how to get men to acknowledge that they have souls to save, a conscience to obey, and a God to Whom they are accountable.

What then, my brethren, can we wish and pray for more ardently, for ourselves and for others, than that God will make us all eagles in the sense in which that image is here used by our Blessed Lord? that our hearts may be consumed with hunger and thirst after justice, that the love of our Lord may so drive us on and on, that we may be unable to rest away from Him, as if we should indeed die if we found Him not? Oh! let us pray that the fruit of that blessed frequentation of the sacraments, and other means of grace, which is our present privilege, but which in the days of the last persecution may be denied us, as it was denied to our forefathers in the time of their persecution, may be a strength and ripeness and robustness of spirit, which may make us able to take long and lofty flights in the service of our Lord—that that interior vigour may be formed in us, which makes little account of the things of this world and even of exterior helps, when such cannot be had! Keen of sight and strong of pinion, and dauntless in courage, and ever ready to die in defence of what is dear to them, dwellers on the lonely peaks with the stars and clouds, and far from the noisy world—such is the picture which we form from what we know concerning the characteristics of the eagles, and our Lord here adds the further trait, that nothing prevents them from finding out their prey or keeps them from it when it is found. Such we may surely say must be the saints of the latter days, and if such must they be, such must be those from whom they come. The poet tells us that the fierce eagles do not give birth to the timid and cowering dove, and neither, we may say, will the timid and soft-hearted dove give birth to the warrior eagle. And so again and again we come round to the same old truth—that the comforts and effeminacies and frivolities and childishnesses of modern life can never be looked to for the training of men who are to fight the last brave fight for God and for our Lord, and that, if there are to be eagles of spirit then their breeding and their nurturing must be now.

SERMON XII.

REASONABLENESS OF THE JUDGMENT.

Et tempora quidem hujus ignorantiæ despiciens Deus, nunc annuntiat hominibus ut omnes ubique pœnitentiam agant, eo quod statuit diem in quo judicaturus est orbem in æquitate in viro in quo statuit, fidem præbens omnibus, suscitans eum a mortuis.

And God indeed having winked at the times of this ignorance, now declareth unto men, that all should everywhere do penance, because He hath appointed a day wherein He will judge the world in equity, by the Man Whom He hath appointed, giving faith to all by raising Him from the dead.

(Words taken from the 30th and 31st verses of the 17th chapter of the Acts of the Apostles.)

I.

WE have often gazed in wonder, my brethren in our Lord, on the famous work of the great Christian painter, in which we see St. Paul depicted as he delivered these simple but most startling words. He was standing in the midst of the assembly of the Areopagus at Athens. We have delighted to follow out the hints which that great Master has given us as to the various attitudes of mind among the listeners on that famous occasion, their perplexity, their half-intelligence, their interest, their acquiescence, their irritation and indignation. If it is not certain that St. Paul stood there as one bound to give an account of himself to men who were judges appointed to deal with innovators in matters of religion, so that even his life was at stake, at least he had among his audience men who wielded immense influence, and who must have been far from pleased at the plain truth which he declared to them in the name of God. If these men were not judges with power to enforce their sentence, at least they were critics little likely to enter readily into the thoughts of that blessed servant of our Lord. They constituted the most cultivated, the most refined, the most intellectual audience to be found in the world. That was, so far, in favour of St. Paul; but, like other men of the same class in other times, they were puffed up and intoxicated by the adulation which they received from their followers and from one another. They were the teachers of philosophy to the Roman world, their words, as is so often the case with such men, were caught up as the utterances of an oracle by a large circle of pupils and admirers, and, if humility be required in those who are to listen patiently and profitably to the words of Divine truth, there is no great likelihood that that heavenly virtue was prevalent among them. St. Luke tells us that all the Athenians and the strangers dwelling among them "spent their time in nothing else but either in telling or hearing some new thing."* And in those few words that blessed Evangelist has painted the frivolity of that so-called seat of learning in colours which are fresh to us even at this distance of time—for, do we not understand the restless curiosity and shallow excitability of such men, a class of whom we have so many thousand specimens among our-

* Acts xvii. 21.

selves—the men who pass from one subject to another without sounding the depths of any, the devourers of half a dozen volumes in so many days, book after book, article after article, novel after novel, as intemperate in their thirst for empty novelties as the habitual drunkard crying out for new drinks, men almost industrious in their pursuit of silliness, and almost serious in their craving for dissipation?

Among such men, then, with whose descendants we are all familiar, did St. Paul stand forth to speak of the Day of Judgment. He began, with his exquisite courtesy and loving skill, by complimenting them on their love of devotion, and he made no higher claim than that of making more clear to them that of which they had already some conception. They had raised an altar to the Unknown God. That was the text from which St. Paul began. He told them how God had made the heaven and the earth, how He had planted the various nations of the world on this globe, all of one race, that they might seek after Him, feel for Him, grope for Him, and so find Him, for He was not far off from any of them. In Him indeed they lived and moved and were. So far, St. Paul must have had the good will and favour and patronage of his intelligent audience, and he may have won them still more when he went on to quote to them one of their own poets in support of what he said. He was a man of letters, then, as well as of modest and pleasant address and demeanour, timid, perhaps hesitating ere he felt himself close to his great argument—this man of no commanding presence, of no self-assertion, this stranger from the distant land of the despised and even hated Jews! And then he spoke so boldly and so plainly and so brusquely that their patronizing feelings towards him were rudely shocked. He told them that they must enter into themselves and set their consciences in order, and prepare to give an account to their Master and their God. The great tidings he told them on the part of this great Lord and Master of all, was that they and all men must do penance, "because He hath appointed a day in which He will judge the world by the Man Whom He hath chosen," and that the proof He gives of this declaration is that He has raised this Man from the dead.

Stern words these, for the Epicureans and the Stoics, and the rest—men accustomed indeed to moral speculations, to dispute of the nature of the soul, of good and of evil, of happiness, of futurity, and the like, but all in an academic and literary way, without practical result—with no care for conscience, no watchfulness over thoughts, no application to their own lives of their theories about virtue, such as men should make who are to meet a Judge and give an account to Him. And you know also how it was afterwards, at a later time in the life of the great Apostle: how in his history St. Luke tells us that the Apostle spoke of the same subjects to the Roman Governor Felix, on whose will his life then depended, and when "he treated of justice and chastity and of the judgment to come, Felix being terrified answered, for this time go thy way, and when I have a convenient time I will send for thee."* A convenient time, my brethren,

* Acts xxiv. 25.

which probably never came for Felix, who was soon removed by Providence from the intercourse which he had begun with St. Paul. A convenient time which thousands of men promise themselves, and but few take the pains to secure, and which we Catholics at least have no excuse if we do not seize, because God has provided in the Church the whole of this blessed season of Advent, before we commemorate the first coming of our Lord in mercy and humility, that we may prepare ourselves for meeting Him when He comes again as our Judge in majesty, and justice, and power.

II.

Surely, my brethren, the truth which the Apostle of Jesus Christ thought it worth his while to urge so suddenly and so forcibly on the attention of these philosophers and their pupils, cannot be one from which any Christian can venture to turn away. And, now that we are at length come to the consideration of the Judgment itself, having passed in consideration many, at least, of the great phenomena in the moral world which, as we are told, will precede it, I begin by reminding you of a truth which has already been set before you with some fulness in the course of these sermons. This truth is that we may fairly conclude that St. Paul was guided by the Holy Ghost, in this choice of subject for his discourse before these philosophers, who knew little of God or of His dealings with men in comparison to the extent to which they were known to the favoured nation, with whom the oracles of God, as he says elsewhere, were deposited

—and St. Paul must have discerned in their condition some features which promised him that his appeal to them in this manner would not be altogether without fruit. That is, we may suppose that St. Paul would not have so boldly and plainly challenged their belief in this doctrine of the Judgment of the world by our Lord Jesus Christ, unless he had known that it was a truth to which there was sufficient witness in natural reason and in the instinctive cravings and guesses, so to say, of the human mind, to make it one from which they would not turn away. These men represented to him the cultivated reason of mankind, as left, in a certain measure, to themselves, as he says in this same marvellous speech, to seek God if haply they might feel after Him and find Him, with conscience and reason and Providence and nature for their guides, helped also no doubt by whatever of the primitive tradition of the children of Adam and of Noe had come down to them unpolluted and undistorted. What then he takes for granted in addressing them, we may suppose that he had reason for thinking either that they knew, or that it was at all events so consonant to reason that they would not turn away from it, and that when put before them it might be expected, with the cooperation of God's grace, to have a power for their conversion and preparation for higher truths which other subjects might not possess.

You observe also that St. Paul lays down two sets of truths in these few words, one set of which are truths of natural religion and the other set of which are matter of revelation. In the first place, you see, he takes it for granted that it is reasonable and right for God to judge the world. And indeed if God made the world and all mankind, as the Apostle asserts to these philosophers, if He made man free, and responsible—for the condition of responsibility is a natural consequence of the condition of freedom—then it is a matter of reasonable consequence that man must give an account to his Master and Lord of the use he has made of his freedom, when the span of his time of probation comes to its natural end. And I find St. Paul elsewhere bears witness to the truth which is the confirmation and proof of what I say, where he speaks of the judgment of God which is to be without respect of persons over Jews and Gentiles equally,* and he says that some of the Gentiles, who had not the written law, still did the works of the law, by the light of nature, though certainly not without the grace of God, and he says of such that they show the work of the law written in their hearts, their conscience bearing witness to them, and their thoughts between themselves "accusing or else defending one another." For it needs no very deep analysis to show us that our conscience is not simply a declaration that this or that is good or bad, or even right or wrong, in itself, but that its voice is a declaration that this or that is lawful or unlawful, forbidden or allowed, worthy of reward or of punishment, and, moreover, that it appeals silently, but most forcibly, to a power greater than itself and greater than ourselves, whose voice it is, and that by that appeal it threatens us with anger and with punishment from God if we disobey, and promises us His approbation and a reward from Him if we

* Romans ii. 14.

obey. Now, I say that this proves to us that wherever there is a conscience—and there is no child of Adam who has not at least this amount of knowledge to guide him through his time of probation—where there is a conscience, there there is a sufficient foundation for this simple doctrine of natural religion, that the Maker and the Lord of all men will judge them all and will reward them or punish them according to their works.

This is the natural truth of which St. Paul makes use, and to which he boldly appeals in these Athenians. But he adds others which are matter of revelation, namely, that God has determined to judge the world by a Man, on a particular fixed day. His assertion is this, that there is to be an end of this world at a given time, and that the judgment is to be by a Man, by our Lord Jesus Christ, and that God has given to the world a proof of this determination on His own part, by means of the Resurrection of our Lord from the dead. St. Paul does not tell them that the Man Who is the chosen Judge of the world, is God Himself, and the Son of God. He does not tell them how He came to die, or what are the ineffable consequences of the atonement wrought on the Cross by the death of the Son of God. But he does declare to the Athenians that the judgment is now to be expected, and that, as St. Peter said in his address to the first Gentile converts admitted to the Church, concerning our Blessed Lord, "God raised Him up the third day and gave Him to be manifest, not to all the people, but to witnesses pre-ordained of God, even to us who did eat and drink with Him after He rose again from the dead, and He commanded us to preach to the people and to testify, that it is He Who was appointed by God to be the Judge of the living and of the dead."*

We have therefore a right to say, my brethren, that this truth to which the Church calls our attention year after year at this holy season of Advent, is a truth which is witnessed to by the moral nature and constitution of man himself, a truth which he might anticipate even if it were not revealed to him, a truth, rather let us say, which every good and virtuous man in the world, under whatever dispensation or creed, does anticipate in his daily government of himself, and of which every vicious man and every wicked man in the world is afraid, and would get rid of if he could. And now I take one great part of this truth, as the subject of our thoughts during what I have to say to-day. I say, one great part, for, as you know, there are stars in the heaven which seem to us single stars, and when we look at them through a powerful telescope they are double stars, or even a cluster of stars. And so this truth of the judgment of God, when we look on it in the light of revelation, I might almost say of reason also, resolves itself into two, which in point of fact correspond to two things which are yet future to all of us, and which may well be separated in our thoughts of what is to come. The first part of this great truth is that which we find in the words of the Apostle when he says, "It is appointed to men once to die, and after that the judgment,"† or when he says, "We shall all stand

* Acts x. 40—42.   † Heb. ix. 27.

before the judgment-seat of Christ."* This is the truth of what we call the particular judgment, which, as we believe, takes place at the end of the life of each man who passes out of this world into the next, and on which, in truth, the fate of each one of us for all eternity must depend. And the other great truth is that to which so many passages of Scripture bear witness, and which, as St. Jude tells us, was the subject of the prophecy of the earliest saint before the Flood, the holy Enoch, who left behind him the prediction that the Lord was to come "with thousands of His Saints, to execute judgment on all, and to reprove all the ungodly for all the works of their ungodliness, whereby they have done ungodly, and of all the hard things that ungodly sinners have spoken against God."† This is the truth of what we call the General Judgment, which is an article of the Christian creed, and which the Church puts before our minds especially at this time.

Surely, my brethren, there is no need to dwell on the immense contrast between these two judgments. It is true that in each we are to give an account to the same Judge, our Lord Jesus Christ, and the subject-matter of the judgment is the same, for it is simply the deeds that we have done in the body. But the first passes in secret, the other before the whole universe, the first is of one single soul only, the other is of the whole world, in the first it is our Lord alone to Whom we give an account, in the other it is to the whole assemblage of the intelligent creatures of God, the angels and the saints and the devils of Hell,

---

* Rom. xiv. 10.   † St. Jude 14, 15.

as well as to all men that ever have been and that ever have to be. In the first we are simply the accused, who have to answer for what we have ourselves done, and in the second we are not only the accused, but we are the witnesses also of the judgment of all others. For the whole history of men and of angels will then be laid bare to all, the history of the world as well as the history of each single child of Adam, and then will be manifested not only our works and words and thoughts, and those of all the human race, but also the acts of God to the whole world and to each individual soul, to His greater glory and to our final enlightenment, according to that marvellous saying of holy David, "that thou mayest be justified in thy words and mayest overcome when thou art judged."*

III.

Now, my brethren, with regard to this last great Judgment, we may surely be certain that God cannot have ordained it without a most wise and just reason, and we know that what God has so ordained must be most profitable for us to meditate on and to make ourselves familiar with. And we have all the more reason for this from the manner in which use of this truth is made in Sacred Scripture and by our Lord Himself, Who made this, as you have been told, the very last warning which He addressed to His enemies when they were about to condemn Him to death as a blasphemer because He made Himself the Son of God. These were the very last words He spoke to

Psalm l. 6.

the Jewish priests in His Passion, " Hereafter you shall see the Son of Man sitting on the right hand of power and coming in the clouds of Heaven."† And I do not know if any truth of the kind was more frequently in the mouths of the Apostles after our Lord than this, or more deeply engraved by their preaching on the hearts of the men of the first generation of the Catholic Church. And it seems to have produced in them two fruits at least of which we have not so much experience in later days, first, their entire unworldliness and detachment from the earthly goods which had before been almost as gods to many of them, and, in the second place, their intense joyousness and peace and patience under adversity and persecution. These are fruits worth gaining, my brethren in our Lord, and well for us if we can win them by our own studies of this last great act of God in His dealings with the world, the act of God in which all those former dealings of His are to be gathered up and consummated.

The early Christians were happy in looking forward to this great day as something which was almost imminent, which at all events, it was their wisdom, in obedience to the warnings of our Lord and His Apostles, to consider as imminent. We have become accustomed to see age after age pass by, and we think of this great day as something yet possibly far distant. How far it may be distant no one knows but God, and there are not wanting signs enough to make us think that it may not be long delayed. But to us, at all events, it is not further removed practically than the

† St. Matt. xxvi. 64.

day of the death of each one of us. That will close the history of his own soul and of the world itself to him as far as his eternity goes. And in the meantime we have a number of holy thoughts and considerations prepared for us by the theologians of the Church, and we shall do well indeed to feed our souls on them, by way of preparing ourselves for the great day, whether it be far off or near. Just as the day of our death, if we make ourselves familiar with it, in thought and prayer, sheds a light on all our life which fits us to meet it, so does the consideration of the last day of the world in which we live, prepare us most powerfully for bearing our part in it as we shall then wish to bear it. I shall put before you in the discourses on some following Sundays some of these considerations, of which I will now only give a short and summary account.

In the first place, then, as regards ourselves. It is true that we are to be judged one by one as we die by our Lord, and that that judgment of His will decide our lot for all eternity. But surely it is quite clear that this is not all that the justice and the glory of God require of us. Our Lord has said, "Nothing is covered that shall not be revealed, nor hid which shall not be known."* In the particular judgment we shall know our state before God, and our Lord will take cognizance of it. But no one will be present but ourselves, and though the issue of the judgment may be known to angels and to saints, and even to the devils, still the grounds of it will not be known, nor all that we have done, and all the forbearance and

* St. Matt. x. 26.

mercies of God towards us. Therefore the universal judgment, if it be only a rehearsal or repetition of the particular judgment, and nothing more, is in a true sense most requisite, in order that all may know all, that Heaven and Earth and Hell itself may see what has been the history of each individual life, what has been the management of itself of each particular soul. And God has not made us units and isolated atoms in His universe. He has placed us in society, and made us live lives which cross and interweave one with another, and none is good or bad to himself alone. He is good or bad, if he be good or if he be bad, to a thousand others also. Now this implies that when all things are to be known, we must know one another, and a great part of the revelations of that day will be this opening to one another of our most secret lives. Therefore if the general judgment were to be nothing more than a repetition of the particular judgment, it would still serve great and essential purposes of the providence and the justice of God.

But, in the second place, I am bold to say that the general judgment will not be merely a repetition of the particular judgment. This seems a strong thing to say, and you may ask how it is that anything will remain for us to be judged concerning, which has not been considered in the particular judgment? I do not say that anything can then be adduced which our Lord had not known and considered in the particular judgment, but I do say that He, in His infinite knowledge, will have taken account then of things which at that moment are still future, and which yet go to make up the account of the soul before Him in the balances of the Divine Justice. You know what the poet puts into the mouth of one of his characters—

> The evil that men do lives after them,
> The good is oft interred with their bones:

and the first part of the saying is true, while the latter requires, by the mercy of God, a correction. For both the evil and the good which men do live after them, and in many cases it may be that men do more harm after their own deaths, or more good, than during their life. Do you suppose that a father who brings up his children badly and laxly, will not have to be responsible before God for the evil of which he has been the parent, and which may go on propagating itself, generation after generation, even to the Day of Judgment? I shall have to draw this out rather more at length hereafter, but do you suppose that a man who has been the enemy of his own soul by his life is not the enemy of the souls of others by his example? Those who have made themselves the enemies or the benefactors of their race, such as, on the one hand, the authors of heresies or false religions, men like Mahomet or Luther, or Henry the Eighth, the men who have written books full of falsehoods against the Church, the poison of which circulates in the veins of whole nations; or, on the other hand, the founders of good works, the builders of churches, and hospitals, and the like—do you think that such men will not find at the day of account that they are confronted by an immense accumulation of evil or of good, which is traced by the justice of God to them ? Well, my brethren, that all this may be made manifest, it is right and just, and even necessary, if all things which belong to the true history of the world are to be made known, that there should be this great revelation of the consequences of sin and the consequences of good.

IV.

Again, my brethren, the Providence by which this world is now governed by God is a wonderful unfolding of justice and mercy and wisdom, in which God deals with men on a large scale, so to say, in which He elevates and brings low empires and kingdoms, and royal houses, and races and societies, as such, and the true Christian history is that view of the events of the world's life which gives the faithful representation and interpretation of the action of the Providence of God in this regard. And in order that this may be perfectly understood to the glory of God, and the illumination of the minds of men, it is fitting that there should be this great day of account, in which everything is made manifest, and the whole of God's dealings with the human race unfolded before the whole assembled universe. This again is all the more necessary because at present the Providence of God, even in its largest display, is so much misunderstood, and the reason why the wicked have been allowed to prosper, and the good have been subjected to so much affliction, requires to be set forth in all its fulness and beauty before all the world. And as God will then judge all the actions, public and private of all men, and of masses of men, in their dealings with the Church and one another, so also must He judge and set right that great power and influence which will have had so large a part in the actions of mankind, the power which consists in the general verdict and manner of judging which we call public opinion. It is a necessary sequel of the decree of God by which we are made to live as members of society, that we should all have a certain influence on one another, and that the whole body should have a most powerful influence on every one of its members, and this influence is exercised by what we call public opinion. Now here is a great power, ordained, we may say, by God, which has been as much abused as that other power, also ordained by God, which consists in the authority of government and law and civil society. And it may almost be said that the government of God would be imperfect, if there were not to be at the final day of retribution some most signal correction of all the mischiefs and all the false maxims and all the lies and all the impostures, of which what has been called public opinion has been guilty, and will be guilty to the end of time, and if, when the very devils of Hell itself are to acknowledge the justice and goodness of God in His Providence, those servants of Satan, who have served him so well by the manipulation of this great engine of evil which we call public opinion, were not to be brought to task, and if any single mind in the whole universe were to remain unconvinced of the beauty of virtue, the honour due to the things which have been most despised and run down in this world—purity, poverty, mortification, humility, meekness, and the like.

Consider, my brethren, how this public opinion has made itself a sort of infallible chair, to the decisions of which every one is to bow, from the Pontiff on the throne of St. Peter to the smallest monarch or princeling in the world! How has it set itself up above pulpits, and councils, and senates, and the wisdom of the learned, and the counsels of the wise, how bravely has it challenged any one who denied its right to be the queen of the world, and how savagely has it persecuted those who have stood up against it! Consider how it has enacted for Christian men and for Christian women a code of laws of its own, to rebel against which was a more dangerous treason than to rebel against the safety of the State or the person of the Sovereign! Consider the number of false heroes and heroines it has imposed on the worship of its subjects, how it has falsified the law of God, and trampled on the conscience of men, calling modesty prudery, and virtue affectation, and humility meanness, and unworldliness folly, how it has made men afraid to seem afraid of breaking the law of God, how it has erected vindictiveness into a virtue, and canonized the nationalism which has brought to the loss of their faith more than one nation of Europe, how it has laughed at the saints and made a mock of the Gospel, how, if it has not restored the worship of heathen divinities, it has at least brought back pagan morality and manners under the name of culture! Well indeed may we ask, is there to be no righting of all the hideous impostures and lies which have been palmed off on poor human society by this false authority, of which we may almost say that it has placed itself in the temple of God, and given out that it is God? Yes, there is to be a terrible righting of all this falsehood in the Day of Judgment, and the triumph of the truth and of purity and humility and the virtues which constitute the imitation of our Lord will not be complete, until the whole world is brought, as it then will be, to one mind, and there will be no tongue to wag, and no heart even to conceive a thought against the law of the Gospel.

Great things these, my brethren, for us to meditate on, and surely we cannot consider them, however imperfectly, without great benefit to our souls. They are all so many rays of the light which will then stream upon us from the face of our Blessed Lord, piercing every cranny and nook in our hearts, and laying bare the most secret influences of our lives. "All things are naked and open in His eyes to Whom our speech is."* Now, dear brethren, He is our Friend, and He will then be our Friend, if we keep Him in our hearts, and look forward to His coming, as did those who first believed in Him. We are soon to kneel before Him in His crib at Bethlehem, and we daily worship Him on the Cross on which He wrought our redemption. Let us join then henceforth to our other devotions to our Lord that which dwells upon the thought that He is to be our Judge and the Judge of all the world. Bethlehem leads us to Calvary. And let Calvary lead us to think of Him as He Himself would have Himself thought of by those for whom He was going to die—"sitting on the right hand of Power, and coming in the clouds of Heaven."

* Heb. iv. 13.

SERMON XIII.

PARTICULAR AND GENERAL JUDGMENT.

Mihi autem pro minimo est ut a vobis judicer, aut ab humano die: sed neque me ipsum judico. Nihil enim mihi conscius sum: sed non in hoc justificatus sum: qui autem judicat me, Dominus est.

But with me it is a very small thing to be judged by you or by man's day, but neither do I judge my own self. For I am not conscious to myself of anything, yet am I not hereby justified, but He that judgeth me is the Lord.

(Words taken from the 3rd and 4th verses of the 4th chapter of the First Epistle to the Corinthians.)

I.

IN these words we see that the Apostle makes mention of three different judgments or tribunals before which he may have to stand and give an account. The first of these three is the tribunal of men, the judgment of men like his friends at Corinth to whom he was writing, and this he calls the day of man, because, as it seems, he has in his mind the great account, which is the day of God, and with this he compares the day, so to speak, of man. The judgment of men is the first of the three tribunals. And next to that St. Paul puts the tribunal of his own conscience, as to which he says that it does not accuse him of anything, and yet that does not justify him. Last of the three he places the judgment or the day of God—" He that judgeth me is the Lord." Now, of these three tribunals St. Paul makes very different account. He does not absolutely despise and make nothing of any one of them, but he says that it is a very small thing for him to be judged by his Corinthian friends, or by any man, or men. Of the second tribunal, that of his own conscience, he makes much more; he places it altogether on a higher level than the judgment of men. But the judgment for which he really cares is the third, the judgment of God, for God is the Lord, the sovereign, the master, and besides He is the all-seeing, the infallible, the most just, and the most powerful. Here, then, we have three judgments to which not only St. Paul, but every one of us must be in some sort responsible, and we have the estimate which we are to form of each settled for us by the Apostle.

And indeed, my brethren, no other estimate could be reasonably made than that which St. Paul here makes. In all judgments and tribunals there are three things which are requisite in order to give their decisions force and weight. First of all, there must be authority to judge, then there must be accuracy in judgment, then there must be power to enforce the sentence that is passed. If authority is wanting, the judgment is not legitimate, it is an usurpation; if accuracy be wanting, the judgment is liable to be false; if power to enforce the sentence is wanting, the judgment is nugatory and inefficacious. Now let us look at these three tribunals of which the Apostle speaks, and see how they stand as to the essentials for a valid judgment. Have men any authority over us? In a certain sense they have a kind of derived authority, for we are made by God responsible to one another and to society in a certain measure and degree, we are bound to obey the laws for the sake of conscience, as this same Apostle teaches us, our conduct as to external things comes under the jurisdiction of the community in which we live, each man, as the Scripture says, has received a commandment concerning his neighbour,* we have duties to our fellow men, and to society as such. Thus we find St. Paul saying that he made it his particular exercise to have a conscience without offence towards God and towards man,† and he says we should forecast and provide what may be good, not only before God but also before men.‡ Within certain ranges, then, the tribunal of men has, in the original institution of society by God, a derived jurisdiction over us. In the second place, it can have but a very imperfect amount of accuracy in its judgments. It cannot read the heart, or understand the motives of our actions, and, as a matter of fact, we know that it is often guilty of great injustice, even in matters which fall under its legitimate ken and scope. Nor, again, in the third place, has it much true power over us to enforce its decrees and judgment. Its power is only external, and if it can even, as our Lord says, kill the body, it cannot touch the soul or the mind, or the heart, and so, He tells us not to fear it. This tribunal, then, is the lowest and the weakest of the three of

---

* Ecclus. xvii. 12.   † Acts xxiv. 16.
‡ 2 Cor. viii. 21.

which we are speaking. It is unreasonable, it is cowardly, it is contrary to our faith, to give it more than the influence which St. Paul allows it, when he says it is a very little thing indeed for him to be judged by the day of man.

What is the authority, what is the accuracy, what is the power of conscience to enforce its decisions? Conscience is given to us by God for our guide, and therefore it speaks to us with His voice. It is the most authoritative thing we have to obey, and if we pay heed to the judgment of men, of which we have just spoken, it is because our conscience tells us that so it must be by the will of God. Moreover, though the judgment of man cannot go beyond the exterior action, the judgment of conscience can penetrate the heart and discern the secret springs of action. It is as much supreme in the interior as the exterior, and no amount of external witness to a false judgment on such matters can in any way paralyze its authority. Again, the authority of conscience is so great, because it is direct from God, that even an erroneous conscience is as authoritative as a conscience which is not erroneous. It is not endowed with any infallible gift of accuracy, but as long as it is clear and decided it must be obeyed. Thus St. Paul tells us of himself that he really thought he ought to do many things against the Name of our Lord as it was preached by the earliest Apostles,* and that he persecuted the Church of God, but that he found mercy, because he did it ignorantly in unbelief.† St. John says in

* Acts xxvi. 9 ; 1 Cor. xv. 9.   † 1 Tim. i. 13.

his Epistle, "If our heart," that is, our conscience, "reprehend us, God is greater than our heart and seeth all things. If our heart reprehend us not, we have confidence towards God."* There is immense mercy in this doctrine. The Apostle might have said, as St. Paul says in the text, that even if our heart reprehend us not, we have not full confidence, at least not full assurance before God, because He is greater than our heart and knows all things. Instead of that, he says that God is content with the verdict of our conscience, even although that verdict is not infallible. Conscience, then, requires to be cultivated, to be instructed, to be attended to, to be obeyed faithfully, and if these conditions are fulfilled, it becomes really enlightened and, in general, a most accurate guide as well as a safe guide. And as to its power of enforcing its decrees, it has a certain interior power which consists in the peace which results from a conscience when it has been obeyed, and the internal torment, greater than any other we can suffer, of a conscience ill at ease or which is continually reproaching us. But in any case it appeals to that higher power Whose voice it is, and so it threatens us with punishment from Him if we disobey, and promises us reward from Him if we are obedient.

In the third place, when we speak of the tribunal of God we speak of that judgment which alone has intrinsic authority, and which is the fountain and source of all true authority and judgment. Here we have the highest authority, the most perfect and

* 1 St. John iii. 20, 21.

infallible accuracy, the most irresistible power to enforce the decisions at which the tribunal arrives. It gives to the others whatever light and whatever authority they have, and it goes far beyond them in illumination. "All things are naked and open to His eyes to Whom our speech is."* The other tribunals are only true and authoritative in so far as they are conformed to this. And, my brethren, there is no time with God as we count time. It is not that He waits until we are dead to inform Himself of what we have done, and to pass His infallible judgment upon it; He judges us instant after instant, and that same judgment which He passes now is that which will be proclaimed to us, and to the whole world, at the two several moments of the Particular and of the General Judgment. These two judgments, then, are moments which we may say are, each of them, necessary in the Kingdom of God, in order that perfect justice may be done and that the truth may be known in its full beauty and its full light. It cannot be imagined that in the Kingdom of God there are to be those mistakes and false judgments and imperfect appreciations of which our minds are now so full. St. Paul does not say that we are never to be able to understand and to judge rightly, but that the time is not yet. Judge not, he says, until the right time. "Judge not before the time, until the Lord come, Who will both bring to light the hidden things of darkness, and will make manifest the counsels of the hearts, and then shall every man have praise of God."†

* Heb. iv. 13.   † 1 Cor. iv. 5.

II.

Now, it will be of great use to us in our considerations of the great Day of Account, if we bear it constantly in mind that both the judgments which we have to undergo, the Particular and the General Judgment, are stages in that perfect rectification of our thoughts, and that manifestation of all things, that are now hidden and secret, which it may be said, is required in the Kingdom of God for the interests of truth and of justice. We have said that in the particular judgment man becomes manifest to himself, that the light of the judgment which God has formed of him and entertains of him will then be turned on his own heart and his own mind, and that in the general judgment this same light concerning each single soul is made the property, not of himself only, but of all the world. He is made manifest to all others, and all others are made manifest to him. And it may be added, that this is not simply a measure of justice for the removing of falsehoods and delusions which at present darken our minds concerning ourselves and one another, it is not a simple vindication of the justice and goodness of God. It is more than that—it is the dawn of a day which shall never set, it is the birth of a new order of things which is to last for ever, the blessings and the woes of which correspond most exactly to the deeds and deserts of each individual soul. This perfect manifestation will live on, so to say, in the rewards of the blessed and in the pains of the lost, and the whole counsel and dealings of God will be, as it were, recorded in those rewards and in those punishments. Then at last, in all their full meaning will our Lord's words have their accomplishment, "Nothing is covered that shall not be revealed, nor hid that shall not be known."* There are no secrets in eternity, and in everything that has ever been will be seen the glory of God.

Now we may see a gradual preparation for this fulness of light, in which we shall then live, in the three tribunals before which, in some sort of way, we all stand, that is, in the right use of each and of the thought of each. For even the judgment of men is not meant to be of no use to us, and when God put man in the world and made him a being to live in society, He intended society and public opinion not to be the depraved and debased influences which they now are. For, in an innocent and happy and holy world, the thoughts and the judgments of the mass of men would have been formed in accordance with the holiness and innocence of that community, and would have been as strong influences on the side of right and truth and justice and virtue, as they have become, since the Fall, strong influences on the side of all that is low and evil. And, even as it is, the judgment of others helps in many respects to form and train and instruct our own consciences, as we see to be the case with the children of good and holy parents and the members of families or communities in which the standard is high and the rule pure. And much more, if we attend carefully to our own conscience,

* St. Matt. x. 26.

if we use this precious guide with reverence and faithfulness, if we cultivate it and obey it and keep it bright and keen by the constant thought of the presence of God and the constant use of self-examination, then it is possible for men like ourselves so to profit by this gift of God as to be prepared by its constant witness for that most severe judgment which we have to undergo when we stand one by one, at the moment of our deaths, before our Lord as our Judge. And in the last place, it is easy to see how this strict account which each several soul has given to its Judge at the particular judgment, is the due preparation of that soul for the other terrible Day of Account, when it is to meet not only its Judge, but the Judge of all the world, and to stand revealed in the light of His unerring truth and justice before the whole universe, before all the angels and all the men whom God has created, there to receive its true sentence and appreciation, which can never be varied or changed or obliterated throughout the whole of eternity. For, indeed, faithful as we may be in the use of our own conscience, we have the word of St. Paul for the truth that to know nothing against ourselves does not certainly justify us, and we must be sure that at the moment of the particular judgment we shall see many things very differently from now, and many things of which we have not a full knowledge or even much knowledge now. And in the same way it may be said, as I shall try to explain, that there are some things which will become more clear to us at the General Judgment, even concerning ourselves, as to which the light of the particular judgment will not have fallen on us as a full and perfect revelation.

It will be enough for us, my brethren, for the remainder of the time which we can give to this subject to-day, to speak chiefly of the first, and as we call it, the particular judgment, which we have all to undergo in the presence of our Lord, and to consider it both in relation to those other imperfect judgments which may precede it in the minds of others, and in our own consciences, and also in relation to that other great and final Judgment of God in the presence of the whole universe to which even the particular judgment itself is a preparation. And as to those former judgments of ourselves and of others concerning us, it is plain that they are very imperfect indeed in comparison with that which God will form of us, or as it is more true to say, which God does form of us day by day and hour by hour, which He is always forming of us, and which will be revealed to us at the last when we stand at our death before Him. You know that it has been a favour occasionally granted by God to some of His most trusted saints, that they should be allowed to see themselves, at least partially, as they are before Him, to see the true character and deformity of their sins, and the true imperfection of that which is least imperfect in them. Thus it is recorded of the Venerable Balthasar Alvarez, of whom St. Teresa was told that he was one of the most perfect souls living upon earth in those days, that he was allowed to see his good actions under the image of a cluster of grapes, of which few indeed there were which were not mildewed or in some other way wanting in perfect ripeness or beauty. And when others of the same high rank in the Kingdom of God, have been allowed to see their faults as they are in the sight of God, it is recorded of them that they have hardly been able to bear the sight. And putting aside the case of special favours and revelations of this kind, which may be vouchsafed to men of strong and robust virtue, who are able, more than others, to abide the shock of the vision of the truth, it is certain that, in proportion as men advance in close union with God and in other high interior graces, they are not the less fearful about the severity of the particular judgment, but more fearful and more strict in their estimate of themselves. And never let us persuade ourselves that, in this or in other things of the same kind, the saints of God have been the prey of exaggerated notions and futile fears. It is a great grace to be able to understand the full measure of human weakness and disorder, a great grace of which few may be capable, but which is of immense value to those to whom it can be vouchsafed. The Divine illumination which spreads itself over such souls is a reflection of the eternal truth, it comes from the face of God, and in whatever proportion it may be in some sort gained by the exercise of interior watchfulness, it is a blessing of infinite worth, because it is some participation of the truth on the subject on which it most of all concerns us to see truly. We are to see ourselves in the true light once for all at the moment of our judgment, and how foolish, then, must we be if we can wish for anything else than that, as far as our poor powers can now bear the sight, we may see ourselves now as we shall see ourselves then!

And, indeed, my brethren, no one can deeply meditate on the circumstances and conditions of that judgment which awaits us, we cannot tell how soon, and which may indeed be on us at any moment, without seeing that every element and every feature of what is then to take place is such as to make us tremble, and such, indeed, as to overwhelm us altogether with terror, save that we have that love of God in Jesus Christ our Lord, of which St. Paul speaks, to reassure us and give us confidence. The Judge is our Lord Himself, Who has created us and has also redeemed us, and as we shall see in another consideration, it will be His example and His precepts by which we are to be judged. No concealment then, no corner or nook of the soul is so hidden, so remote, but will be flooded by the calm keen light which will stream from His Divine Face. Ah, my brethren, it sounds severe enough to say that we are to be judged by the precepts and by the example of our Lord, but as a matter of fact, it will be this simple sight of Him that will be to us the representation at once of His precepts and example, and of our own conformity to or difference from them. There will be no need of more than His simple presence to rectify all misconceptions, to drive away all delusions, to convict all consciences. "With the hearing of the ear I have heard Thee," says holy Job, "and now my eye seeth Thee. Therefore I reprehend myself, and do penance in dust and ashes."* A perfect instantaneous rectification of all minds—but alas! not a perfect rectification of all wills. There will be souls, thousands on thousands, who will stand before our Lord, who will at once have their judgments and intelligences set right as to themselves and all that they have done, and who will have for their greatest eternal torment the ineffable anguish of the reproaches of the enlightened intelligence against the will hardened for ever in its perversity. There is nothing in any self-judgment, however severe, that we can pass on ourselves, that can have an effect of illumination and conviction like the presence of our Lord. No, nor can we even accuse ourselves with the vehemence or the perspicacity with which the charges that can be brought against us will then be urged by the evil spirits, who will have no moment left after that to plot for and contrive our ruin. No help, no resource, no intercession in that strict hour of justice.

III.

And observe, my brethren, that the illumination of the intelligence of which I am speaking will not consist merely in this, that a new and more piercing light will be thrown upon a field of which we have already some knowledge, though it be dim. It is not merely that the light will be fiercer, but also that it will bring under its range a number of objects of which we may have taken little heed and had but little thought. Such, for instance, will be the benefits of God to us, in return for which we shall have treated

---

* Job xlii. 5, 6.

Him with such scant gratitude—an immense accumulation of gifts, natural and supernatural, spiritual and material, blessings in the Church, graces, inspirations, movements, warnings, the time given us to profit by them, the grace to use them well. Such, again, will be the standard by which we ought to have measured ourselves, the law of God in its full application to our lives and opportunities, the duties of our state and of our personal vocation, the special helps by which we have been surrounded to enable us to walk swiftly along the path by which God has chosen to lead us. Again, there will be a special illumination as to the character and individual desert of our multitudinous thoughts, imaginations, desires, words, actions, an illumination which will contrast, so to say, one side of our character and conduct with the other. What we have been to our bodies, what we have been to our souls, what to the world, what to God, what as to temporal things, what as to eternal goods, our slothfulness, our indifference, our negligence, our contempt, in the one case, will be set, in that light, over against our vigilance, our energy, our industry, our zeal, in the other. The defects and flaws in what is good will be as manifest as the unsuspected foulness and depravity of what is bad. The sins we have caused or aided in others, the sins of which we have been barely conscious, the long endless roll of omissions—all will be unfolded then. What more is needed than this simple enumeration to convince us of the truth of which we are speaking—the truth of the immense distance between the strictness and penetrating severity of the Particular Judgment, and the comparative dulness and lightness of any judgment that we can, even with all our present graces, pass upon ourselves?

We must remember, my brethren, in all our considerations of this great subject, that, though we are naturally inclined, in our anticipations of that judgment of our Lord which will then be passed upon us, to think more of the fiery trial to which all our actions, interior and exterior alike, will then be subjected, as burning away the greater part of our works as worthless, rather than as proving them to have been, so to say, of that genuine metal which can stand even such a fire, still our Lord, in His descriptions of that day, does not speak in that way, but that, on the contrary, He dwells more especially on the blessed words of reward and encouragement which He will then utter to His faithful servants. Yes, this is the wonderful power of the grace of God, of the provisions which our Lord has left behind Him in the Church for the strengthening of our human weakness, that there are to be many who will hear from His blessed lips those happy words, "Well done, good and faithful servant!" And the higher we rise in our thoughts concerning the justice and the severity of God, the more do we learn to understand the fulness of the work which our Lord has wrought for us, the beauty of the fruits of His grace in the poor human hearts and souls who surrender themselves to the guidance of His Holy Spirit. Yes, it is possible, by the faithful use of our means of grace, and especially by the faithful use of the tribunal of our own conscience, to meet our Judge, even though He be our Lord Himself, with confidence, and not to be disappointed of our hope that we have done away with our deficiencies, with our debts of pain, and have laid up some store of good works with which to rejoice His Heart

But now I am insisting more on this one point, that as we may prepare ourselves for the strict judgment of our Lord in the particular judgment by the faithful use of our own conscience, so also does that particular judgment itself prepare us in a marvellous way for the other great ordeal through which we have to pass at the moment of the Universal Judgment. What can we fear after that first judgment by our Lord ? It is true that it may be a terrible thing in itself to have stand before the whole intelligent universe which God has created, and there to be revealed and laid bare as we have been revealed and laid bare to ourselves in the particular judgment. In itself it is a terrible thing, and such as might make the bravest heart quail. But then we shall have had the experience of the former revelation to prepare us for it. You remember how the blessed Magdalene knelt unmoved and indifferent in the presence of so many neighbours, who knew of what a kind her life had been, at the feet of our Saviour in the house of the Pharisee, and how gibes and sneers were not wanting, the whispers of ridicule, the pointed finger of contempt. Do you suppose she cared at all, that blessed penitent, for what they might say or think of her ? she who had lived upon admiration and homage, and had been only too ready to let human respects influence her even to sin ? I think she cared not one jot for them all, and that the reason why she was so indifferent was that she had been manifested to herself even before she came into that room, and that every moment that she knelt there, in the presence of Jesus Christ, was a fresh and deeper revelation to her of what she really was. In her self abhorrence and contrition, the whole world was nothing to her except something that could help her to greater humiliation, and give her an opportunity of atoning to the injured honour of her God by the public profession of her penitence. It was not in her to despise any one but herself. But she could not have wished to be in the sight of the Pharisee and his guests another than she was in the eyes of Him Who was all in all to her. Surely there will be something of this kind in the General Judgment—we shall go to it strengthened and enlightened by the sight of our Lord, and burning only for whatever may conduce to His glory in the manifestation of ourselves to the whole world.

And yet, once more, my brethren, there is a difference between these two great acts of God, and it cannot even be said that the last of the two will not reveal more than has been revealed in the first. In the first place the souls of men will then be reunited to their bodies, for good or for evil, and the reunion is to last for ever. Whatever has been the lot of the soul in the time between these two judgments, it has been alone, and without the companionship of the body, though it has been suffering or receiving comfort for the deeds done in the body. After that time they are never more to be separated, and the joys of one will be the joys of the other, the pains of one will be the pains of the other. The mere sight of the bodies of the just, shining like the sun, will be a revelation to all the world of what they have done. And the mere sight of those loathsome carcases in which the souls of the wicked are to suffer for evermore, will be in itself a declaration, on the part of their most just Creator, of what their deserts have been. One single glance now of those glories and those infamies might be enough to convert half a world. And there will then begin an infinite variety of pleasures and rewards, of pains and punishments, exactly and most justly proportioned to the deserts of the souls and bodies to which they will be allotted, and this of itself will be a new revelation of the justice and the power of God, as well as of the merits of man. Then at last it will be seen by all and understood by all, what is the worth of sensual indulgence, what the value of self-restraint, what the crown of purity, what the retribution which will fall on the following of the lower passions, then it will be seen what glory can be purchased by mortification, then it will be known what is the home which gluttony and lasciviousness have been building for themselves. It will be known, because in the bodies themselves of the just and of the wicked, the eternal sentences will be written, and the simple sight of that glory on the one hand and foulness and ignominy on the other hand will proclaim to the whole universe what shall be the eternal pleasures and the eternal pains. If there were nothing new but this in the General Judgment, it would be a revelation not unworthy of the justice and the sovereignty of God, an explanation of the Passion of our Lord over which the Angels might rejoice—a revelation and an explanation for which we shall all have been in part prepared by the first judgment which we have already undergone.

But there is much more. It seems a strong thing to say that there will be things manifested then which have not been manifested at the former judgment, but if the statement require explanation, it will be at once seen to be true when it is explained. No doubt there can be no alteration of the judgment pronounced by our Lord at the moment of the death of each child of Adam—that judgment is given once for all, and it can never be revoked. But yet both for those on whom our Lord has looked with favour and for those who have forced Him to banish them from His presence for ever, there will be matters concerning which He has had to think in giving sentence which cannot be fully made known to them as they are known to Him until the great day of the Universal Judgment. For, my brethren, the particular judgment will inform us of our own sins in our own souls, but will it inform us of the influence which we have exercised for good or for evil on the souls of others? Will it tells us, without any imperfection, or inadequacy, what has been our work on those with whom we have lived? You know how many kinds there are given, in our books of catechetical instruction, of sins in which we may be partakers in others, and how many ways there are also of helping on the souls of others in the path of virtue. How difficult it is for us to trace out for ourselves the evil or the good that we have to put to our account in the souls around us, and what is far more, in the souls of those who come after us! There are those who have trembled indeed at the thought of that one word of our Lord in His parable of the wheat and the cockle: "Let both *grow* together until the harvest." He does not say, let them remain, or abide, but let them grow—as if He would have us note that both evil and good in this world have a fertility, and a productiveness, and a self-multiplication, which can only be signified by the image which He uses, and as if this were to be the secret of the history of the Church in her struggle with the world, that she has in each generation to reckon with the influence of those who are then living, and at the same time to cope with the maxims and traditions and principles of evil which have been left behind them, by thousands of poor souls who have long since passed away to stand before their Judge. We often have occasion to thank and to praise God for the good which He allows us to reap from the work of His servants who have passed away—it is one of our joys, and one of the glories of the Church, that others have laboured, and that we have entered into their labours. In their own day we say, they have fought the good fight, they have built up the Church of God, they have handed on the glorious traditions of the faith and of Christian virtue, they have kept intact the deposit which they received from their fathers, and have passed it on, richer, more precious, and more beautiful than ever to their own children. Alas! it is equally true that there have been the sowers of the evil seed as well as of the good, there have been men who have left behind them lessons and principles of evil manners, of false doctrines, of rebellion against the Church, they have lowered the standard of morals, they have poisoned literature, they have corrupted art, they have debauched the imagination of the young, they have popularised licentiousness, they have ridiculed modesty, they have done their best to deprive vice of its loathsomeness and virtue of its dignity. And they pass away, the lascivious painter and the immoral dramatist, the leaders of immodest and tyrannical fashions, along with the founders of heresies and the originators of schisms, and it is difficult to say which of the two classes have left most misery behind them for mankind. They are canonised in the world of letters, or of art, or of society, and their souls are in Hell. Nor will it be till the great day of the Universal Judgment of the world that it will be known, what is the amount of evil of which these men and women have been guilty, how many souls they have slaughtered, how much of innocence they have ruined, how many hearts would have been pure but for them, of those who are for ever to be their companions in the most terrible torments of body and of soul.

IV.

Ah, my brethren, these thoughts open to us a whole world of considerations concerning the revelations of the last great Judgment, when we shall be confronted with what we have been guilty of, not only in ourselves and in others during our lives, but even after our lives have come to their end. Better for us to have been the instruments of letting loose upon the world some pestilence or famine, to have poisoned the rivers of a whole country, or fired a great city, or broken down the dyke which keeps the waters of the ocean from overwhelming some smiling land, than to have been the authors of a licentious fashion of dress, or a lascivious dance. The ruins of war and famine can be repaired, the destroyed cities can be restored, the abundance of a few seasons soon does away with the traces of inundations, or earthquakes, or the fiery streams of the volcano. But the evil example of one may become the dominant fashion of a generation, just as the slander against the ministers, or the morality of the Church, which was first excogitated by some recluse in a community tainted by heresy, becomes an axiomatic truth in the literature of a whole nation and of half the world. The world is now full of these gigantic inheritances of falsehood or of laxity, and the evil which men do in this way is far greater after their death than it has been during their life. Who can suppose that he will have the blessedness of passing out of the world and leaving nothing behind him but good? Who can be without fear that he may find at the last day that he has done more evil than he thought of, even when he stood before the Son of Man?

But, as I have said already, there is another and a more glorious revelation to look forward to than this. It is true indeed, as holy David teaches, that we cannot understand our sins, that we must pray for pardon for sins that we know not, and for what we have occasioned in others. Yes, that is true, but it is not the whole truth, and even if we have great reason to fear that we have a long account to give of the sad influence of our lives upon those of others, that is only one ground the more for practising ourselves, not only in contrition and penance, but also in good works and holy deeds, which may balance by a catalogue of good the mournful list of our evil. This is what St. Paul insisted on, when he had been speaking to his Corinthian friends of the doctrine of the resurrection of the body: "Therefore, my beloved brethren, be ye steadfast and immoveable, always abounding in the work of the Lord, knowing that your labour is not in vain in the Lord."* God is more ready to reward than He is to punish, and a thousand unknown mischiefs that we have left behind us, may be cancelled in His eyes by the diligence in good works for His service of which we are capable. In any case, we must cast ourselves at His feet, and own that we have no hope but in His mercy, when that last moment comes. Let us do it now, my brethren, as that blessed Magdalene of whom I have spoken, but let us do it, like her, to rise from before those blessed feet, and go forth to a life of active service and devotion and zeal and mercy and charity, and He, Who said afterwards that one act of hers should be spoken of in the whole world, may find it in His gracious Heart hereafter to crown the labours of our penitence in the face of that mighty assembly of men and of Angels!

* 1 Cor. xv. 58.

SERMON XIV.

THE WAYS OF GOD MANIFESTED.

Quod ego facio, tu nescis modo, scies autem postea.
What I do thou knowest not now, but thou shalt know hereafter.
(Words taken from the 7th verse of the 13th chapter of St. John's Gospel.)

I.

THESE words take us back, my brethren in our Lord, to that most touching scene in the supper chamber at Jerusalem, when our Lord was kneeling at the feet of His chief Apostle, and St. Peter was resisting with all his energy the act of honour which He seemed to be receiving from his Master, Who would fain wash his feet and those of the other disciples. "What I do thou knowest not now, but thou shalt know hereafter." Our Lord went on to explain to them some part at least of the significance of His action, for He told them immediately that it signified the cleansing of their souls by the application of His Sacred Passion, which was then imminent. He explained to them also another signification of this action, for He told them also that if their Lord and Master washed their feet they ought also to do the same one for the other. And the theologians of the Church have found further significations for that gracious action of our Lord, for they have remarked that He did this a little before the time at which He instituted the Most Blessed Sacrament, and that by this action of His He signified the necessity of the utmost purification of the soul on the part of those who were to be admitted to that sacred banquet. These are some of the meanings of that action of our Lord, which are made known to us either by Himself or by the holy Christian doctrine which He has left behind Him in the Church. And we cannot but doubt that there may be others which are not yet made known to us, and that when all things that He did and said are explained to us in the light of Heaven, we shall see many other beautiful and deep meanings in this as in His other actions and sayings. Thus He is better than His word. We do know many things, but not all, even now, and we shall know them all and feed upon their endless beauties hereafter.

But now to-day I only take these words as a text which may apply generally to all that God has done for us and for others, to the whole of His dealings with men and angels, and with the whole universe, which He has created, and which He governs by His Providence in a way which is now in so many particulars hidden from our eyes. All this is to be unfolded before us at the Last Day, as well as our own doings and the doings of all others like ourselves to God. Then there will be the most complete and most magnificent manifestation of all, and then the words of our Lord to St. Peter will be most abundantly fulfilled, "What I do thou knowest not now, but thou shalt know hereafter;" or again, of those other words of which we spoke last Sunday, " There is nothing covered which shall not be revealed, nor hidden which shall not be known." When St. Paul speaks of that Last Day as the coming of the Lord, he says that He will then bring to light the things hidden in darkness, and will manifest the secrets of hearts. The manifestation of the secrets of hearts is the manifestation of what we are and what we have really been, the manifestation of the things hidden in darkness will be the manifestation of what God has done and what He has been, and these two things together make up that perfect and complete revelation of all things which it is the will and decree of our good God that we should all have when we enter on eternity. This then is the subject of our thoughts this morning.

II.

We all know, my brethren, the intense delight of which our minds are capable in the contemplation of the works of God. We all know to what an extent His beauty and power and wisdom are made manifest to us in the exterior creation of which we form a part, and the beauty and good of which we have the privilege, along with the angels, of in some measure understanding. And those who have time so to occupy themselves, find an unending pleasure in the study, as we call it, of nature. It is but natural that it should be so, for God has made our minds for the intelligence of the great things He has done in the universe; He has, as it were, given us the key of His works, and intends us by our knowledge of

S

them to rise to the understanding of Himself. But it is quite certain that the moral and spiritual world is a higher region in the Kingdom of God than the physical universe, and that He has displayed and exercised His great and most glorious attributes far more in that first world than in that which I spoke of second. The beauty of a single soul, to those who are enabled to see it, is a greater beauty than that of all the worlds of light, and of all that we see around us in the material universe. If it is so great a pleasure and so elevating a pursuit to study the visible works of God, it must be far more noble, and far more elevating, to study God in His works of the moral and spiritual order. And if this is true of the beauty of a single soul, it must be much more true of the whole universe of souls, so to speak, which God has created. We know that our delight and wonder at the works of God in the physical creation are caused, not only by what we there see of His wisdom, and power, and love, in the manner in which He has made and provided for each creature or each class of His creatures, one by one, but much more by what is disclosed to us of the same marvellous attributes of God in the harmony, and combination, and arrangement, and mutual dependence, and balance, which He has made between the various orders of His works. For this it is that makes up what we call the world, which the ancient students of nature called by the word, which signifies beauty, adornment, or order, for this very reason, because they saw in it so much of beautiful arrangement and wisdom.

Now if this is true of the order, and harmony, and symmetry, of the material universe, and if these give us a higher idea of the wisdom and providence of the Maker of all things than even the most beautiful of His works taken singly, we may say the same with even more truth of the spiritual and moral world of which we are speaking. We know, each one of us, that our lives are bound up with the lives of others in a most wonderful way, and that the actual result and outcome of all is in each case linked by a thousand ties with the lives of those across whom we have come in our path through this world. So that it may be said that God has arranged each single life of all His millions of children, not for itself alone, but with endless and countless relations and influences on others or received from others, and all this is an exercise of His wisdom most beautiful, most perfect, and most worthy of study and thankfulness. And the history of the whole race is the combined and connected history of each single soul with that of all other souls. Here is a marvel and a wonder far surpassing anything that can be found in the material universe, because souls are free, and the elements are not free. And all this is to be revealed to us at the last day, so that we may truly say that we are in a certain sense to judge, not only one another, as we shall do when the whole of the secrets of each single heart are made manifest to all; and not only angels, as St. Paul says, for we shall then know, not only the whole history of men like ourselves, but that also of the other spiritual beings who are so like us in nature —but also the works and the doings of God Himself will be made manifest to us for His glory and for our instruction, to furnish us with matter for eternal praise of Him in His dealings with His creatures, and for the perfect justification of Him in the eyes of the whole world.

Now we may say, in the second place, that this manifestation of the works and dealings of God with His spiritual creation will be by far the greatest and most wonderful of all the manifestations which are to be made at that last day, and I cannot but think that it was something of this truth that made the early Christians, of the age of the Apostles, long with so much eagerness for that last day. St. Peter tells us that the angels in Heaven desire eagerly to know, and watch with the most intense interest, the workings of the Holy Ghost in the Church. And well may they do this, for there can be nothing in all the range of their knowledge which can manifest to them more perfectly the character and the attributes and the counsels of God. And what the angels so much desire to study and contemplate, that must surely be the noblest and most blissful occupation of the children of God. And observe also, that this action of God is not something distinct and separate from the story of each soul as it will be unfolded to the gaze of men and angels at that last day, but it will be something without which the story of each single soul will be altogether imperfect and unintelligible. St. Paul tells us that in God we live and move and are,* and we know that the true life of every soul is a long continued intercourse and as it were pleading of

* Acts xvii. 28.

God with it, and that we might as well leave out the consideration of the influences of the blessed sunlight, or the air, or the rain, on the growth of a flower or a plant, as attempt to give an account of the history of a soul without considering the workings of God in it, and for it, and on it. And there is the same beauty and wisdom about this action of God, the same manifestation of His glorious and loving attributes and character, whether the soul of which we are speaking is the soul of a sinner or the soul of a saint. I suppose, if we could read the true spiritual history of some great servant of God, St. John or St. Peter or St. Paul, we should be entranced with the greatness and magnificence of the sight laid bare before us; and if we could at the same time read the record of all that God has done for that soul, the secret workings of His grace, the action of the Holy Ghost, the manner and degree in which the merits of the Precious Blood of our Lord and the grace of His Sacraments have been applied to it, the effects of the custody of the angels and the prayers of the saints and the communion of blessings of which the children of the Church are partakers—that again would be a most entrancing spectacle.

But not the less so would it be to trace out the dealings of God with a soul such as that of Judas or Caiaphas or Pontius Pilate—a soul that has resisted grace, that has been raised high in the favour of God, and then has forfeited His favour and fallen most miserably, that has turned out an apostate and a traitor, that from the service of God's altar has passed into the ranks of the heresiarchs, or the authors of schism, and that after having been destined for one of the highest thrones in the Kingdom of Heaven, has had to take its place in eternity among the rebel angels themselves. For God is never more great or more tender or more beautiful, than He is in His dealings with those whom He foreknows to be doomed by their own faults to be the objects of His eternal wrath, and, if at that Last Day His redeemed shall go into Heaven with their hearts all glowing at the sight of His goodness to themselves and others like them, they will not be less convinced of His justice and His mercy and His patience in His dealings with those who are to be for ever lost. Yes, and these poor sufferers themselves, the architects of their own unending ruin, will have to acknowledge that He has dealt with them with an extreme of tenderness and forbearance, of which perhaps there will be no greater examples even in His dealings with His saints.

III.

This is a great subject, my brethren in our Lord, and it stands to reason that it is a subject with which we are at present altogether unable to cope. When St. Paul has answered in a certain manner the difficulties which had been raised in many minds, among the Christian Jews, on account of the rejection of their nation and the admission of the Gentiles in their stead to the privileges of the Christian kingdom, he breaks into the well-known passage, "O the depths of the riches, of the wisdom and of the knowledge of God! How incomprehensible are His judgments and how unsearchable are His ways! For who hath known the mind of the Lord? Or who hath been His counsellor? Or who hath first given unto Him, and recompence shall be made him? For of Him, and by Him, and in Him, are all things: to Him be glory for ever, Amen."* And, after all that we can gather by way of explanation of the ways of Providence from Sacred Scripture and the sayings of the Fathers, there will always remain a great deal more than what we can understand; and indeed, we may most truly say that God would not be God if we could understand all that He does. What we can gather comes to this in the main —we can see certain great principles which must be observed in our thoughts concerning God and His dealings with His creatures, and we can feel sure that much which we do not understand is the application of those principles by Him. But whether in any given case He follows one law of His dealings or another law, what is the particular reason for this or for that among His multitudinous acts to individuals, that is beyond our ken. And now, just as we can gather, from what our Lord said afterwards to His Apostles, a considerable light as to His meaning in the action to which the words of the text refer, although He said that the full intelligence of that action was not to be given to them at that time, so we may most profitably dwell a little on some of the principles of the government of God which are not altogether unknown to us, and so enhance in our own minds the greatness of that full revelation of His

* Rom. xi. 33.

works which is to be made to us at the last day.

It is not as if there were no real difficulties, even to Christians, in the daily government of God. We do not doubt that all He does is and must be wise and just and good, but it is the same with some of the things which we see in Providence as it is with the articles of our faith—that is, we know that they must be true and we believe them because we have the authority of God for their truth, but we do not understand them, we take them on faith. And so it is with many things in the government of God—we take them as just and good and wise, as we ought, because He has done them, but we do not fully understand them, and the full understanding of them is reserved for that great revelation of the ways of God of which I am speaking. And those who are not Christians, and many who are Christians, but without intelligence in the ways of God, and without due reverence for His infinite majesty, are often found to rail against and writhe under the arrangements of His Providence, against which they murmur and complain almost blasphemously. It is in answer to such complaints that we find so much in Scripture and in the Fathers of explanation of the ways of Providence. Not that either the Apostles or the Fathers themselves thought that they could fully comprehend the ways of Him who is above all flight of human or angelic thought, but that they thought it right to furnish those for whom they wrote with certain principles by which to silence objectors and on which they might at the same time feed their own souls in thankful contemplation of the Divine works and ways.

Thus we find St. Paul, in more than one place, laying down the principle of the sovereignty of God as an answer to the cavils of those who questioned His justice and wisdom. "O man," says the Apostle, "who art thou that repliest against God? Shall the thing formed say unto Him that formed it, Why hast Thou made me thus? or hath not the potter power over the clay, of the same lump to make one vessel unto honour and one unto dishonour?"* And indeed this is one of the most constant mistakes which people make in their judgments of God. They forget that He is absolutely free in the distribution of His gifts, that He may choose whom He wills for the great exhibitions of His favour, and that though it is against His nature to be unjust, or cruel, or tyrannical, He is not bound, and He will not bind Himself, to give exactly the same favours to one as to another. Another simple answer to the complaints which are so often made against Providence is one which is but the commonest and simplest matter of reason. Such complaints might be made against the maker of any complicated machine or the contriver of any long and combined system of action, like the campaign of an army, or the order of some great drama or anything of that kind, and the answer is that we can only see a part at a time and that we are unable to judge of it until we can see the whole. God's dealings with the race of man, with nations, and with individual

* Rom. ix. 20, 21.

persons, are a great whole, beginning in time and reaching on to eternity, and it is but necessary that He should do many things, in the course of this great complication and combination, of which we do not see the purpose at the moment when they are done. These are general principles, and by means of these we can answer a great number of the difficulties of which I am speaking.

But there are a score of others which men put to themselves in their wayward, foolish way of finding fault with the decrees of God, and which will not receive their final solution until we see all things which are now hidden uncovered in the light of day. Why do we not know whether we are in grace or out of the grace of God? Why are even the servants of God afflicted with the perpetual doubt whether they shall be saved? Why are the wicked, the heirs of misery, not forewarned of the doom that awaits them? Why do we not know when we have to die and how long we have to live? The hour of our death is the one most important moment for us, on which eternity depends, and why do we not know when it is to come? Why do the wicked prosper in the world? Why are the just afflicted in the world? Is it not the world of God, and has not our Lord come down for the purpose of redeeming it, and why then is vice rampant and sin unpunished and virtue persecuted and humility laughed at and the whole favour of the world given to the enemies of God? Why do the good die young, when they might live on and be so great a benefit to the Church and to the world, and on the other hand the wicked live to a green old age, prospering all their lives, and by their prosperity, leading others to blaspheme, and loading the earth with the moral and physical ruins which they cause all around them? Why are children snatched away even before baptism, why do they suffer for the sins of their parents, while hoary headed sinners are spared to live out their days? Why is the grace of perseverance denied or not granted to many who have begun well, and many others who have offended God for many long years, saved at the very last by a deathbed repentance? Why do the servants of God themselves fall, and why are any, whom God has made capable of eternal happiness, plunged for ever into Hell?

IV.

Such are some of the questions which are constantly arising in the minds of men as they speculate on the action of God in the government of the world, and I suppose that there are few who have not at some time or other listened to the doubts which such speculations suggest. Now, I am not here to answer these questions to-day, for though there is not one of them which has not a good and sufficient answer in Scripture or in the doctrines of the Church, time would fail us altogether, even if I were simply to rehearse what is found concerning them. But I use them as showing that there are whole realms, so to say, of the works and ways of God which are at present shrouded to us in darkness or which are only lit up, as I have said, by the general principles of God's government of which I speak. I use them to show that though we know much about God, there is much more that we do not know, and that the general principles which we can at present gather are in themselves so beautiful and so satisfying, as to assure us that, when all things are revealed, the result will be an immense increase of that glory which consists in the recognition of His ways on the part of his intelligent creatures.

Thus we can see that there is no one of the difficulties which we have just mentioned which does not point to some great law of His love and wisdom. In those which consist in complaints as to our ignorance, whether of our present state in His sight or of our final perseverance and glory, surely it is easy to see that it would be no mercy on His part to assure men beforehand either of their glory or of their damnation. This difficulty is founded in part on a mistake, namely, the idea that eternal happiness and eternal misery are, so to say, fixed quantities, equal in all cases, which can neither be diminished nor increased. This is not so. For each sin has its own eternity, and each good and meritorious action has its own eternity, and to save a sinner from one single sin which he would otherwise commit, is to benefit him by a whole eternity of immunity for punishment corresponding to it, and to hinder a just soul from one single act of virtue is to impair his glory for ever in the same proportion. Now, it is easy to see that if men knew now what their eternal lot was to be, the just would run the risk of greatly diminishing their glory by carelessness or presumption, if they did not altogether forfeit it, and the wicked would be deprived of their one best hope of diminishing their punishment in the next world by carefulness and the endeavour to do some works of penance, and by the restraint which their conscience now exercises over them. In the case of the uncertainty of the hour of death, we can see again that all the blessings which our Lord attached to the virtue of vigilance and holy fear would be taken away, if the moment of death were revealed to us beforehand. And indeed the revelation would defeat itself, for as it is the just are secured a holy death by being always uncertain of the moment when it would come, and the wicked are preserved from an immense number of additional sins by the fear of death.

In the case of the prosperity of the wicked and the afflictions of the just, the very fact that so it is in the world which is governed by God, is a proof that the good things of this world are not true goods, that God desires His elect to win their crowns by suffering and by the practice of all the virtues which make up the character of our Lord, despised and rejected and afflicted, and the whole light which His example has shed on the path to Heaven would be thrown away if virtue was to be rewarded here and if God was to be served by the hope of temporal goods. Where would be the great Christian truth of the Cross? Do the just die young when their life might be of so much good to the world, and do the wicked live on to the end of a long life, causes of mischief and of ruin? But we are told in Scripture that the good are often taken away lest the beauty and purity of their souls should be marred, and the wicked are left to live on and prosper partly because they have a few good works which can be rewarded in no other world but in this, and partly because God uses them for the chastisement and correction of His own children.

Do children suffer for the sins of their parents? Yes, they do, and it would be a lesson lost to fathers and mothers if this were not so. Yes, they may suffer even eternal loss of banishment from the presence of God in Heaven; and yet it is not the doctrine of the Church that any one will be punished in Hell for sins not his own, or that those who lose the supernatural happiness of the saints of God, without any fault of their own, will know what it is they have lost. Do the just often fall, and are the life-long sinners sometimes saved? Certainly, and if the just never fell through their own negligence, where would be, again, the truth of the necessity of continual vigilance and prayer? And if the sinners were never saved at their end, where would be the glory of God in the salvation and sanctity of Peter or Paul or Magdalene or that blessed thief on the Cross, the first trophy in the world of spirits of the power of the redemption of Jesus Christ?

The government of the world by God then is a scheme of infinite beauty and magnificence, and the answers of the saints are but the sign-posts which point out some of the principles in which it is conducted. All shall be made manifest in the last day, and all will begin their eternity with the full knowledge of this, as of the other great things that shall then be revealed. Now we know that He is good, wise, merciful, all powerful, all holy, but not how good, how wise, how holy. Now we are like the saint of old who had a vision as of some part of His majesty, covered by the hand of God as He passed by, that he might not see what no one may see and live. "Now we see through a glass in a dark manner, but then face to face. Now we know in part, but then we shall know even as we are known."*

* 1 Cor. xiii. 12.

SERMON XV.

THE BOOK OF LIFE.

Et vidi mortuos magnos et pusillos, stantes in conspectu throni, et libri aperti sunt; et alius liber apertus est, qui est vitæ: et judicati sunt mortui ex his quæ scripta erant in libris, secundum opera ipsorum.

And I saw the dead, great and small, standing in the presence of the throne, and the books were opened, and another book was opened, which is the book of life, and the dead were judged by those things which were written in the books according to their works.

(Words taken from the 12th verse of the 20th chapter of the Apocalypse of St. John.)

I.

THIS is the vision of the great day of account given by the blessed Apostle and Evangelist St. John. And you see, my brethren, that he tells us that there are two accounts opened in that great day, the one, we may say, written by the hand of man, the other written by the hand of God. I have spoken to you already about the contents of the first of these books, and of the great manifestation which awaits us, first at the time of our particular judgment, when we shall see ourselves as we are and have been, in the light of God, and again when, at the General Judgment, we shall be manifested as we are and have been, not only to ourselves, but also to the whole intelligent creation that God has made, and when we shall see all secrets made manifest, the secrets of the hearts of others as well as our own, and the still more marvellous revelation of the ways and dealings of God with ourselves and with all others. We are all of us, day after day, and hour after hour, writing in the first of these books the account that shall be opened against us in the Day of Judgment. When the good Christian kneels down at night before his Crucifix, and calls to mind all his thoughts, and words, and deeds, and omissions throughout the day that is drawing to a close, he sums up as it were the page of that day which shall be opened again to meet him at the Day of Judgment. Well indeed for him, if he makes up his accounts as a prudent householder, and if he uses his opportunities, which no prudent householder would be willing to forego, if he had such, of cancelling whatever there may be against him, by acts of contrition, by penance for his sins, by the use of the sacraments, and by repairing at once whatever there may be to be repaired! In that case he need not fear when the page is to be opened again at the Judgment Day—he may find there, indeed, what he has done or said amiss, but he will find the other side of the account also, he will find that his shortcomings have been fully balanced by his exercises of sorrow and penance, wiped away altogether by the infinite merits of our Lord and the most faithful mercy of our God.

That is the first book which will be opened as to every human life, the book of conscience. Then it will be seen what has been the true character of every life in the sight of God, and according to that character will be the decision of the Judge Whom

T

no one can deceive and no one can escape. But you see, my brethren, that the blessed St. John tells us of another book which shall be opened then, and he says that according to that book also will be the decision of our condition for all eternity. He calls that book the book of life, and he says, a few lines further on in this same passage, that "whosoever was not found written in the book of life was cast into the pool of fire." This second book then also has an influence, and a decisive influence, on our state for ever, and what is it? What can be more important for us than that we should know what that book is? It is something, you see, not the same with the book of our own writing, it is not the book of our thoughts and words and deeds. It is the book of life, the writing of God—it is that book of which St. Paul speaks in one of his Epistles when he says of St. Clement and others, that "their names are written in the book of life." It is that book of which our Lord spoke before, in words which that blessed Apostle may have had in his mind, when he said that about his friends and the book of life, for our Lord told the disciples who had come back to Him after they had worked miracles in His name, "Rejoice not in this, that the devils are subject unto you, but rather rejoice in this, that your names are written in Heaven." How is this, then, my brethren? Are there two different standards by which we are to stand or to fall for ever? Is it not enough, that we are to be judged by our works, or after that are we to be again tested by another book with which we have had nothing to do?

No, certainly, we are not to be tried by a book with which we have had nothing to do. But in this difficulty, as it seems at first sight, there is, as is always the case with such difficulties, a most precious and most salutary truth. You know that all this revelation to us concerning the great day of account, is conveyed in Sacred Scripture in words and images which are taken from the forms and proceedings of human justice. Now, in every case or cause, where there is an accused, or a man who stands to be examined, and put to the proof, there are two things which have to be considered in the administration of justice to him. There is the account of the facts, which we call the evidence, on which those who have to decide his fate must base their judgment, and, when the facts have been ascertained beyond doubt (as must be the case in all the judgments of God), there is also the law or the rule by which the facts must be measured, and according to that law or rule the judgment must proceed. Thus we say in matters of human justice, either that a man has been condemned or acquitted according to the evidence, or according to the law. We say this indiscriminately, and we are right, whichever of the two terms we use, for the evidence decides the action or application of the law, and the law gives the true legal interpretation of the evidence. And so in this great judgment of God of which we are speaking now, there are these two books, as the Scripture speaks, there is the book of our own writing, which is the book by which we stand or fall, and there is the book of God's writing, which contains the law, the rule, the test, the measure, according to which the actions of our lives are good or bad, worthy of eternal reward or of eternal hate and punishment. And thus again it remains true, that every one whose name is not written in the book of life shall be cast after that judgment into the pool of fire.

II.

What then, my brethren in our Lord, what is this book of life? The holy writers of the Church answer this question in many ways, but the diversity between them is more apparent than real. The blessed St. Anselm tells us that the book of life is the life of our Lord Jesus Christ, which is the standard, so to say, by which all men are to be judged, while others tell us that the book of life is the record written by the will of God, by which certain men are chosen and predestined to life everlasting. Now I say that, for our purpose to day, the difference between these two interpretations is nothing, and that they come to the same thing, for this simple reason, that those are written by God in the book of life who are conformed to the image and example of the life of our Lord. If they are made heirs to eternal glory, it is because God has written them in the book of life, and if God has written them in the book of life, it is because they have been conformed to the life of our Lord. He is the way and the truth and the life, and no man cometh to His Father but by Him. He is the one pattern, and the one measure, and the one standard, and the one test, and the one example, by which all men are examined and measured and judged—only, thanks be to God, He is more than a standard and a test and a measure and a pattern, because He not only enlightens us and teaches us and shows us the path of life, but He also gives us the strength and the courage and the power to walk along the path after Himself. Those who are like Him are the predestinated, and those who have no likeness to Him cannot be predestinated. This is the doctrine of the New Testament in a score of places, of which one will be enough for my purpose, that in which St. Paul says that "to them that love God all things work together unto good, to such as according to His purpose are called to be saints. For whom He foreknew, He also predestinated," what to, my brethren? "to be made conformable to the image of His Son, that He might be the first-born among many brethren, and whom He predestinated them He also called, and whom He called, them He also justified, and whom He justified, them He also glorified."*

The book of life, then, is the pattern, the example, the life of Jesus Christ. It was what it was in the counsels of God for this especial purpose, that He might be our pattern. If we have borne the image of the earthly, we shall also bear the image of the heavenly, if we have suffered with Him, we shall also reign with Him. For, my brethren, you have often been told that, if it had been God's sole purpose in the Incarnation of His Son to redeem the world, one drop of blood would have been enough for that. Our Lord might have suffered and nothing more. But such was not

* Rom. viii. 29, 30.

the will or the design of God. You see St. Paul says that our Lord was to be the first-born among many brethren, not, he says, among many redeemed, or many delivered from captivity, or rescued from the bondage of the devil, or saved from eternal perdition, though all these things might have been said with truth—but many brethren, who are conformed unto His image and His likeness. For the Fathers tell us that man was originally created that he might be a kind of copy of his Creator, as St. Leo says, and in order that man might know Him, Whom he was to copy, his Creator became man like him, took on Him our nature and lived among us, and so, made it possible for man to become like his God. This is what determined the whole course and order of the life of our Lord, and His life was what it was that we might all of us, of whatever age or condition or rank or calling, find in it a perfect model and pattern by which we might direct our lives. The life of our Lord was arranged by God for that purpose, and it is equally true to say that our life is meant by Him, above and before all things, to be a repetition and copy of that perfect original.

This enables us to see better than before, what God has done for us in giving us His Son, and how He has arranged everything for the greater and eternal glory of that most beloved Son. First, He has made Him the Redeemer of the world, and this in itself is a glory ineffable and without compare. Then He has made Him the pattern and example of all those who are ever to find favour in His sight. He is the beloved Son, in Whom He is well pleased, and all who are to please Him must be like that First-born of His love. Then again, He is not only the pattern of all good and the example to whom all must be conformed, but He is also the Judge of the whole human race— as He says Himself, the Father has given all judgment into His hands because He is the Son of Man. And He is not a Judge Who has to conform His judgments to a rule or a law or a book or a code, distinct from Himself, He is the law, and the rule, and the code, and the book of life. This is another great and infinite glory, because it makes Him the measure by which the whole intelligent creation is to be finally estimated and rated at the most solemn moment in the history of that creation, when the time of probation and trial is to be summed up, and all the choices and the wills of all human souls brought to the test on which the whole of their future existence is to depend for its character, of infinite bliss or of endless and limitless woe. And out of this glory is yet another to grow, which is to last on throughout the endless ages of eternity—for there will be no glory in Heaven of all His Saints which is not founded on His infinite merits, which is not the fruit of what He has done, the reward of faithfulness to His pattern, and all the multitudinous beauties and splendours of the Saints, infinite as they are to be in their variety and contrasts and harmony and combination, will be but reflections and copies of His perfections, Who is not only the meritorious cause of all, but also the source of all and the original of all.

This then, my brethren in our Lord, is another

great manifestation, which we must add to those others of which we have already spoken, as awaiting us at that last great day, when all secrets shall be made known. Not only shall all the hidden things of our own hearts and lives, and of the hearts and lives of all others like ourselves, be displayed in the open day of the presence of God, not only shall the whole most beautiful counsel and action of God to us, and to all others, and to the whole human race, be laid bare to sight in their full proportions and details, but also there will be this third great unveiling of the character and the life of our Lord by which we and all men shall be judged. That will be the measure and the rule and the norm of the judgment which shall be made of every one. Now as to this marvellous truth, there are many things which have yet to be said on which I shall not enter to-day, reserving them for another occasion. But to-day I will add one more thought to those on which we have been dwelling, a thought which may seem to be an answer to a possible difficulty, but which, like all true answers to such difficulties as meet us in our consideration of the great works of God, may be found to contain fresh truths and to add much to our intelligence of things which are so much above us.

III.

I suppose, then, that among other things which may seem hard to our comprehension on this great subject of the day of account, we may have sometimes placed the immensity of the mass of knowledge concerning God, ourselves, and others, which is to be poured in upon us on this great occasion. What human mind can stretch itself to the intelligence of all these wonders? And what space of time can suffice for this solemn recital and judicial consideration of so large a multitude of subjects? Now I answer this in this way. I have already said that the Sacred Scripture uses, in all these matters, the poor language of men, and sets forth the great truths of the spiritual world in the words and images of this human life which we lead here and now. We hear of books, and of the throne, and of the dead standing before the throne, and of the judgment being made out of the books. A long process truly, my brethren, if all the deeds and thoughts and words of each child of Adam were to be recited, one after another, in that great assembly! No, the books which are opened are the consciences of men, and the light which shall make all things clear on that day is the reflection on our minds of that knowledge of us which God has. So also the illumination which shall show to us all that God has done, and intended, and been, in His Providence to each one of us, is but the reflection of the Divine light upon our minds, driving away all shadows and flooding every cranny of our intelligences with its own piercing brightness. Everything in that great day, as the doctors of the Church tell us, is instantaneous and immediate. You know that St. Paul tells us that the resurrection of the dead, the reunion of the souls of all men to their bodies, which is then to be, is a thing which is accomplished in a single instant of time. He says that it shall be done in the twinkling of an eye. Our Lord also tells us of His own coming, that it shall be as when the lightning shines out of the east and appeareth unto the west—so shall the coming and the presence of the Son of Man be. So also will be the illumination of the consciences and the minds of all as to these great subjects of manifestation of which I speak. No need of long examination, or the recital of proofs, of the adducing of one thing after another to make the conclusion clear to all. No twilight, or dawn, or gradual break of day, but one single flash of light, laying everything bare in the clearest sunshine.

Only that illumination will come, but it will not pass away, in the twinkling of an eye, or as a lightning flash. It will remain on, for ever and for ever, as a soft strong light without change and without shadow. For we have but the poorest and faintest ideas of the immense intensity and keenness of spiritual perception into which these feeble minds of ours shall wake up, when we are called from the dust to stand before our God. The difference between the gloom of the arctic night, and the full blaze of the tropical noon, between the gropings after knowledge in the mind of the infant in the cradle, and the full-blown intelligence and well-stored mind and memory of some master of human science, is great indeed, but not so great as that which will have to be passed over, in order that our minds may take in the glorious truths which are to meet us in that birthday of our new existence. And as it is with the enlightenment of our minds concerning ourselves, and concerning God, so will it be with the revelation of the character and virtues and perfections of that blessed Sacred

Humanity of our Lord Jesus Christ, by which we are all to be judged at that last day.

Do you suppose, my brethren, that, when we shall see our Lord coming as our Judge, it will be but the outward form of the Son of Man in His majesty and glory that we shall behold ? That indeed will be an entrancing sight, but that will be but the least portion of what we shall gaze upon. We shall see the beauties of His Soul, His interior perfections and virtues, a far nobler and greater sight than any that can be taken in by the eye of the body. We shall see His Sacred Heart, with all its affections and glories. We shall read at one glance the whole character and interior of that most beloved Son in Whom the Father is well pleased. And again, my brethren, do you suppose that when men, one by one or all together, are to stand before that throne, it will be their bodies alone that we shall see, and that their hearts will not be manifested and their characters read in that light of Heaven ? It would not be the light of Heaven, the light of the presence of God, if that could be so. And if this be so, then there will be no need of more than a single glance to tell us and the whole world, who are conformed and who are not conformed to the image of the First-born among many brethren. We know brothers and sisters in this life by their likeness one to another—we say that they have the same face, or the same figure, or the same eyes, or the same hair, or the same voice, and that we should know them in a moment. But the brethren and sisters of our Lord will be known then in a moment, and without the possibility of any mistake as to their resemblance to Him, the resemblance of the soul and of the heart. He tells us that the just shall shine like the sun in the Kingdom of their Father. No doubt their glorified bodies will be as resplendent as the sun, or more resplendent than the sun, but the true glory of the saints will be the glory of their souls, which will shine through those dwellings and tabernacles of surpassing loveliness, with which they are to be linked for ever, tabernacles, as St. Paul calls them, not made with hands, eternal in the heavens. And the light there is not of the sun or of the moon or of the stars, but the source and foundation of all is this, that the Lamb is the light of that blessed city. And what is this but to say that there is no light there but that which comes from Him, and no glory there but that which is a participation, first of His image, and then of His glory?

This is that great and eternal illumination of the whole world of which the first lighting up of the universe was a figure, when at the beginning of all things God said, "Let light be, and light was," and the whole creation at once become radiant in that new mantle of brightness. But, if that was so beautiful a change, and if its effects as they have remained on ever since in this lower world are the source to us of so much blessing and joy, far greater and more magnificent are the blessings which will abide for ever in Heaven, from the illumination of the spiritual creation by the light of the Incarnate Son. "For God," says St. Paul, "Who" of old "commanded the light to shine out of darkness, hath shined in our hearts, to give the light of the knowledge of the glory of God in the face of Christ Jesus." *

My brethren, as we kneel to day,† and during this holy season, before the crib, in which our Lord is represented to us in all the humiliation and poverty and suffering of Bethlehem, let us remember that He took all that upon Him, and all that followed upon it in His life on earth, in order that we might be made like Him now, that we might be made like Him hereafter. Let us say to ourselves, "that life which began in those circumstances of pain and contempt and obscurity, is the life by which I shall be tried by-and-bye, in the day when we shall all be judged, and our lot in eternity decided." And let us make our prayer to-day as the Holy Church bids us, asking of God for the sake of His beloved Son, that as we rejoice in His first coming to be our Redeemer, so also when He comes to be our Judge we may see Him without fear, *venturum quoque judicem securi videamus.*

* 2 Cor. iv. 6.
† This Sermon was preached on Christmas Eve, being the Fourth Sunday in Advent.

SERMON XVI.

THE SAINTS OF GOD.

Cum autem venerit Filius Hominis in majestate sua, et omnes Angeli cum eo, tunc sedebit super sedem majestatis suae, et congregabuntur ante eum omnes gentes, et separabit eos ab invicem, sicut pastor segregat oves ab haedis; et statuet oves quidem a dextris suis, haedos autem a sinistris.

And when the Son of Man shall come in His majesty and all the Angels with Him, then shall He sit upon the throne of His majesty, and all nations shall be gathered together before Him, and He shall separate them one from another, as the shepherd separateth the sheep from the goats, and He shall set the sheep on His right hand and the goats on His left.

(Words taken from the 31st, 32nd, and 33rd verses of the 25th chapter of St. Matthew's Gospel.)

I.

WE have seen last Sunday, my brethren in our Lord, that the judgment of all mankind is to be made according to a certain rule and standard, and that that rule and that standard is the life of Jesus Christ. He is the book that is to be opened, the book of life, and all that are found written therein, that is, all who are like Him, are to reign with Him for ever, and all who are not found written therein, that is, all who are not like Him, not conformed to His image, are to be cast, as St. John tells us, into the pool of fire. Now this is either a terrible truth or a consoling truth. It is a terrible truth to those who have no consciousness in themselves that they are striving, day by day, to make themselves conformed to this blessed image of the Incarnate Son of God in which our only hope of salvation lies. It is a consoling truth to those who are using all the means and opportunities of grace, and seriously setting themselves to the task of the imitation of our Lord. It is a joy and a blessing to know the path along which we have to walk. This is that blessing which was promised by God of old to His people—"I will not cause your teacher to flee from you any more, thy eyes shall see thy teacher, and thy ears shall hear the word of one admonishing thee behind thy back, this is the path, walk ye in it, and go not unto the right hand nor to the left."* And all the more because our Lord's example comes to us enforced by all His love for us and all His loveliness, and it is an example that carries with it the grace and strength which can enable us to follow it. Following this we are safe. "There is therefore," as St. Paul says, "no condemnation for those that are in Christ Jesus, who walk not according to the flesh." The Christian knows what he has to do, and he knows, moreover, the immense helps with which he is provided to enable him to do it. And yet, my brethren, I suppose that there is no more common danger to us than the thought that the requirements of our God are beyond our strength, and even when we think of the loving character and gracious example of our Lord, we are inclined to say to ourselves, as the Apostles once said to our Lord after He had taught them the Christian doctrine about the difficulty of salvation for the rich—"Who then can be saved?"

* Isaias xxx. 20.

II.

Now, my brethren, such fears and even, in a certain sense, such anxieties concerning our salvation and the issue of that great trial for which we are all preparing, are well enough when they are spurs to exertion and helps and motives for resolution and for courage. But it is turning our Lord's love against Himself if they foster in us the spirit of despondency, and make us fold our arms in indolence and in despair. No one can question that it is the teaching of our Lord that salvation is a difficult thing, a thing that requires exertion and energy and determination and effort. But it is not the same thing to say that a thing is difficult and to say that it is not within the reach of all who make up their mind to have it. Our life is full of things which are difficult in themselves, and which yet are done or gained by thousands and thousands. It is difficult to get on in the world, to succeed in a profession, in the ordinary objects of human ambition, and the like—nay, we are all doing day after day things which we have learnt by education and as the fruits of our civilization, which yet are in themselves most difficult and even impossible except to those who know how to do them. Difficulties appal none who have the knowledge and the means to surmount them, and who are willing to give the labour and attention which the process requires. And so our Lord seems to me to lay down this double doctrine concerning salvation, both that it is difficult and that it is within the power of all who will to have it. You know how He answered the Apostles on the occasion which I just now quoted. He said the things that are impossible with men are possible with God. Look at the picture which He has drawn of the great Judgment Day in the passage from which the text is taken—there is to be a division as of the sheep from the goats, but it is not said that the goats outnumber the sheep, and He tells us by the very image He uses that both those on His right hand and those on His left hand had the same opportunities.

Or look again at the parable which almost immediately precedes this description of the Judgment Day —the parable of the Ten Virgins, five of whom were prudent and five were foolish. It was not the difficulty that prevented the foolish virgins from gaining the blessed lot which the others gained—it was their folly. Look at the parable of the Wheat and the Cockle—there our Lord says that at the end of the world the angels shall go forth and gather the wicked from the midst of the good—that does not seem like the account of one who had before his mind the vision of a few saved among a multitude that are lost. So it is in the parable of the Wedding Banquet—there is one out of many rejected because he had not on a wedding garment, that is, because he had not provided himself with what all the others had been able to provide. So it is in the parables in which our Lord speaks of the servants who have pounds or talents given to them to traffic with for the advantage of their lord—those who make profit and are rewarded are more in number than those who do not make profit and are punished. In all these places there is one concurrent witness to the truth of which I speak

—that the gaining of salvation may be difficult, but it is difficult to those who will not exert themselves, and whether it be the case that among Christians few or many or lost, the number of the lost depends not on the difficulty of the enterprise, but on the cowardice and foolishness of those who fail.

And surely, dear brethren, it is in a certain sense disloyal and ungrateful to our Lord, Who has in His infinite condescension and love taken on Him the office of being our pattern and example for the very purpose of showing us how to live and to please His Father, to make of the very beauty and perfection of His example a ground for complaint that we are to be judged by an impossible standard. And you will say to me at once, that it is a hard condition that we are to be measured by the standard of infinite perfection, and that our thoughts and words and actions are to be held worthless unless they are conformed to those of our Blessed Lord. What, we may say, are the thoughts of poor creatures like ourselves, immersed as we are in the gulf of worldliness, and temporal cares, and interests, are our thoughts and desires and imaginations and aspirations to be measured by those of that most pure Heart, which from its first birth into existence in the womb of the glorious Virgin Mother, was on fire with the one desire of bringing about the glory of the Father and the redemption of the human race, at the utmost cost to itself! We know what the desires of Jesus Christ were even in His Mother's womb, and know how the whole of the painful life which intervened between that moment and the last in which He breathed out His Soul into the hands of His Father, was but one continual strain after the Divine glory and a continual exercise of the most heroic interior virtues. And are we to be measured by that standard, and if we do not come up to it, are we to be cast into the pool of fire? We know what were the words of Jesus Christ, how full of love and charity and meekness and humility and all perfection, always most gracious and most truthful, and most edifying, and most gentle, and are our thousand utterances day after day to be brought up to that standard and measured thereby? We know what were the actions and deeds of Jesus Christ, of Him Who taught first by example before He taught by word, that the blessed on earth and in Heaven hereafter are the poor in spirit, the meek, the mourners, the hungry and thirsty after justice, the merciful, the pure and clean of heart, the peacemakers, the persecuted for the sake of justice, and we look over our own lives and we see there a continual practice of the faults most contrary to these, almost as if His teaching, by which we live or profess to live, had been the reverse of what it was. Are these virtues of our Lord even in honour among men as they might be even if men did not practise them to the full which His imitation requires? Ah, my brethren in our Lord, if this is the book of life, if those who are to be saved must be conformed to this pattern, we are tempted to say with that wicked prophet of old who was forced by God to bless what he would fain have cursed, and to predict what he did not wish to see—"Alas, who shall live when God doeth these things?"

III.

Certainly, I do not say that we see around us a world, even a Christian world, which lives by the example of Jesus Christ. We all know that if the judgment which is to come could be but once rehearsed before it comes, it would clear up an immense multitude of delusions and scatter to the winds a number of impostures and tricks by which men deceive themselves, and will go on deceiving themselves, as a matter of fact, until the day itself comes to take them unawares. The world will always be very much what it is—it will be the realm and the kingdom of the concupiscence of the flesh and the concupiscence of the eyes and of the pride of life, it will be the dominion of him whom our Lord speaks of as the prince of this world. But I am speaking of Christians, who know the example and the teaching of our Lord, who obey His laws and who live in the sunshine of the faith and of the truth—and to such I say that we are bound to hope and to believe that when the book of life is opened in the face of Heaven and Earth, we shall find there the names of millions of such as we call ordinary Christians like ourselves, and like those among whom we have lived.

My brethren, do we ever kneel around the dying bed of a Christian friend, without exercising this hope? It is this that gives wings to our prayers, and makes us so anxious that those whom we love should have the benefit of the adorable Sacrifice of the Mass offered for them—not that we believe them to have no need of our prayers, but because our

Christian hope forbids us not to believe that they have died in a state of grace, and that the precious Blood of our Lord has begun, and will continue in them, that blessed process of final purification which may be needed to make them perfectly fit to stand before the face of God for ever. My brethren, this has been the tradition of the Church from the first, it comes to us with all the weight of the constant instinct and practice of all the generations that have preceded us in the enjoyment of the Christian privileges and the means of grace, and we may be sure that it will go on beyond our time, and that, when we ourselves come to pass away, when it is said among our friends, that so and so has gone, either suddenly or after a long visible preparation as it may please our blessed Father to arrange for us, our friends also will gather around our bed or around our bier, and will say for us the same holy prayers in the same holy hope and confidence in the mercy and providence of our God. Surely, my brethren, these things would not be so in the Church of God, if it were true that but few, except heroic Christians, were to be able to conform themselves to the image which God has set before them as their pattern and model. And I say, that however much it may be right, and according to the intention of our Lord, that we should impress on ourselves and on others the first truth of which I have spoken, and which cannot be denied, that the imitation of our Lord is difficult, there would not be the constant traditional practice and feeling in the Church, if the other truth also were not firmly established in her heart, that an immense number of her children are able, by the mercy of God, to accomplish this difficulty.

Now as to this it might be said, in the first place, that the salvation of the world is the work and the enterprise of God, it is the special end and object for which He has done the grandest thing that He has ever done at all, in Heaven and in Earth, and that it is not the way of God to undertake great things which He does not bring to an accomplishment. To say this, it is only to say in other words what St. Paul says in the passage which was quoted to you last Sunday—" What shall we say to these things? If God be for us, who is against us? He that spared not even His own Son, but delivered Him up for us all, how hath He not also with Him given us all things?" Surely it is not easy to think that God will let Himself be defeated, even by the malice of Satan and even by the obstinacy of the perverse human will, to such an extent as to contrive all this great economy of the Incarnation and the Passion and the Catholic Church, and then find at the end of all that it has been done in vain.

And again, my brethren, if it be an incongruous thought to conceive of God that He would undertake so great an enterprise as that of the salvation of the world, and let it be defeated, it is also the same to think that He would take that very means which He has in His wisdom taken for the accomplishment of His great object, and do it all for nought. I mean that it is hard to believe that God has become Man and set Himself to win our hearts to Himself by all the sweetness and condescension of the Incarnation, that He lived among us in order that He might set us this perfect example, of which we are so faint-hearted and so ungenerous as to complain that it is only too perfect, knowing all the time that no one would follow Him along the path of beautiful virtues which He has marked by His own footprints, in order that men might be happy here, at peace with themselves and with their God, and, by their happy practice of what He has thus marked out for them, might prepare themselves to reign with Him for ever. Can we think of our Lord that He would not only die for us on the Cross, but moreover leave behind Him in the world the whole marvellous system of the Catholic Church, with all its precepts and teachings and sacraments and ordinances brimming over, so to say, with graces and spiritual forces, a system coextensive in its multitudinous arrangements and provisions with human life in all its stages and fortunes and developments, only to see the whole arrangement fail, or at the most remain a witness unparalleled in the whole history of the world of the perversity of men, in refusing the most careful and wise and copious and tender provisions made for them by their God? No, this cannot be, and more than that, this has not been. For the whole of history since our Lord's time, as the whole of prophecy before, tells us a different tale, for it tells us of the imitation of our Lord's example by thousands and thousands of His saints.

IV.

From the very beginning of the ordinance of prophecy in the world, it has been said in these descriptions more or less clearly what St. Jude quotes from the prophecy of the holy Enoch, that " the Lord cometh with thousands of His saints." And indeed it may be truly said that the presence of the saints is necessary in the great day of trial and manifestation, for the confusion of the wicked, as well as for the consolation of the just. Well, my brethren, and who are the saints of God? Have they been men and women of different mould from ourselves? We know indeed only a small part of the history of some few of them —we know that by far the greater number of that immense multitude have lived hidden from mortal sight, at least that their sanctity has never been proclaimed by the Church on earth, whose calendars are yet crowded and overcrowded by the number of those who in various parts of the Catholic world have been deemed, by the holy instinct of the Christian people, to be worthy of that special veneration which belongs to heroic virtue, and have been honoured by God, in return, by those manifestations of their power with Him which He has vouchsafed to grant, as an authentication, so to say, of the accuracy of the instinct which has led to that veneration. And if we cannot gather any certain conclusions as to their numbe rfrom that of those whom we know in this way to be among the saints of God, at all events we can gather two things which are enough for our purpose now, namely, we can gather that the number, even of great saints, is very large, and we can gather also that they have been taken from all classes and conditions of men. We know thus much at least, they have not all lived in the deserts, they have not all been consecrated to the service of the altars of God, they have not all renounced the use of their earthly possessions or their homes, they have not all passed their days in the exercise of prayer or of practices of penance. If they had done this, they would have imitated only a portion of the example of our Lord. No, the saints of God (in the largest sense of the word), as far as we know them, have been, as I say, men and women like ourselves, they have been young and old, they have been rich, and poor, and learned, and unlearned, and high in position, as the world counts position, as well as lowly and obscure. Humanly speaking, they have often been as weak, and as feeble, and as unstable, and as heavily weighted, so to say, with difficulties for the attainment of salvation as any of ourselves can be. Had they been persons of singular and exceptional dispositions or characters or histories, then it might be said that some characters and some dispositions and some circumstances were so unfavourable to sanctity as to present insuperable difficulties to the attainment of salvation. The lives of the saints teach us nothing of the kind. There are among them kings and queens, there are among them soldiers and courtiers and statesmen and men of every profession, merchants, artisans, labourers, mechanics, those who have had an abundance of the good things of this world to tempt them, as well as those who have received from Providence the blessed privilege of poverty and of affliction. All ranks and conditions of men are there, as if God had willed it on purpose that all ranks and conditions might hope to add to their numbers and to share the crowns which they have already won.

You may have heard, my brethren, of the great St. Augustine, how he tells us, in his history of his own conversion, that he had a great interior struggle with himself, and that one of his chief difficulties lay in what seemed to him the impossibility of living according to the requirements of the Gospel law in the matter of purity. And then at last he said to himself, thinking of so many whom he had known and heard of, who had honoured God in perfect continence and chastity, "Can you not do what these and these and these have done?" This is another of the great blessings conveyed to us in the Providence of God by what we know of His saints. We are inclined to say to ourselves, If it were not for my strong passions, or if it were not for my peculiar disposition and violent character, or if it were not for the very great extent to which I am so constantly tempted, as if the devil had a particular power to hinder my efforts after salvation, I might hope, but, as things are, I find the battle so difficult that I fear sanctity and salvation are not for me. Here again the saints meet us, and silence our complaints, while they add immense strength to our courage. They would tell us now, as we shall see at the last day, that these very seeming difficulties have been to them the occasions of their sanctity. They will say to us, that if they had not been so strongly tempted, they would never have known their own weakness, and so have been driven to prayer and reliance on God, that if they had not had that strong natural character to conquer, and those violent passions to subdue, their virtues would have been no more than the natural virtues, such as we see sometimes in children and in persons who do not attain any great height of perfection. They will tell us that they owe their crowns to the fierceness of the battle which they had to fight, to their natural dispositions, their wild and indomitable passions, the violent temptations from without to which they have been exposed, these have been the very things which have been to them the occasion of their greatest victories, and if they had been treated otherwise in the Providence of God, they would not have the same glorious crowns in Heaven which they now possess. And we may say the same of other things which we are accustomed in our pusillanimity to complain of as matters which make it more than ordinarily difficult for us to serve our God faithfully. We complain of adversities, of the hardness of our lot in this world, of the unkindness with which we are treated by men, even those who have been the objects of love and benevolence on our part—all these things, we are inclined to say, as the patriarch Jacob said, "All these things are against us," and make us almost despair of winning our crowns. Well, when the saints of God shall be revealed in the Day of Judgment, we shall see that these very circumstances of life, these calamities, these adversities, these disappointments, these ingratitudes, all this rough treatment at the hands of men or of Providence of which we are inclined to complain, are just the very things out of which the heroic virtues of the saints have been formed and made perfect.

V.

Consider for a moment, my brethren, how this must be so, if we believe at all in the particular Providence of God. He is the Father of all, and He distributes to all their natural gifts, He knows all their dispositions, and the temptations to which they are the most liable, and He guides their lives as a father guides his children in their way through the world, or rather with a love, a power, and a wisdom, which are not to be found in any earthly father. No doubt He chooses very different gifts indeed for different souls, and He places them in very different circumstances and positions of life. But He observes two rules, not only with His saints, but with every single soul of His children, first, to give them the graces which their state and their duties require, and secondly, not to let them be tempted beyond their strength. Of course it is possible for men to throw themselves out of the path of life in which God desires them to walk, but even then He does not forsake them until they have first and long forsaken Him. I am not saying that God makes it impossible for any to be lost, but that He makes it possible and more than possible for all to be saved. And we have already spoken of the revelation which will meet us at the last day of the tender and particular Providence of God over each soul of man, and what we already know of His immense goodness and tenderness is a security to us that we shall find in that day that the things of which men complain most as the dangers to their salvation, if they are not matters of their own choice, in which case no complaint can be made against the Providence of God, are just the things which, if they had been faithful to Him, would have turned out for their greater and more glorious sanctification. Every sinner who has thrown away his own chance of the glories of eternity will be confronted there, not only by the revelation of the goodness and mercifulness of God in his regard, but also with the sight of a number of men of like passions, or of like difficulties of character, or of like external circumstances with himself, and he will see that they have used these things as means to advance in the service of their God, while he has neglected them or used them to his own perdition.

But, my brethren, I am now using the examples of the saints for our encouragement, and not for the confusion of those who may find themselves in that last day among the goats on the left hand of our Lord. You may remember in the words which follow after those of the text in that chapter of St. Matthew, that our Lord there shows to those that are lost as well as to those who are saved, that they have each had the same opportunities. The difference has been that some have used them and others have neglected them, and now this leads me to the last point on which I need speak in this consideration on the day of account. I have said that the saints of God have been taken from every state and rank and age, from every country and race and nation, that they have been men and women like ourselves in every respect as to their character, or their dispositions, the strength of their passions, or the circumstances of their lives—and that so they are illustrations of the truth of that saying of St. Paul in the passage more than once referred to, that all things work together for good to those who love God. And yet there remains one subterfuge for discouragement, one hiding place in which the spirit of pusillanimity may entrench itself. And it is this—that perhaps the saints of God had some very singular providence of His over them, by which there were secured to them more abundant supplies of Divine grace than we have, for their conflict against the same difficulties and the same temptations. My brethren, it is not well to pry into the special favours which God may bestow on those who are so very dear to Him, and who reward, if one may so speak, His special tenderness and care by a special correspondence and faithfulness. But in general we may say at once that it is not so—that the victories of the saints have been won by means of those common ordinary means of grace, faithfully used, which are open to us all. I might indeed say more, for there have been many of the saints of God, notably in countries like this, in which persecution has raged, who had not a half of the spiritual advantages which we enjoy and of which we think so little. But I set that aside, and I say it is true in general that the saints of God, the members of that immense multitude which the seer of the Apocalypse saw before the Throne of God, men of all peoples and tribes and nations and languages, had no more at least of the means of grace to help them to Heaven than we have or may have whenever we choose. They had the same example of our Lord and of others who had gone before them in the imitation of our Lord to follow as we have, they had the same holy teaching of the Catholic Church, the same word of God, the same sacraments, the same prayers, the same Holy Sacrifice of the Altar as we have, the angels guarded them, the earlier saints prayed for them, they had the blessings which belong to the communion of saints, they had in prayer the key of Heaven, they had faith which showed them the nothingness of the world. Even to enumerate the common means of grace, as we call them, is enough, because there is not one of them which does not contain a power far more than sufficient to carry a poor child of God safely, through a more difficult world than this, to the embraces of his Father. If we could ask them, how they came by their crowns, they would tell us by the use of the same weapons which we have in our hands. For what more can any one want but the merits of Jesus Christ, than the application of the Precious Blood to the soul, than the Heavenly Food of the Body and Blood of our Lord, than the power to ask of God with the certainty of being heard, the power to turn everything into a means of advancement and of the expiation of sin or the increase of merit?

VI.

Therefore, my brethren, I say in conclusion of our considerations of this great subject, what St. Paul said to the Hebrews, who were at that time quailing before the terrors of earthly persecution and of difficulties of every kind in the maintenance of their Christian profession : " Lift up the hands which hang down, and the feeble knees, and make straight paths for your feet, lest any one halting go out of the way." The consideration of the great day of the Lord is not meant by Him to make us timid and cowardly, but manly and resolute and confident and courageous. It is meant to dash away the esteem of temporal things, the fear of human opinion, to show us the imposture of the world, to put an end to slothfulness, and to raise us above the intense frivolity and littleness and childishness of which human life becomes so full, when its great end and object is forgotten. We must accustom ourselves to the light which streams from that day on those who contemplate it in the spirit of faith. That light will change our whole lives, it will give us new conceptions concerning God, and ourselves, and the future for which we are in preparation. It will make us see beforehand, in some measure, how great and beautiful and tender and merciful are the dealings of God with us, how great He is in His justice and in His provisions for His children. It will make us see how rich we are already in the abundance of the means of grace and salvation by which we are surrounded. It will make us understand how intense must be that happiness which is in preparation for the children of God, how glorious that existence into which we shall wake up, to exercise therein for ever the faculties of that new life, of which we shall have the first taste and use in that great day of account.

SERMON XVII.

ALL THINGS MADE NEW.*

Et audivi vocem magnam de throno dicentem: Ecce tabernaculum Dei cum hominibus, et habitabit cum eis. Et ipsi populus ejus erunt, et ipse Deus cum eis erit eorum Deus. Et absterget Deus omnem lacrymam ab oculis eorum, et mors ultra non erit, neque luctus, neque clamor, neque dolor erit ultra, quia prima abierunt. Et dixit qui sedebat in throno, "Ecce, nova facio omnia."

And I heard a great voice from the Throne, saying, Behold the Tabernacle of God with men, and He will dwell with them, and they shall be His people, and God Himself with them shall be their God. And God shall wipe away all tears from their eyes, and death shall be no more, nor mourning, nor sorrow, nor crying shall be any more, for the former things are passed away; and He that sat on the Throne said, "Behold, I make all things new."

(Words taken from the 3rd, 4th, and 5th verses of the 21st chapter of the Apocalypse.)

I.

IN these words the Beloved Disciple of Jesus Christ describes the state of things which shall be established when his Lord comes for the second time. And now, in the midst of the joy of the Feast of His first coming, it is our business this afternoon, my brethren in Jesus Christ, to dwell for a short time upon what the Holy Scripture tells us of some chief features of that second advent of His which is to close the history of this present world, and be

---

* Preached on the Sunday within the Octave of Christmas, being the Feast of St. John the Evangelist.

V

the opening scene of the new history of our race, redeemed in Heaven. I say it is the close of the first creation, and the opening of the second, and that, when we consider it, we should not separate the latter aspect of it from the former aspect. We see that this lies at the root of the difference between our own common way of looking at our Lord's second coming, and the way in which the Christians to whom the Apostles wrote looked upon it—that to them it was rather a beginning than an end ; and to us, commonly, it is rather an end than a beginning. An end is done with and gone, a beginning lives on in that to which it gives birth. Of the two features, I say, the earlier Christians dwelt more on the one, and we are more inclined to dwell on the other. Their thoughts of what they looked to were more distinct and penetrating, they had a firmer grasp of the realities of the world to come than we have. And yet, if they had altogether forgotten the terrible part of the second advent, they would not so well have fitted themselves to be partakers of its glories and its blessings. So also, my brethren, in our preparation to meet Him as our Judge, we must not forget to dwell on the great and marvellous blessings which our Lord will bring in His train. He Himself, in His discourses and parables, has dwelt on both one and the other topic, and His Apostles and Prophets have done likewise. They have taken the greatest pains to describe for us the blessings which await us under a wondrous variety of figures, so that there is hardly anything precious and pleasant in this life which Jesus Christ, or His servants, have not used as an image to prepare us for the delights of the life which is to come. And so this evening, under the guidance of that beloved Disciple—at once Apostle, Evangelist, Doctor, Prophet, Virgin, Martyr, and the special child of Mary—whose Feast we are keeping, we will first of all take one more final glance at the series of events which, according to Sacred Scripture, are to happen at the end of time, and then we will dwell for a while more particularly upon those features in the prophecy on which the hopes and confidence of Christians are meant to rest.

II.

And here again, before leaving the subject, let me add one or two words as to the manner in which we are to explain unfulfilled prophecy in general. There are certain rules which we must keep in view if we would do this with safety, one or two alone of which need be mentioned now. In the first place, we are very likely to deceive ourselves if we aim at fixing the exact time of future events with any precision. We have seen how our Lord has expressly told us, with regard to the end of the world, that the Father keeps the times and seasons in His own power, and that it is not for us to know them.[*] And moreover, even if this were set aside, we must remember what I have already had occasion to mention, that God's mode of estimating time is very different indeed from our mode. A thousand years are to Him as a day, and a day as a thousand years. In the second place, we may remind ourselves of this

[*] Acts i. 7.

—that not only is the time of the end of the world uncertain to us, but that also the order of the several events which make up, as it were, this great scene of prophetic vision, is frequently not clear. We know that a certain number of great things will happen, but which is to be first, which is to be last among them, we do not know. The Prophets of God often predict one and the same thing in many different ways, and thus visions which may seem to form a consecutive series are, in truth, prophecies of one and the same event. Again, they often predict a part of some great history, and not the whole—as St. Paul says to the Corinthians, "We know in part, and we prophesy in part."* Thus it may not always be easy to combine the fragments, as it were, which they severally furnish to us, into any certain order.

Now I say that the matter before us in these discourses gives us more than one example of this uncertainty. We know, for instance, that there are to be signs in the sun, and in the moon, and in the stars,† disturbances in the physical order of the world, in land and in sea, before the last coming of Jesus Christ. And yet again we are told that that day is to come as a thief in the night, as a snare, at a time when men least expect it. The day of the Son of Man is to be like the days of Noe, or the days of Lot, when the coming Flood was not thought of, and the destruction of the Cities of the Plain was expected by no one. There are two ways of explaining this, but we are unable to decide between the two; we are unable to say whether these great

---

* 1 Cor. xiii. 9.   † St. Luke xxi. 25, 26.

signs of which we are told are to go before the rising of Antichrist, and that after his victory the world is to be in apparent peace at the moment of our Lord's coming, or whether, as it seems to have been in the days of Noe, the warnings of God, however great and signal, will be utterly disregarded by the men of that generation, so that, notwithstanding all the signs in heaven and on earth, they will be sunk in utter security and forgetfulness of God's threats, under the dominion of the enemy of Christ. In that case, the signs would be contemporaneous with the absolute recklessness of men as to their future fate; and we know too well the hardness of the human heart under great calamities to be surprised at the prediction. It has often been seen that, when God has visited the world, or certain particular countries, with the great plagues which have left their mark on the history of the centuries in which they have happened, men, instead of being converted by the visitation, have given themselves up all the more recklessly to the extravagances of vice and debauchery. And we all know how truly our Lord has said of those who are not touched by the ordinary and appointed ministrations of warning, that they "would not be converted, though one went to them from the dead."*

This, then, is one of the points as to which uncertainty hangs over the prophecy, at least as to the order of time. I will mention one other great feature of the vision, as to which there is a difficulty of the same kind. There are many passages in Scripture which speak plainly of the future destruc-

* St. Luke xvi. 31.

tion of the world in which we live by fire.* It is hardly possible to allow that these texts can be fairly interpreted in any merely figurative sense, and I will give for this only one amply sufficient reason. St. Peter, in a passage which I have already had occasion to quote, compares the future destruction of the world by fire to the historical destruction of the human race in the days of Noe by the waters of the Deluge. He says: "The world that then was, being overflowed with water, perished. But the heavens and the earth which are now, by the same word are kept in store, reserved unto fire against the Day of Judgment and perdition of the ungodly men."† Now, my brethren, as you know, it might not be forbidden to us to think that the Deluge, though universal as to the destruction of mankind, may not have been universal in extent over the whole globe, which may not then have been inhabited in all its parts.‡ But though we might not see reason for condemning those who consider that the Deluge may have been partial in this sense, we should contradict Scripture if we were to say that it was figurative. And it would be inconsistent with the plain sense of the words of St. Peter to explain the fire of which he speaks as being less literal and real than the Deluge with which he compares it. The earth, therefore, is to be burnt up by fire; but here, again, the facts of the future that is coming upon the earth are more certain than their order. We cannot say for certain when this conflagration is to take place; whether it is

---

* *e.g.*, Isaias li. 6; Psalm ciii. 32, xcvi. 3.
† 2 St. Peter iii. 6, 7.   ‡ See Note to this Sermon.

to be before the Judgment Day, and so, perhaps, the means of the death of the generation of men that is in possession of the earth at the latter days, or whether it is to take place after that great day of account, or, as some have thought, partly before and partly after.

This, then, as well as the great signs of which I have before spoken, must be counted among the great features of the prophecy, although we are not absolutely certain as to the order in which they are to be arranged. And as to the other wonders of that time, what need is there for me to recur to them to-day? We know that all mankind shall rise, though, as the Apostle says, not all shall be changed.* Some shall rise to honour, some to ignominy, some to glory both of body and soul, others to eternal shame and suffering in both. The Angels shall go forth, and separate the wicked from among the good; then shall be the manifestation of the consciences of all to all, the perfect rectification of all judgments, the absolute vindication of all the dealings of God with souls, the triumph of virtue and right, the speechless self-conviction and exposure of all that has been wrong and vicious; then shall the eternal sentence come home to the hearts of all, witnessed to and acknowledged by every conscience singly, and proclaimed aloud, as to every child of Adam, in the hearing of Heaven and earth—"And these shall go into everlasting punishment, but the just into life everlasting."†

* 1 Cor. xv. 51. † St. Matt. xxv. 46.

III.

And now, my brethren, as we must select some one or two out of the number of thoughts which crowd upon us as we survey, however briefly, this chain of great and marvellous events so closely linked together, the rapid unfolding of which is to be the history of the last few years of the world, I will choose some which seem most in keeping with the holy and happy season now upon us, some which are most frequently suggested to us by the language used by the holy Apostles, and by the tone of thought which they inculcate upon their disciples. No doubt the coming of Jesus Christ is the "great and terrible day of the Lord." Who, as Malachias says, "shall be able to think of the day of His coming, and who shall stand to see Him? For He is like a refiner's fire."[*] Who can think of the signs in the sun and in the moon and in the stars, of the shaking of the powers of the physical universe, of the plagues and woes of the latter time, of the earth burnt up as a scroll, of the terrible voice of the Archangel, of the dead summoned to judgment, of the throne set and the books opened, of all the tribes of the earth wailing because of the sign of the Son of Man in the heavens—who can think of all these things without fear and dread, such as breathe in the strains which the Church puts into our mouths as we sing her last hymn over the bier of the departed? *Quantus tremor est futurus!* or, *Quid sum miser tunc dicturus?* or, *Rex tremendæ majestatis,*

[*] Mal. iii. 2.

Qui salvandos salvas gratis, salva me, fons pietatis!
And yet, my brethren, there are other strains, which, as I may say, ring more frequently in our ears as we listen to the words of Jesus Christ and the blessed Apostles of His Gospel. As we sing the *Dies Iræ* we are thinking how to expiate to the utmost what remains there may be of the debt which man owes to God's justice, and so we do well to fill ourselves with the emotions of fear and awe which suit the temper of humble and earnest pleading for the dead by means of the Holy Sacrifice. But God's justice is a justice of reward as well as of punishment—of restitution, renovation, crowning and blessing for the sake of Jesus Christ, Who is not only the end of the old creation but the Beginning and First-born of the new. And so our Lord says to us: "When these things begin to come to pass, look up and lift up your heads, because your redemption is at hand."*
And so I find the latter times spoken of by the holy Apostles. I find St. Peter speaking of them as the times of the "restitution of all things;" "when the times of refreshment shall come from the presence of the Lord."† And St. Paul's Epistles are full of hope and longing expectation of the appearance of Jesus Christ. It is a thought always before him and those to whom he writes, so that, as I have shown you, he had even to warn his disciples at Thessalonica that they were not to look immediately for the "glory to come which is to be revealed in us."‡ As to himself, St. Paul is looking forward to

---

* St. Luke xxi. 28.
† Acts iii. 20, 21. ‡ Rom. viii. 18; 2 Thess. ii.

the crown of justice which the Lord, the just Judge, will render to him in that day, and "not only," as he says, "to me, but to them also that love His coming."* Those that love the coming of our Lord will certainly desire it and long for it, and the feelings of fear and awe which its terrible features naturally arouse will be swallowed up in those of loving expectation. And to love and expectation, as characteristics of the feelings of Christians with regard to the latter days, we may add, on St. Peter's authority, a still more surprising quality, that of perfect tranquillity and peace. "Seeing then," he says, "that all these things are to be dissolved, what manner of people ought you to be in holy conversation and godliness," in the daily practice of virtue, and in religious exercises of devotion? "looking for," and not only that, but "hasting unto the coming of the day of the Lord, by which the heavens being on fire shall be dissolved, and the elements shall melt with the burning heat!" But he says, "We look for new heavens and a new earth, according to His promises, in which justice dwelleth. Wherefore, dearly beloved, seeing that you look for these things, be diligent, that you may be found undefiled and unspotted to Him in peace."† Joy, longing desire, careful and diligent preparation, such are the feelings, and such, if I may so speak, is the attitude which the coming of the day of the Lord is to find in us, if we are like the Christians to whom the Apostles wrote. Let us, then, consider one by one a few of the elements of this joyous anticipation and desire.

* 2 Tim. iv. 8. † 2 St. Peter iii. 11—14.

In the first place, my brethren, we have already seen that the New Testament bids us look on the coming of our Lord, not only as the end of all the misery, and the conflict, and the uncertainty of this life; not only, again, as the great day of account, when the throne is to be set and the books opened, when the great separation of good from evil is to take place, and the eternal rewards and eternal punishments will be awarded—but particularly, and before all, as the dawn of a day whose sun shall never set, as the beginning of a life of blessedness and of a new order of things, which shall never change nor end. Nor was this expectation a merely general and vague expectation, but it had its anticipations of the renovation and glorification of human life and existence in every particular in which it is now liable to infirmity, decay, and corruption. The coming of our Lord was to bring them, in one word, "life from the dead"—a new, restored, blessed, endless life, answering in all its features, though raised so infinitely higher in respect of its happiness, to the life of which we have experience here and now. We, such as we are, are to be made blessed in every respect. My brethren, if we divide the life we live into portions, as it were, according to the several parts of our compound being, the occupation of all our faculties on the scenes in which we dwell, the objects before us, the companions in whose affection and society we live, we find that in each of these departments we have powers and capacities of happiness which are disappointed and dissatisfied now, and we can only imagine ourselves happy when, in all these respects, we have what our nature craves for and is intended for by God. The mind, the soul, the heart, the body, have each their life—a life of uncertain, insecure, imperfect, and transient pleasure here, at the best; a life in most cases, with much of positive pain and misery mingled in it. We are set in the midst of a universe of which we have not the key, the powers of which are often hostile and fatal to us; and we are made dependent one on another, endowed with immense faculties of loving and understanding our fellows, and yet with a wall of division raised between us, with no power of reading one another's hearts, and with pettiness, selfishness, and other evil passions within us, to prevent us from reaching out of ourselves to perfect sympathy one with another.

Well then, I say, that the coming of our Lord was looked upon by the Apostolic Christians as the healing of all these wounds at once and for ever, as placing us in a condition of ineffable bliss in every one of these particulars. I do not speak now of the glory of the soul made perfect and confirmed in grace, the will for ever united to the will of God, the intelligence filled with His light, the whole heart and mind beatified by the sight of Him. This blessedness of the soul may be given before the time of the resurrection of the body and of the general judgment, and those who die in grace become heirs of it when they die. Only, let us observe that in the next life it will not be with the children of God as it is here. Here, if a Saint is visited by special favour and for a short time, as St. Paul was caught up into Heaven and heard unspeakable words, it is as he says, "whether in the body or out of the body I cannot tell"—there is too great a strain in ordinary cases for bodily life and sense to retain their full vigour and activity, they are rapt in ecstasy and overpowered by it. They seem dead, and without perception of anything but God. This is on account of the weakness of our present existence, even in the highest Saints: though we read nothing of this kind in what Scripture tells us of our Lord's Humanity and of His Blessed Mother. It will not be so in the next life, even though our union with God there is far closer and is permanent. Then the blessedness of the soul will overflow on to the body without impeding its full life and activity and enjoyment. One part of our compound nature will no longer be a drag upon the other, but both will share in the same immortal life, the same heavenly strength and beatitude. As the Angels calmly, and with perfect ease and tranquillity, see and enjoy God and know all things in Him, and yet while they are rapt in the contemplation of Him they converse one with another, and at the same time watch over the universe which is committed to their charge and guard us upon earth, whispering holy thoughts, warding off dangers, guiding our footsteps, and keeping back our infernal foes, always with God, and always with us, as holy Raphael journeyed with Tobias, and yet said, "I am Raphael, one of the seven who stand before the Lord,"*—so in the next world with us, the beatific vision and possession of God will not absorb

* Tob. xii. 15.

our faculties or impede the other functions of our Divine life, rather it will be the principle of that life in all its fulness and activity of enjoyment, of the life of the glorified body, of the life which occupies itself in the companionship of the Saints, in the contemplation of God's creation, in the reading of the marvellous secrets of His providence and His mysteries, in the perfect possession of all whom we love in Him.

Yes, my brethren, these bodies of ours are no longer to be prisons to us, full of danger, but are to glow with the perfect life which Jesus Christ brought with Him from the grave. The early Christians knew this well. They looked beyond the destruction of all things to the new and beautiful and happy creation which had been begun in Jesus Christ, and which was to burst into full life and bloom and glory at His second coming. They looked back for a moment to the days of Paradise, and they found that in each particular of blessedness in which the state of innocence had surpassed that condition of misery in which we now are enchained, that state of innocence again was to be far surpassed in the new Kingdom of Christ. Let us begin with the body, to please and pamper which we are so often tempted to forego the future glories of the children of God. "Who shall deliver me," says St. Paul, "from the body of this death?"* Who shall deliver me from the evil law in my members warring against my soul? Who shall deliver me from sickness and pain, and weariness, and death! "We ourselves," he says, "even

* Romans vii. 24.

we who are regenerate, or who have the first fruits of the Spirit, even we ourselves groan within ourselves waiting for the adoption of the sons of God, the redemption of our body."* "For we know," as he goes on in another place, "that if our earthly home of this tabernacle be dissolved, we have a building of God, a home not made with hands, eternal in Heaven. For in this also we groan, desiring to be clothed upon with our habitation which is from Heaven."† "This corruptible must put on incorruption, and this mortal must put on immortality."‡ The coming of our Lord was to them the time when He would "reform the body of our lowness made like to the body of His glory,"§ when He will give to each one of those who rise again to that wondrous change, which is to be the lot of His Saints, a body like to His own as it is now in glory, a body like to His when He showed Himself in His majesty to the Apostles on the Mount of Transfiguration.

It is, therefore, a little thing, too little for God to do for us for the sake of our Lord, to give us back again the integrity and health and bloom and beauty of our first parents before their fall. It is too little to destroy the conflict of sense and conscience, to root out the principles of concupiscence, to endow us with perfect impassibility and freedom from pain. That was the gift of an innocent and untried nature, but now we have to inherit the fruits of conflict and of conquest for God through Jesus Christ. "It became Him," says the Apostle, "for

---

* Romans viii. 23.   † 2 Cor. v. 1, 2.
‡ 1 Cor. xv. 53.   § Philipp. iii. 21.

Whom are all things and by Whom are all things, Who was bringing many children into glory, to perfect the Author of their salvation by His Passion."* It was fitting that when God undertook to raise a vast multitude of the human race to the dignity of His sons, and to bring them into His own glory, that He should provide that that glory which was to be so nobly won and the crown of so many great gifts, should have the full merit of the Passion of Jesus Christ and of the sufferings of His followers to enhance its beauty and its intensity. Here then, my brethren, is the Christian answer to those who are so fond of what is called the full development of our natural being, who consider the perfection of man to consist in healthy animal life, whether moral or not, who ask, why God has given us our bodily instincts and cravings if they are never to be satisfied and always to be mortified? They are to be mortified and kept under now, that our bodies hereafter may rise, not to disgrace and ignominy, but to glory and brightness and immortality, glowing with life and beauty; real flesh and blood, as our Lord after the Resurrection had real flesh and blood, but spiritualized, made heavenly and deathless, and destined to endless enjoyment in the exercise of the marvellous gifts then bestowed upon them.

IV.

Again, my brethren, the Christians of the Apostles' time looked to our Lord's coming as the renovation and restoration of the physical universe itself, in

* Heb. ii. 10.

which our lot is cast. St. Paul had taught them that the present state of things, even in the physical universe, was a penal state, a state inflicted upon the creation by God in consequence of the fall of man—man, who had incurred death for himself and brought his earthly home and the world itself into the servitude of corruption. The change and decay and succession and waste, which all nature undergoes, are consequences of sin, and we look forward, as St. Paul says, "to the revelation of the sons of God"* as the time when "the creature shall be delivered from this servitude into the liberty of the glory of the children of God;" or we look, as St. Peter says, "for new heavens and a new earth in which justice dwelleth."† My brethren, we all know that nothing that man can frame or imagine can be compared for sublimity beauty, delicacy, gracefulness, and grandeur, to the natural works of God, and yet we are taught that the mighty mountains, and the boundless sea, and whatever there is that ravishes our eye or ear in tree or flower, in plant or bird or animal, is to be supplanted at our Lord's coming by creatures more noble, more beautiful, more wonderful, than any that the earth has yet known. When God made this varied universe out of nothing, He did not make the best that He could make, and for the dwelling-place and home of His children through Jesus Christ He will make new heavens and a new earth, to which these shall be as nought. And this is one Christian answer to those who ask why religion sets so little store upon physical knowledge, why she looks, as it

---

* Romans viii. 19. † 2 St. Peter iii. 13.

seems, coldly and unfavourably upon those who give their lives to the investigation of the secrets of nature, why she accounts all their acquirements as nothing in comparison to a single holy thought, or to a cup of cold water given to a traveller for the sake of Jesus Christ. I do not say there are not other answers, but this is among the answers; that all these things are, as St. Peter says, "to be dissolved and come to nought." At present they help us by their use, and by the knowledge we may gain from them of the goodness and the power of their Maker. They serve our mortal life, also, and are to be received and used with thankfulness and joy. But still the children of God have a fairer and more majestic home in store for them, filled with creations of His power and love far more marvellous, and their intelligence is hereafter to feed itself upon their contemplation, and their life is to be diversified by the use of the new creation. But then they will read and know, and understand and enjoy, without fear of presumption and error, without the possibility of mistake, obscurity, or impurity of intention, because they will see and comprehend all things around them in the light of the vision of God Himself.

And once more, my brethren—only to touch most shortly upon what, next to the possession of God, will be the greatest joy of the new state of existence —as we are made to love and to be companions one to another, to live, as it were, outside ourselves, open to a perpetual interchange and flow of influence and sympathy, to feel loneliness as a privation, and brotherly love and mutual intelligence as our greatest blessing—so it will be in our regenerate state, when this our life of isolation and separation will be at an end. There will no longer be barriers and veils of separation and diffidence between us, but we shall each rejoice in and profit by the gifts of all others as if they were our own. And this blessed society which awaits us in the next world was the frequent contemplation of the Saints, and is set before us as a motive of hope and exertion by St. Paul. "For ye are come," he says, "to Mount Sion, and to the city of the living God, and to the company of many thousands of Angels, and to the Church of the first-born who are written in the heavens, and to God the Judge of all, and to the spirits of the just made perfect, and to Jesus the Mediator of the New Testament."*

V.

Surely, my brethren, it is nothing strange if, with the Babe of Bethlehem before us on the knees of His Immaculate Mother, we raise our hearts and send forth our thoughts, as did the Christians of old, to that most blessed consummation and restitution of all things which is the great end of His coming amongst us at all. "He that spared not His own Son, but delivered Him up for us all, how hath He not with Him also given us all things?"† What is simply reasonable, in looking forward to what is coming upon our race and upon the earth in which we dwell, but that we should pass by the things which are transient, and dwell rather upon the things

* Heb. xii. 22—24. † Rom. viii. 32.

which shall abide and shall never change? Heaven and earth shall pass away, but the words and the work of Jesus Christ our Lord shall not pass away.

There shall come plagues, and woes, and tribulations, and persecutions, and apostacies—but they shall pass. The civil system of the world, the principles which hold society together, shall be sapped and undermined; but this also shall pass. There shall come the enemy of God, the rival of Jesus Christ, the most vaunted and the most fascinating of the world's heroes, armed with powers such as never yet have been placed in the hands of one man; he shall seduce and subdue the nations, he shall wage terrible war against the Saints of God, he shall prevail for a moment, but he shall not seduce the Elect—and he too shall pass away. There shall come that great apostacy on which we have lately reflected, the restoration for a time of the hideous reign of unregenerated nature in all its savage voluptuousness and refined cruelty under a new form of paganism—but that shall pass. The birth pangs of the new creation shall be terrible, earthquakes and incursions of the sea, the sun turned to darkness and the moon to blood, the stars falling, the world shaken to its foundations; the death of the human race will be terrible, the burning of the heavens and the earth with fervent heat—but all this shall pass. The awful Day of Judgment will come, the resurrection of the dead, the opening of the books, the eternal separation, the rewards and punishments allotted by the mouth of the Son of Man. But even the Day of Judgment will pass away, and be at an end; and then shall break forth that eternal and most glorious morning, the new creation and condition of things wrought by the infinite wisdom and the power of God for the sake of those who love Him. Heaven and earth purified and renovated, the souls of the Saints filled with Divine intelligence and indefectible and boundless love, the mind enlightened by the light of God's countenance, the will and heart ennobled and beatified by inseparable and closest union with Him, the body endowed with the gifts requisite for the ceaseless exercise and enjoyment of its new spiritualized existence—bright as the sun, deathless, painless, incapable of fatigue, decay, or feebleness, having changed its subjection to the trammels of space and natural laws of motion for the freedom and activity of angelical life. Mutual knowledge, society, companionship, love, confidence, tenderness, endearment, the union of heart with heart in the possession of those whom we love; these things, at the earthly shadow of which we so often grasp in vain, to our hurt and disappointment, and, it may be, to the staining of our souls, will then for the first time become truths and realities in the perfect union of the children of God in all the marvellous variety of their individual perfections, and in the daily play and working of their glorified faculties of heart and mind. The Christian people will then indeed be a holy nation, a community, a society, a family, in which all will be wise, all great, all lovely, all powerful, with the riches of the wisdom, and the might, and the power, and the beauty of God their Father. What their dwelling will be, what their thoughts, what their occupations in the exercise of their new life—of these we can no more know, or, rather, far less, than the savage of the ice-bound north can know what is the social life, what are the enjoyments, and resources, and refinements, and natural blessings of the civilised communities who possess the fairest regions of the world, and inherit all the achievements and conquests of humanity; or than children in their nursery can guess of the intellectual delights and lofty dreams of the poet or the sage. Only we know that as we have this varied and marvellous being given to us by the hand of our God and Creator, every part of our nature, every faculty of mind, and heart, and body, will have its own ineffable beatitude in the Kingdom of His glory. We are now Thy sons, O God, and it doth not yet appear what we shall be; but we know that when Thou comest we shall be like Thee, for we shall see Thee as Thou art!

What wonder, then, if Prophets and Apostles, my brethren—yes, and our Lord Himself—should have exhausted all the poor and stinted resources of human language to paint the delights of the City of God! Eye has not seen them, ear has not heard them, the human mind has no ideas that answer to them, the imagination of man lacks the colours in which these glories are to be painted. These are "secret words which it is not granted to man to utter,"* and we must be caught up into Paradise with St. Paul before we can begin to take them in. A little while, and we shall know them; the night will pass, the day will break, the shadows flee away.

* 2 Cor. xii. 4.

Till then, let us feed ourselves on hope, and on such strains of that heavenly music, such rays of that Divine light, as have found their way into the darkness and confusion of this our place of exile. Let us listen to such words as his with whom we began this evening, telling us of "the river and water of life, clear as crystal, proceeding from the throne of God and of the Lamb. In the midst of the street of that city, and on both sides of the river, was the tree of life, bearing twelve fruits, yielding its fruit every month, and the leaves of the tree were for the healing of the nations. And there shall be no curse any more, but the throne of God and of the Lamb shall be in it, and His servants shall serve Him, and shall see His face, and His name shall be on their foreheads; and night shall be no more, and they shall not need the light of the lamp nor the light of the sun, because the Lord God shall enlighten them, and they shall reign for ever and ever."*

NOTE.

The opinion casually expressed at p. 326, that it would be allowable so to explain the Scriptural narrative of the Deluge as to leave room for the supposition that its universality related only to the human race and the parts of the earth inhabited by man, may seem to require some explanation. The reader is referred to an appendix to some articles which appeared some years ago, under the title "Cosmogonia Naturale comparata col Genesi," in the *Civilta Cattolica* (vols. 50, 51, or Serie x., vols. 3, 4, 1862), and particularly to vol. 51, pp. 30—36 and 291 seq.—which will be found abundantly to justify the statement in the text.

* Apoc. xxii. 1—5.

SERMON XVIII.

THE GREATNESS OF DEATH.

Multoque plures interfecit moriens, quam ante vivus occiderat.
He killed many more at his death, than he had killed before in his life.

(Words taken from the 30th verse of the 16th chapter of the Book of Judges.)

I.

WE have all heard of this last exploit of the hero and champion of the chosen people, whom God raised up to deliver them from the oppressions and encroachments of the Philistines. The character of Samson seems to us, in many ways, strange and even grotesque among the great company of the judges and heroes of Israel, because the few incidents which are related of him take their character from marvellous displays of the preternatural physical strength with which God endowed him. But I am only speaking to-day of the close of his career, when he was in bondage and deprived of his eyesight by the cruelty of his enemies, and when, by a heavenly inspiration, we cannot doubt—because his gift of marvellous strength came back to him for this last struggle—he laid hold of the pillars on which the theatre rested in which he was made a show of to amuse his enemies, and shook them so violently that the roof fell in, and a great multitude of the enemies of the holy people died in the ruin which ensued. And so, of all his exploits of this kind, his death was the greatest. He slew more in his death than those whom he had slain in his life.

And what the Sacred Scripture says of this ancient hero, we may say, my brethren, of that Christian death in general of which I am to speak to you. Death is, or may be made, greater than life. Life is worth little, except as leading up to death. The crown of a good life is a good death, and without a good death a good life may be made worthless and a failure. Ordinarily, in God's mercy, a good death succeeds a good life, but this is not an unchangeable law without exception. Sometimes, by the special mercy of God, death reverses and cancels the whole of a miserable life. Death is a moment, and life is a little span of many moments at the beginning of an existence which has no end, and the whole of that endless existence is to take its colour and character from that one moment of death. Death is the greatest of our opportunities, the noblest of our actions, the occasion of the most heroic virtues. Its importance is so overwhelming that, in the mercy and wisdom of God, its moment is hidden from us, that we may expect it at any moment. It is of immense importance how we live, it is of paramount and sovereign importance how we die. Death is great in what it teaches us of God, great in itself, great in the blessings and occasions which it places in our hands. The very thought ennobles and elevates us, it fills us with the holiest fears and the holiest hopes. It enables us to think greatly and to act greatly. It makes heroes of common men, it makes Christians into saints. Well may we pray about it whenever we say, in our Lord's words: "Thy Kingdom come, Thy will be done." Well may we make it the subject of a special invocation every time we salute the Blessed Mother of our God in the words of the Church: "Holy Mary, Mother of God, pray for us sinners, now," at the present moment, but especially also "at the hour of our death." We ask the help of thy gracious prayers, the aid of thy all-powerful love, we ask it now, that we may be pleasing to thy Son, but, O gracious Queen, Mother of our Saviour, Virgin most Powerful, there is one moment which we cannot forget even now, the moment which will decide our eternity, when we shall need thee more than ever, "Pray for us sinners, pray for us at the hour of our death!"

II.

Nothing is truly great but God, and God is great in all that He does and in all that He appoints. In this sense, He is not greater in one of His works than in another. But we may call an act or a decree of God great in comparison, if it displays to us more of God's greatness, His Majesty, His Power, His Wisdom. In this sense, death is a marvellous witness to the greatness of God. He has written so many truths concerning Himself in the universe in which we live, and in that revelation of His laws and His ways and His will which is contained in His providence, in His government of the world, that St. Paul tells us that it was inexcusable in the old heathen—and if in them, how much more in the men of our time who are such poor copies of the ancient heathen?—not to know Him, honour Him, worship Him, and serve Him. And now we know that the whole of this mighty universe is smitten by its Ruler with the sentence of decay and corruption, and that we ourselves lie under the sentence of death, a sentence which we see executed with inevitable rigour on every child of Adam, however much the manner and the time and the circumstances of its execution in particular cases, display the Mercy and Compassion and Forethought and Tenderness of God. Death then is great, inasmuch as it is an act of the Power, the Dominion, the Justice of God.

All the more is this so, because death was not, as we may say, in the first counsels of God. "God made not death, neither hath He pleasure in the destruction of the living." "God created man incorruptible, and in the image of His own likeness He made him, but by the envy of the devil death came into the world."* It is the choice of God to make His spiritual creatures free, and that implies that they can to a certain extent thwart His first designs concerning them—and then He chooses also to bring good out of evil, instead of not permitting evil, and to make the very penalty of sin a lesson, a warning, an instruction and so a blessing to His creatures. He does this, not by great and sudden catastrophes, as when He drowned the whole race of man in the Deluge, or swept away by a single

* Wisdom i. 13, ii. 23, 24.

chastisement the dwellers in the Cities of the Plain, or the armies of the Assyrians—but by a continual, silent, almost imperceptible, action, removing one here another there, young or old, rich or poor, conspicuous or humble, men who are the support of nations or Churches, by the side of infants, and the aged, the imbecile. Not an hour passes but many die, and yet all seem to pass away without being missed by the world at large, in such a way still that we know by certain experience, that of all the hundreds of men that are now living and moving on the face of the earth not one will live after a certain number of years, and that the place of every one of these will be supplied by others, who are in their turn to pass away. And yet, this removal and substitution, of millions on millions of men, is arranged by Providence in such a manner that the shock is never felt too strongly at any moment, and that human life, and human society, and the course of history, and the stability of States, and the continuity of intellectual progress go on unhindered. Wave after wave breaks on the shore, but the ocean remains the same. And at the same time that man remains while men perish, the administration of the decree of death is so guided by Providence that the blow falls on each one at a particular moment, selected in the Wisdom of God, with full forethought and consideration for that which is best for each individual soul. And so, while it remains true, as the Wise Man declares, that God made not death, still it is also true that when God permitted death, and adopted it as a punishment for that misuse of life of which man had already been guilty, He made it a remedy, a boon, a work in which He would display His most wonderful attributes, wisdom and mercy, as well as power, sovereignty and justice. And this is the first greatness of death, that it displays so magnificently the greatness of God.

But what is death in itself, that it can be called great, apart from the revelation or declaration which it makes to us of the greatness of God? We speak, my brethren, of death as a thing, or even as a person, as if it had an existence and a power of its own, and thus to speak is only in accordance with the language of Scripture and the ways of thought of all mankind. Thus, as I have said, we are told that death comes into the world, we are told that death is the last of our enemies which shall be destroyed, we are told of death coming, and reigning, and subduing, and relieving. But what we mean by all this is that death is a decree and an act of God's almighty power. It is as much so as life. "By the word of God the heavens were made, and all the hosts of them by the breath of His mouth," and by the same word and will and breath of God His creatures cease to be, and that ceasing is death. If we want to see how great death is in itself, we must ask ourselves what it is that God does at that moment which we call death? What God then does is, to dissolve the union which He has established between the soul and the body. The soul is indestructible and immortal, the body is dust, and unto dust it returns. This union between the soul and the body, which makes up human life, is, if I may so speak, the very central wonder and marvel of God's creation. The physical creation of God is full of marvels and beauties, and the spiritual creation of God is far more marvellous, and far more beautiful. But in man these two orders of creation meet and are united, by a union more close and intimate and vital than exists elsewhere. It is not merely that an immortal spirit dwells in a material frame, or uses it for a time, and then departs from it, leaving it as it was. The material part of man has no life at all apart from the soul. The soul is the form of the body, making it what it is, its life, and yet it is distinct from it. The body is not the mere instrument of the soul, it is the organ through which alone in our present condition, the soul lives, acts, energizes, thinks. Philosophy has strained its intelligence in vain to discover the link of this union, which is so intimate and so essential, between elements which belong to two different worlds. And sometimes it errs in making the soul too independent of the body, and at other times it errs by denying the distinct existence of the soul and the body. It is this union which is the cause and origin of all the marvellous energies and achievements which make up human life.

Well, at the moment of death, God destroys this union. The body returns to dust from which it sprung, the spirit goes to God, Who made it. For a time only, but completely for a time. And this is the other great marvel of death, that a separation so complete is yet to end in a perfect reunion. God does not end altogether the work which He has done, the life which He has made. But He ends, by the separation of soul and body, as He began it by their union, this present life, that is the time given to the free spirit to work out, by the use of its own will, its own eternity. Up to that time, the soul has been writing, day after day, hour after hour, in the book of God, what it has chosen to write. If it has written evil at one time, it can write good at another time. If it has persevered long in good, it may still at the end write evil. If it has accumulated an immense weight of evil during a long life, it may still, at the end, cancel all by a page of repentance and contrition. Up to this time it has been free to change, and to choose, as Moses says, life or death, good or evil, Heaven or Hell. It may change and range about, as the vane which marks the wind flickers to and fro, and is never still. But at the touch of death the poor fluttering will of man is fixed for ever in one direction, and the last indication of its choice determines the whole of its eternity. Man has all that time been building, as the Scripture says, the house in which he is to dwell for ever, and now it is finished and settled and he enters upon it.

We talk of great turns and crises in the history of single souls or great bodies of men, and we speak of supreme moments, in which issues of immense importance are decided. A battle is fought, and the course of history is changed for a century. A political question is settled, and the life of a whole nation is altered. A man of genius makes a great discovery, a happy guess at first, and it becomes a certainty, and the human race is enriched with a new treasure of knowledge, or science, or art. Knowledge, science, art, political and social life, the course of outward events for a century, the form of government of an empire, the destruction or the foundation of a dynasty, what are all these passing and temporal things to the decision as to the eternal lot of an immortal soul? They are playthings and bubbles by the side of the issue that is being decided, thousands of times every day, in the world in which we live, by that silent process of death of which we think so little. This is a further greatness of death —it fixes for ever the changeful will of man, it decides in one single moment the issue between two alternatives, the space between which is infinite— yes, we may use the word infinite of the difference between an eternity of good and an eternity of evil, and all those other alternatives, the decision between which is thought so momentous in human history, are as nothing by the side of this.

III.

But God does still more than this at the moment of death. He does still more, because a time of probation and choice might end, and a decision as to eternity might be made, and yet the soul as to which it is made might be left as it was, except that it is confirmed for ever in evil or in good. But death is also a mighty truthteller and a mighty convincer, and to know what passes in the soul at the presence of death we must take into consideration all the delusions that then vanish, all the blindness that is then dispelled, all the truths which are then poured in upon the soul with a light that nothing can resist. My brethren, there is no teacher, no preacher, no doctor, no apostle, so eloquent, so mighty, so convincing as death. What should we say of a man who had the gift, by a breath, or a word of his mouth, of driving away the mental delusions and follies of all the maniacs and lunatics in the world, or of giving sight to all the blind, or of flooding with knowledge and learning the minds of all the ignorant? Certainly we should say that he had a great gift. But the gift of death is greater. My brethren, we should need the pen of the philosopher merely to enumerate all the delusions which may reign in the human soul, delusions not as to trivial matters, but as to matters which concern the eternal life or death of the soul itself—the delusions as to God, the wild errors of heathenism, the false religions, the systems which deny all religions, the religions which are chiefly imperfect rather than false, the religions which, pretending to be Christianity itself, are blasphemies against God's goodness, or denials of His mercy in the Incarnation, or rebellions against the Church, or misrepresentations against the revealed doctrine, or destroyers of the sacraments, or slanderers of His grace, or impugners of His word. Or, again, who shall count up the false glosses and maxims which rule the conduct of men as to the moral natural law, the successful tricks that are played upon conscience, the euphemisms, the impostures, the pharisaisms of which men persuade themselves or seek to persuade themselves? Or who shall count up the various ways in which the world, and common opinion and practice, the self-interest of classes guided by human passion, impose on the minds and hearts of men false laws of injustice, impurity, vindictiveness, and other deadly sins? Who shall number the illusions of trade, of political life, or of professions, of the mart, the Parliament, the club, the theatre, the ball-room, the press, the bar, the pursuit even of knowledge, not less than the hunger for wealth? Some one has said, that every man is mad somewhere, but at least it is true to say that all but the saints of God are more or less deluded. The degrees of culpability and responsibility are various, for men are slaves of tradition, and of education, and of the society in which they live, and of their opportunities of knowing the truth—but yet, how many are there, even among those who profess to serve God, from whose eyes the hand of death will find no delusions to brush away?

But, many or great, blameable or innocent, fatal or excusable, of whatever kind or of whatever degree, all delusions will go then. The sinner who has so clung to the inventions of his passions or his interest, that he has persuaded himself to live a bad life in the midst of the greatest light and the highest privileges, will doubt no more then. He may have held out against the ministers of the Church, and the warnings of conscience, against the prayers of the saints, against special warnings vouchsafed to him by Providence, but then he will give way, when it is too late. Men whom no power on earth or Heaven could undeceive before, will be undeceived then. Blessed in comparison they, whose mistakes have been involuntary and who have not contributed to their own blindness! But scales will seem to fall from the eyes even of those who have served God, for the realities which concern Him and the soul, and the value of time, and the importance of eternity, and the power of prayer, and the treasure of grace, will shine forth in a new light, when the veils of sense are riven, and the voice of the world silenced. And it will seem, even to the enlightened, that they have never known even the things which they have known.

And yet the work of death is not exhausted by the destruction of delusions. Death is not simply the greatest destroyer of falsehood, and impostures, it has its positive revelations to make as well as its negative. For death is the opening of a new world, the gate of a new life. There is a poem in our language which speaks of the wonder of the first Man, when he saw, for the first time, the sun sink in the west, and the pall of night cover the whole face of that glowing and beautiful world into which he had waked up a few hours before, and of which he had been told that he was the master and lord. Adam might have thought, the poet says, that that loss of day, and that overwhelming shroud of darkness, had destroyed his world and the life he was to lead therein. And then he found, as he looked up into the night, that darkness had in truth illumined him, and that day had deceived him. For in the vault of heaven above him, he could now see the multitude of worlds of which his universe was made up, suns and planets, and satellites, myriads of orbs, more splendid and mighty than his own, palaces and kingdoms of light, a sea of glory and beauty which had been hidden from him in the day. Such is the blinding of life, such is the enlightening of death. The pale light of this life of care and struggle and feebleness and misery, hides from us the true universe in which our souls are to live for ever. Those who know this world and this life best, those who reckon even highest the great achievements and conquests, as they are called, of human virtue and human genius, think but little of them, even in themselves. Life has little to give us here. Its only value is that, here and now, we can purchase eternal goods and lay up treasure in Heaven. But its greatest mischief is, that it veils for us the truths and the realities which are spiritual and eternal. It dulls our ears to the voice of God, it weakens our eyes to gaze on the truths amid which our soul is made to live. We are as blind men, groping about in a palace that belongs to us, and we have no idea of its treasures and its beauties, until the touch of death comes to make us see.

IV.

These, my brethren, are some of the greatnesses of death in itself and in its manifestation to us of God. If those things are true, I need not say more on that other point—that death has a marvellous gift of ennobling and elevating us. I speak now only of the thought of death, the familiar contemplation of this inevitable but most precious truth. Those who live with great men, or who take a part in great deeds, or who study great works, and give themselves to great pursuits, these men gain accordingly some share of the greatness of their friends, or their teachers, or their studies, or their actions. The mere resolution not to fear the risk of death, nerves even the bad to deeds great in their badness, and the good to deeds of true heroism. My brethren, apart from goodness or badness, what is the characteristic of human life and human society as we see them in all around us, nay, as we see them in ourselves? Is it not their pettiness, their triviality, their small aims, and ambitions? Yes, life is made up of a crowd of trivialities, a swarm of vanities—emptiness, childishness, frivolity, a waste of time and thought and energy upon nothings, which cannot satisfy the undying mind which must be fed. Vanity of vanities, vanity of vanities! And yet this life of ours was not given us to be wasted in blowing bubbles or in playing with toys. It was not given us for elaborate fooling and newsmongering, for building castles on the sand. Human life in truth is not trivial—its daily round of small duties and successive occupations is invented for us by God, that we may practise virtue, and serve Him, and conquer ourselves, and use grace, and fit ourselves for an immortal life. It is the want of this great truth that makes life so trivial and so miserable. "Oh," says the Prophet, "that they would be wise and would understand, and would provide for their last end! How should one pursue after a thousand, and two chase ten thousand!"*

* Deut. xxxii. 29, 30.

Death is the first of the great truths, the truth from which the others follow. Death alone interprets life ;. —but it not only interprets life, it makes life great and it makes life noble. Yes, we can be great and noble now, if we live as men who are to die—as men who are to die, but to whom death is not to be only the end of all that is foolish, and transitory, and childish, and frivolous, but the opening of the gates of eternity, where all is grand, and noble, and peaceful, and enduring, where the minds and hearts of the children of God, so feeble in themselves, are strengthened to the contemplation of the most clear Truth, and to the enjoyment of the most pure Love.

SERMON XIX.

THE SACREDNESS OF DEATH.

Et pro eis ego sanctifico me ipsum, ut sint et ipsi sanctificati in veritate.

And for them do I sanctify myself, that they also may be sanctified in truth.

(Words taken from the 17th verse of the 19th chapter of St. John's Gospel.)

I.

WHAT does our Lord mean, when He speaks of sanctifying Himself, that those whom He loves so much may be sanctified in truth? We can understand easily enough how His followers and children can be sanctified through Him in truth, because it is through Him and from Him that all grace proceeds: "He was full of grace and truth, and of His fulness we have all received," and He it is Who sends us the Holy Ghost Himself, the Sanctifier, to dwell in our hearts. That is easy enough—but how does our Lord sanctify Himself? He uses the word sanctify, as we are told by the holy writers of the Church, in the sense in which it occurs elsewhere in Sacred Scripture, of the sacrifice of Himself in death. More than once in Sacred Scripture does it bear this meaning, signifying that death consecrates, as it were, what it touches, and consecrates it to

God, the Author and Master of human life. Thus in the Old Testament all the first-born of Israel are said to be sanctified to the Lord, by which is meant that they belong in a special manner to God, Who had taken them as His own portion when He slew all the first-born in the land of Egypt, and it was in consequence and in acknowledgment of that sanctification, that all the first-born of the chosen people, our Lord among them, as the First-born of His Mother, were to be presented in the Temple, and a ransom paid for them by sacrifice, in order, as it were, to buy their lives back from God.* Our Lord, then, speaks of His death as a kind of sanctification or consecration, not that anything in life or death could make Him holier, Who was the source of all holiness, the ineffably Holy One with all the Holiness of the Divine Nature, but that it was a sacrifice of His life to the Father, and as such a consecration. Now this, dear brethren, is not confined to our Lord. What He has done in particular to hallow and consecrate all Christian deaths, is a part of this great subject which I reserve now for a future discourse. But setting that aside for the moment, I say that death in itself, that all deaths, have by the decree of God this sacred and consecrating character, and it is of this that I shall speak to-day. I find this set forth by the Church in one of the hymns which she puts into the mouths of her ministers in the daily office, when, at the ninth hour, when the day has turned to its decline and the shades of evening draw on, she bids them say,

* Exod. xiii. 2, 14, 15.

Largire lumen vespere,
Quo vita nunquam decidat,
Sed præmium mortis sacræ
Perennis instet gloria.

Grant us light at eventide,
That our life may still abide,
And, a sacred dying's meed,
Endless glory may succeed.

A sacred death! This may have, as the Church tells us, so great a value in the sight of God that it may purchase as it meed an eternal glory! Death, then, is not only a great thing, but it is a religious act, a sacred thing, it is something which is consecrated, something which belongs to God.

You will say to me perhaps, my brethren, that life is a sacred thing as well as death—that "whether we live, we live to the Lord, or whether we die we die to the Lord,"* that "whether we eat or drink or whatever we do, we are to do all things in the name of our Lord Jesus Christ."† Certainly—and I say that good Christians who live in this way, who look to God and behold Him Who is invisible, as St. Paul says, in all the actions of their daily life, they are preparing themselves by a sacred life for a sacred death. They will be the first to understand how great is the truth of the sacredness of death. And I say further, that this truth is so deeply imprinted on the natural religiousness and conscience and instinct of man, that even those who live in such a way that they cannot be said to recognize the sacred character of life, even those do acknowledge that death is solemn and sacred. The anticipation

---
* Rom. xiv. 8. † 1 Cor. x. 31.

of death, of the approach of death, hushes them and saddens them and makes them almost worshippers. Strife is at an end, the loud tongues of slander, reproach, cavil, criticism, are silenced, no one cares to revile, to insult, to speak against the dead. The presence of death chases away frivolity, and worldly gaiety, the dance, the song, the whirl and reel of dissipation; even the schemes of vice and crime, the plottings of debauchery, the cravings of lust, are paralyzed when death is near, for death sends into the soul a gleam of cold clear light which seems to fall from the eye of a Master, and a Judge, and a God.

II.

The first element, if I may so say, in the character of anything that we call sacred, is that it is set apart, withdrawn from common use and common life, and made to belong to God alone. Now let us see how this idea applies to death. Death belongs to Him, because it is the end and cessation of life. He alone can give life, He alone can take it away. It is true that death follows naturally on certain causes which are allowed by Him to have the power of ending life. But no one may put these causes into operation but Himself. It is a sin against God to take away human life, even our own. God gives to society, for its own protection and for justice, the power of doing this, whether in the administration of justice or in lawful war. But outside this permission it is a crime. And if man has the right and power to take away even the lower life of the inferior animals, it is because man is made by God the lord of this lower world. Death then belongs to God alone, and when it comes to us in what is called the course of nature or providence, whether it is by slow decay or rapid disease or accident as it is called, it is the act of God putting an end, then and there, to a human life. Thus death is most truly described by the common language of simple Christians, when they say that God has taken away this or that person, or this or that soul is gone to God. The Scriptural descriptions of death are so many beautiful images—"The silver cord is broken, and the golden fillet shrinks back, and the pitcher is crushed at the fountain, and the wheel is broken upon the cistern, and the dust returns into the earth, from whence it was, and the spirit returns to God Who gave it."*

Here again is another element in our notions of sacredness, the element of the presence and nearness of God. It is at the moment of death that God and man meet for the first time. I do not mean that God is not always and everywhere present, that we are not encompassed as it were, by Him all our lives, and that He is not always present in the very innermost shrine of our souls. In Him we live, and move, and are. But the veils of sense hide our God from us. We are as blind men groping after Him, we hear of Him, we are told of Him, we trace Him in His marks and His foot-prints, but we do not see Him. This it is that holy Job says of himself, which thus comes true of all of us, the foolish, the

* Eccles. xii. 6, 7.

thoughtless, the slave of the world and of sin, as well as of the saint and the innocent: "With the hearing of the ear I have heard Thee, but now mine eye seeth Thee, therefore I reprehend myself, and do penance in dust and ashes."* Then it is that all men are like those favoured saints of old, who have had some special vision or intercourse with God—as when Moses in the wilderness, "hid his face, for he durst not look on God"†—or when Elias in the cave of Horeb, after the wind and earthquake and fire had passed, heard "the whistling of a gentle air, and covered his face with a mantle, and stood at the entering in of the cave" to hear the words of God.‡ Or rather, even those terrible and thrilling manifestations of God were but representations, they were the work of angels who were in the place of God. But at the moment of death not saints alone but sinners, all of us, whatever our spiritual state, whatever the condition of our conscience, we are to stand in the presence of God, with no bodily veil or cloud between the soul and God Who gave it! And so, my brethren, whatever reason we have for holding certain times or certain places sacred in our life, those same reasons apply with far greater force to the moment of death. We call the times or the places of prayer sacred, or the temples in which God dwells in His sacramental Presence, and in which we meet to celebrate the Holy Mysteries, and to pray and praise God together, or to listen to His words, or to receive the sacraments—these are all very sacred and holy, but not less sacred

---

* Job xlii. 5, 6. † Exod. iii. 6. ‡ 3 Kings xix. 13.

and holy in its way is the moment of death. And the sacredness of death is more awful and solemn and subduing, because then we are alone with God. Solitude itself is sometimes appalling and frightening, especially when we feel ourselves absolutely alone, and without human help or companionship in the dead of the night, or in some great scene of nature, or with the stars above us, but that awful sacred loneliness of death is the most solemn of all. No doubt we hope to be aided then, we hope to have the sacraments of the Church, and the priests of the Church, and the prayers of our friends, and the help of the Angels and Saints, and of Mary the Mother of God—but still we shall die alone, we shall wake up alone in the presence of God, we and no one else, not our nearest and dearest. We all have to give an account to our Judge one by one, all that we have said and thought and done from the first moment of our lives. At the moment of death, we meet our God, we give in our accounts then, and we await His award.

III.

But I am not now speaking of judgment, but of death in itself. And so I shall not go on to enhance the sacredness of death by the consideration of the great account which is required and rendered then. The end of life and of the time of our probation, would in any case have brought us to the moment of our judgment, but I am speaking of death as it is, death that came into the world through sin and by the envy of the devil, not as it might have been, or as the end of life might have been, if the state of innocence had lasted and if man had never been chased out of Paradise. But even then, there would have been judgment. And now, looking at death as it is, as it is the penalty inflicted on a fallen race for sin, I find two other elements of a sacred character in it which will be enough to occupy our thoughts for the rest of our time to-day. We have seen that death is sacred, inasmuch as it belongs in an especial manner to God, and inasmuch as it brings us close to God, and into the very presence of God, in a way of which we have no other experience. And now further, death is a sacred thing, because it gives great glory to God, and because it is a great instance and exercise of His justice.

You may remember, dear brethren, the words of the blessed Evangelist St. John, when he is speaking of that tenderly loving prediction made to his friend St. Peter by our Lord, after He had in that solemn manner given to him the charge to feed His lambs and feed His sheep. Our Lord then predicted to St. Peter the manner of his future martyrdom, almost describing the crucifixion he was to undergo at Rome for the faith and service of his Lord, and St. John then says of our Lord: "This He said, signifying by what death he should glorify God."* He does not say, you see, signifying that He should glorify God by his death, but by what particular kind of death he should glorify God. And the words of St. John imply that all Christian deaths glorify God, and that it is not a question whether we shall glorify

* St. John xxi. 19.

God by death, but only by what special kind of death we shall give Him glory. It is not, then, the privilege of apostles and martyrs and other saints, to glorify God by their deaths—all deaths give glory to God, and in this truth lies another element of their sacred character. How is this? It is because death in itself, and as it is what every human soul must pass through at the end of its life, is a great vindicator of the rights of God against what is rebellion against Him, and a great vindicator of the truth of God against what belies Him and questions Him—as holy David says in his Psalm of Penance, *Ut justificeris in sermonibus Tuis, et vincas cum judicaris*—" That Thou mayest be justified in Thy words, and mayest overcome when Thou art judged."*

Before man sinned, the warning went forth, which Satan persuaded him to disregard, " In the day in which thou eatest thereof, thou shall die," and the tempter said, " Ye shall not surely die." Now the truthfulness of God and the mendacity of the father of lies require that the word should come true, and that every man should die. And every single death of a child of Adam, of the babe of an hour of life, or of the aged sinner of a century, testifies to the truth of God and the falsehood of Satan. But again, when man chose to sin, he rebelled against his Lord, and from that moment that beautiful Kingdom of God which He had made for Himself in man became a Kingdom divided against itself, a scene of rebellion and discord and warfare against God. Pride rose up to defy God. Sensuality broke loose, and de-

* Psalm l. 6.

graded and debased and defiled the nature which He had made pure and upright. Avarice, selfishness, greed of temporal goods, hardened, perverted, blinded, man, and bent him down. Charity was extinguished, anger and cruelty were raised in its place. These are the enemies of God in man, and in death God acts like a great King, Who by a single word or touch tumbles in the dust all who have lifted themselves up against Him. The soul has sinned against Him, by the use it has made of the body, of the objects of sense, of the world in which it was set to serve Him. The soul itself is indestructible, but at the moment of death it undergoes a complete humiliation before the Majesty of God. All human pride is brought to nothing, and those things which have been the instruments or the occasions of sin are reduced to dust. The world of sense vanishes. The strength of the mighty, the wealth of the rich, the greatness of noble race, knowledge, or talent, or power, or beauty, or grace, or excellence of any kind of which our poor human nature can plume itself—all are cast down and come to dust at the foot-stool of the throne of God. The moment which brings the soul into His presence puts an end to all false greatness, to all pretences and shams and impostures. All become nothing, emptiness, vanity, corruption in His Presence. Men may make even gods in this life of money, or pleasure, or power—and when the touch of death comes, these idols which they have worshipped are broken to pieces before them. The flesh which has been indulged, is chastised by falling to dust and becoming food for worms, and all things else that men have delighted in and set their hearts upon are annihilated. The slave of avarice becomes poor, naked, miserable, and has to leave all his goods and possessions. The justice of God falls on everything which has been His enemy in the soul of man, everything that has been set up in His place, everything for the sake of which His law has been forsaken and His rights despised. You may remember how, in one of His parables, our Lord describes the King who returns from a far country to take account of his servants, and how He makes him say, "As for those mine enemies, who would not have me reign over them, bring them in hither and kill them before me."* This is what takes place at death. All on which execution is then done has been the enemy of God. The soul may have served God, and if it has, the world of sense, and the body, and all that it has possessed and used have been the instruments of its service. But still they have been instruments which have had to be conquered, they have been the home of every evil inclination, every low appetite, and it is for the justice of God that they should be destroyed.

But, my brethren, this leads us to another point in what I call the sacredness of death, which is more consoling and more encouraging to us. No doubt if we love God, as the Angels love God, it must be a joy to us to see His justice satisfied, to see His truthfulness proved, to see Him glorified by the confusion of whatever has gainsaid Him, or the humiliation of whatever has raised itself up in proud

* St. Luke xix. 27.

rebellion against Him. In this sense we may imagine them to rejoice in the physical calamities which are inflicted from time to time to God's enemies, nay, even in the destruction of the whole world which is to close the history of man, and to usher in the new heaven and new earth unsullied, unstained by iniquity. In this sense we may say that the Angels rejoice for His sake, at the sight of death, as the loyal subjects and children of the great King, at the vindication of His authority and the punishment of His enemies. Yes, but the Angels have not to die themselves, and yet there have been Saints who have said that the Angels, if they could form a wish against the arrangements of His will, might even wish that they might be able to taste of death in order that they might honour God thereby. Now, what is denied to the Angels is the necessity of nature to us. Take then, as this last feature about death which makes it so sacred, if we understand it as we ought, that although we cannot avoid it, although it comes to those who shun it and flee from it, as well as to those who court it, still, such is the goodness of God, we have the power of accepting it, or making it voluntary, and so meritorious and most acceptable and pleasing to God. Our Lord said of His own life, "No man taketh it away from Me, but I lay it down of Myself, I have power to lay it down and to take it up again."* We cannot say this—and yet we can do in this, as in everything that happens to us by the will and providence of God, we can make it as much an act of our own will as if it depended on

* St. John x. 18.

ourselves. And by doing this, we can share, in our poor and humble way, that perfect sacrifice of Himself into the Hands of His Father which our Lord made at His own death. Did He not say in the garden, "Father, if it be possible let this chalice pass from Me," as if to let us see that He too chose to take up and share that natural reluctance and shrinking from death which any one of us may feel? And did He not say after that, "Not My will but Thine be done," as if to teach us to overcome the shrinkings of the flesh by the vigour of the spirit, and place ourselves unreservedly in the Hands of His Father? And on that surrender of our Lord, my brethren, are founded the holy and willing deaths of all His true children.

I do not speak of the martyrs alone, or of the saints. God, the Master of life and death, sometimes takes weak men and women like ourselves, He has taken them from all ranks and ages and conditions, and without requiring in them beforehand any consummate sanctity, but simply Christian faith, and then He has put them to the test, to confess their faith under pain of mortal sin, and by confessing it, to suffer excruciating tortures and to die. This sacrifice, which He has actually exacted of some, He might exact of all, just as the service of the country may require the sacrifice of the life of every single soldier in the ranks as it does actually require the sacrifice of the life of many. But what God does not actually require of us, though He might, that it is our wisdom voluntarily to offer to Him, and we do this by accepting our death whenever it comes, and however it comes, willingly, and making it a free sacrifice to Him in perfect conformity to His holy Will. Then indeed death is made a sacred thing, it is not merely sacred in itself, and independently of us, in all those ways of which we have been speaking, it becomes an act of worship and of religion, it gives glory to God by this beautiful act of submission, of resignation, of love for Him and His glory, by which it is accompanied. We are not all priests, we are not all ministers of the altar, we are not all called to the life-long martyrdom of consecration to God by vow in an apostolic and penitential life. No, but once at least in our existence we may make ourselves priests, and martyrs, and confessors, and consecrated to God, when the time comes for us to pass out of this world, and we rise up, as Abraham did, in the strength of faith, and take our life and being in our hands, as he took his one child Isaac, and present ourselves on the holy mountain of sacrifice, ready to give up our life for His glory, bidding Him take back what is His own, rejoicing in the triumph of His glory, in the destruction of all that has rebelled against Him, in the humiliation of the proud human flesh, in the reducing to dust of all that has hindered His perfect service in the existence of His creature.

This is the holiest and most blessed sacrifice of which our poor humanity is capable. It requires no priestly unction, no apostolic mission, no religious consecration, no martyr's vocation. Yes, and so meritorious is it, so full of love and of conformity and of imitation of our Lord, that I do not fear to say that such a death may be made so sacred, as to have a marvellous power of expiation from the Sacrifice of our Lord. In the old Christian times, when religion penetrated every department and corner of life, it used to be considered that those who died by the hand of justice, with all the spiritual aids which religious charity could provide, wiped away, by that involuntary sacrifice, the guilt of the crime for which they suffered, and died holy deaths. The place of execution, the act of execution itself, both were considered holy. And no doubt it has often been true that such sufferers, when they have been perfectly contrite and resigned and submissive in their suffering, may have been heirs of the crown of that blessed penitent who hung by our Lord's side and said, "Lord remember me when Thou comest into Thy Kingdom," and who heard those gracious words, "This day thou shalt be with Me in Paradise." The death-bed of every Christian is the place of solemn submission to God's justice, and all who render up their souls to God may do that last act of their lives with faith, hope, confession, and contrition, and resignation, and love, before which the gates of Paradise will roll back at once, through the merits of Him Who has tasted death for all men.

IV.

Let me sum up in a few words, dear brethren, what I have now said, in such a way as to make it as practically useful to us as possible. We have seen that our Lord speaks of His own death as a sanctification or a consecration, and we have endeavoured to trace out how the same character may belong to all Christian deaths. And if it be true, in the first place, that death is sacred because it brings us for the first time face to face with God, alone with God, without veil or cloud between Him and us—does not this truth shed a light upon all our lives, each moment of which leads us up to death, does it not show us that we do not understand life truly, and our relation to God truly, unless our life is really led with God alone?—unless, within all the outward show and stir and bustle and strife of life, our hearts and souls and minds are fixed on Him as the one centre and end of our being, as Him to Whom we belong, Whose eye at all moments watches us, reading all our thoughts, understanding all our aims? My brethren, that one truth will make you like the saints.

And again, we have considered the further truth, that death gives glory to God, because it vindicates His truthfulness, it asserts His dominion, it chastises and destroys that which has been rebellious against Him in His Kingdom. It is a great triumph of His over the world, the flesh, and the devil, it puts down pride, and reduces to dust anger, avarice, sensuality. And what is the import of this truth, but that death must be dreadful to those who are on the side of these enemies of His glory, but that it can have nothing dreadful at all to those who are the friends of His glory? The sting of death, as St. Paul says, is sin—and where sin is not, there the sting of death is not. Then brethren, even for our own happiness and peace in this world and in the next, this life of faith, and hope, and charity, the life of self-conquest and virtue and purity and detachment and humility is the life of blessedness; and if we so live now that God may be glorified in our lives, it will be nothing but the crown of our happiness that He is to be glorified in our deaths.

And lastly, as we have seen that death may be willingly accepted and embraced, and that when we accept and embrace it we have an opportunity of winning from God the very highest graces, such as those which make the words true, "Precious in the sight of the Lord is the death of His saints," and that this is true, not of what we call heroic deaths only, or rather, every Christian death may be made heroic by the exercise of the virtues which belong to that blessed moment which is the end and crown of life— my brethren, what is the lesson of this truth, but that we should strive and pray for ourselves, and others, that we may have intelligence to see all the opportunities that are offered us, and grace and will to use them? This I take to be one true reason why God so constantly warns us of death, and yet leaves it uncertain, and why we are so continually urged by the Church to prepare ourselves for that last moment. It is not only that we may be in a state of grace when we come to die, that we may persevere to the end in the faith and the service of God. That is an ineffable grace, but it is not all. Our Lord would have us miss no beauty, no perfection of virtue, of which life and death are capable. And so we may take this third truth and apply it thus. As, from the sacredness and loneliness of death we learn to live in God's presence, as from the consideration of the glory which death gives to Him, we learn to mortify ourselves in the practice of virtue, so also, from the thought of the sanctity of which death is capable, we may learn to practise ourselves in heroic and special exercises of resignation, humility, mortification, and charity, such as may make our death most precious and most holy.

SERMON XX.

THE HAPPINESS OF DEATH.

Mihi enim vivere Christus est, et mori lucrum.

To me to live is Christ, and to die is gain.

(Words taken from the 21st verse of the 1st chapter of the Epistle to the Philippians.)

I.

I HAVE had to speak to you, my brethren, about those features of death which give to it its greatness and its character of sacredness. And now, that we come to the subject of its happiness, that character of death may be said to be already partly proved by what we have already considered concerning it. For if death be great in what it reveals to us of God, if it be great in itself, in its nature, as the end of life and the beginning of eternity, in its power of dispelling illusions, in its revelation of truths, in its effect upon us, as is shown in the effect of even the constant thought of it—then it cannot surely be in itself an unhappy thing to die. Again, if death be a sacred thing, if it belongs to God, if it is an approach to God, a going to God, putting us face to face and alone with God, if it glorifies God, if it does honour to His justice and vindicates His truth and humbles His enemies, and much more, if it gives us an opportunity of making to Him the most perfect sacrifice, and paying to Him the most complete homage to our own immense gain—then again, if all these things are true, it must be a happy thing to die, it must be a gain to die.

Of course, it requires Christian faith and Christian hope to die happily. Of course death cannot have any magic charm to destroy the mischief that a soul may have been heaping up during a long life, death cannot alter the great eternal truths, or our relation to them, it cannot silence the voice of conscience, or still the pangs of self-reproach, it cannot cancel the past, at least it cannot of itself cancel the past, and so it cannot change the influence of the past on the future, it cannot make the Holy of holies love wickedness, it cannot give peace to the soul which is at war with its Maker and itself. It cannot be a happiness, except in a relative sense, to die, when death seals the sentence of a miserable eternity. The happiness and the gain of death, as we see in the words of St. Paul, are for those who can say with him, "To me to live is Christ." And yet, before we pass on to this our main subject, there are some remarks to be made, even on the deaths of the wicked, which show us at least that God does not act with them simply, as it were, out of vindictiveness when He takes them out of the world, but that, even then, He is not unmindful of mercy.

Death is certainly a happy thing to the just, and its happiness to the just and holy is proved abundantly by what we have already seen. For those are the persons who are able to avail themselves the most fruitfully and faithfully of the good counsel of God in bringing them to the hour of death. Death is to them their greatest opportunity, and therefore it is happy. I shall speak a little more before I close as to the other reasons for which it is true to say that death is happy indeed to the saints—and when I say it is happy to the saints, I mean to all those who love God and live in His grace, though they are simple, ordinary Christians, as we term them, men and women who have not been called to leave the world, or practise the evangelical counsels, or live that high and hard life, as it seems, which looks to so many as a kind of living death. Death is a happy moment on many accounts for the simple Christian soul, who has walked in humility and peace along the path of the Commandments. But there is yet another thing to be said about the goodness of death, as it is administered by God in His particular providence, and this is, that even to the enemies of God death may have a merciful character, as we say that God is merciful when He punishes less than men deserve, or when He keeps them from sins which otherwise they would commit, or takes away the occasions and powers which they would abuse, or when He waits a very long time for their penitence, which never comes. For mercy may be shown in punishing lightly as well as in forgiving or rewarding, in alleviating chastisement as well as in taking it away, and in this sense it is true that death may be a sentence of anger, tempered by mercy, even to the enemies of God.

II.

We are told in Scripture that God made man immortal, in His own image and likeness, and that it was by envy of the devil that death entered into the world. This does not mean that man had a natural gift of immortality, but that he was capable of living indefinitely, until the time came for his trial to be accomplished, and then he would have passed into that other state of existence which is to be his for ever, without that dissolution and corruption and misery which we call death. And the means by which this continual existence of man was preserved, was, as the Fathers tell us, the Tree of Life. And as long as his life was innocent, it was happy, and as soon as he lost his innocence, he became miserable. Now to perpetuate the miserable existence of a sinner, in the sense in which it would have been perpetuated if death had not intervened, would be to multiply sin, to perpetuate unhappiness, and to prepare an immense accumulation of guilt for the future punishment of God. And so some of the Fathers tell us, death was a merciful invention of God, at the same time that it was a decree of His justice. And man was driven from Paradise, as we are told in Scripture, lest he should put forth his hand as before, and eat of the Tree of Life and live for ever. One worst part of the condition of the fallen angels is that they cannot die. And even with us, surely a sinful life, a life at war with God and with our conscience, is a true misery, an anticipation of Hell, and surely it is a mercy and not a scourge that such a life should be cut short. The Scripture tells us again of some of the saints of God: "He was taken away lest wickedness should alter his understanding, or deceit beguile his soul. For the bewitching of vanity obscureth good things, and the wandering of concupiscence overturneth the innocent mind."* And if that be true of the saints, and if it be true, as is implied in the passage, that God foresees that this or that person, who is now dear to Him, will, if he lives longer, fall away, it must also be true that many sinners may be cut off by death, when God knows that if they lived longer they would offend Him more. And as it is the mercy of God, in the case of the just who are snatched away while yet undefiled, that saves them, as it were, from themselves, so it is the mercy of God, in the case of the wicked, who, if they live, will be still more wicked, which saves them from themselves. And in this way we come to see how that may be true, which some of the saints of God have said concerning His providence in death, that every one, even the sinner, is called away by death when it is better for him to die than to live.

And if there may be in this way an exercise of mercy, even in the death of the impenitent, to the impenitent themselves, much more clear is it that the decree of death is a merciful decree for the human race in general since the Fall. For as it is, the world is intensely wicked. As it is, the fear of God, the voice of conscience, the danger of death, all the terrors of God's justice and all the pleadings of His grace, have little enough power to check even enormous

* Wisdom iv. 11, 12.

sins—general depravity, the mad revellings of sensuality, cruelty, tyranny, pride, the oppression of the weak, the grinding down of the poor, the hard treatment of those who are unable to help themselves in this life. If there were no such decree as that of death, the struggle of life would be far more intolerable than it is, and the greatest support of conscience, the one great daily interference of God which reminds men what they are, that dust they are, and unto dust they must return, the one great leveller and equalizer of all under the varieties of human conditions, would be swept away. If the merciful law of death could be abolished and abrogated, the world would become ten times more the ante-chamber of Hell than it is.

III.

But, my brethren, our business this afternoon is not with speculation as to the degree in which it may be for the comparative happiness, or the lesser unhappiness, of the enemies of God, or this poor world over which Satan has had so much power, that the decree of death should fall on this or that person, or, in its turn, on the whole race, generation after generation. Our business is with those who have the faith and the hope of Christians, and we have to see how to them death may not only be an occasion of great thoughts and actions, a sacred holy time, when they may give great glory to God, and add immensely to their own eternal reward, but also a happy time, a time of peace and content and rejoicing and exultation. And here again, we may say, our Lord has begun the lesson for us, and if I were to choose a part of Scripture which might be read over and over again by those who wish to live in the light, as I may so call it, of a good and happy and holy death, next to His Sacred Passion, I should choose those chapters in the Gospel of St. John which contain the long discourse of our Lord to His Apostles after the Last Supper and before He led them forth to the Garden of Gethsemani. No sooner is the execution of the treason of Judas certain, no sooner is the door closed upon the traitor himself, whom our Lord sent out so mercifully, hiding from all the rest the wickedness which he was meditating, while at the same time He was most tenderly and patiently warning him again and again—Judas is no sooner gone forth into the night, as St. John tells us, than our Lord breaks out as into a strain of joy. "Now is the Son of Man glorified, and God is glorified in Him. If God is glorified in Him, God also will glorify Him in Himself, and immediately will He glorify Him." And all through that tender discourse He hardly mentions death, though the thought is ever in His mind. He speaks once or twice of His suffering, but His usual word for what He is going to do is that He is going to His Father, and going before them to prepare a place for them. "I go to My Father, I go to My Father, I came forth from the Father and am come into the world, again, I leave the world, and go to the Father." The words come over and over again, like a sweet phrase in some solemn strain of music, and in that simple truth that death is a going to the Father, there is contained for us a whole mine and treasure of happiness.

And it is not our Lord only Whom we have as our teacher as to the thoughts which should occupy us when we feel death at hand,—as it is always at hand to the prudent sensible Christian, always near, always approaching, a familiar thought, and because it is familiar, a thought full of intense peace and joy —it is not only Jesus Christ Himself, Who pours Himself out in love and rejoicing for our sakes at the near approach of His passage to His Father, but, so it is ordained in His goodness, all the rays of light and consolation which stream from His countenance, as to this or other parts of the Christian course in which we are to follow Him, all are caught and reflected to us again, as in a glass, in the writings of His Apostles, and especially of St. Paul. And if I were asked, again, to name a part of the Apostolic writings which might be put by the side of those chapters of St. John of which I have been speaking, I should take those Epistles of the blessed Apostle which he wrote when he was himself expecting death. St. Paul is a man whose character shines out of every page he writes, he is always overflowing with affectionateness and sympathy, open, vigorous, even impetuous, frank, generous, full of brightness and happiness, even when he has to speak of matters of discouragement or reproof, and infinitely tender, noble, considerate, delicate. He was twice, at different times, almost under the sentence of death at Rome, and his life each time was absolutely at the mercy of that cruel Roman Emperor whose name has survived as a synonym for wantonness and maliciousness in cruelty beyond all compare. The first time St. Paul was spared for further labours and sufferings, for the Church, and it was during that captivity that he wrote the Epistles to the Philippians, the Ephesians, the Colossians, and Philemon. The last time he saw that he was not to escape, and it was then that he wrote his Epistles to his dear child in Christ, St. Timothy, and perhaps to St. Titus also. In all these Epistles there is a strain of solemn joy and intense happiness at the prospect of death, which seems to be given us by God in Sacred Scripture that we may learn what is the Apostolic and Christian spirit at the approach of death.

The text is taken from one of the letters which St. Paul wrote during his first captivity. He speaks first of the uncertainty of his lot, but of his resolution that whether in life or death he will be a faithful servant of his Lord, "I know," he says, "that this shall fall out to me unto salvation, through your prayers, and the supply of the spirit of Jesus Christ, according to my expectation and hope, that in nothing shall I be confounded, but with all confidence, as always, so now also shall Christ be magnified in my body, whether it be by life or by death." Whether he lives or dies, it is immaterial, but it is his expectation and hope, which their prayers will obtain for him, by the grace of the Holy Ghost, that he will magnify our Lord in his body, whether by life or death. "For to me to live is Christ, and to die is gain." His whole life is what it is by the grace and virtue of our Lord, as he says in another place, "I live, but not I, Christ liveth in me." His whole life is Christ, again, because the life and example of our

Lord present the one pattern and model on which his life is shaped. And, again, his life is Christ, because the one end and object of all his thoughts and desires and actions is to make Christ known and to advance His Kingdom. What can be happier than that? What can be happier and better than to live a life so heavenly, so Divine, so radiant with grace, so fruitful, so meritorious, so glorious to God? We are told of apostolic men who have declared that if they had the choice between going at once to Heaven, secure of eternal happiness, on the one hand, and on the other hand, of labouring on in this world, for God's glory in the salvation of souls, uncertain all the time of their own salvation, they would choose the last, trusting their sacrifice to their God, the Master and Lord for Whom they make it. St. Paul himself, at one time, as he says, was willing to be separated from God, an "anathema," as far as such separation could be, for the sake of his brethren. And hence he says clearly, "To me to live is Christ, and to die is gain." He says, as if balancing the two alternatives, if he is to live in the flesh, "this is to use the fruit of labour," he will have the blessing and happiness and reward of further labours for Christ, but which he shall choose he knows not—he is straitened between two, "having a desire to be dissolved and to be with Christ, a thing by far the better." Thus, again, he cannot refrain from telling them that he thinks death better than life. "But to abide still in the flesh is needful for you." And, so far as he is concerned, he lets charity decide the choice, "Having this confidence, I know that I shall abide and continue with you all, for your furtherance and joy of faith, that your rejoicing may abound in Christ Jesus for me by my coming to you again."* In this case, then, the Apostle declares, as I have said, that it is better for him to remain and carry on still further the work which he has been doing for God. But, later on, at the time of his second imprisonment, that out of which there was to be no exit for him but death, he breaks out in those well known words to St. Timothy, "For I am even now ready to be sacrificed, and the time of my dissolution is at hand. I have fought a good fight, I have finished my course, I have kept the faith. As to the rest, there is laid up for me a crown of justice, which the Lord, the just Judge, will render to me in that day, and not only to me, but to them also that love His coming."† Here, then, putting these two passages together, we have the reasoning, so to speak, on which St. Paul taught himself to love and desire death. And by examining this we shall be able to see in what consists the happiness of a Christian death.

IV.

The motives which are contained in St. Paul's words are divided by some holy writers in this threefold way. First, they say, the Apostle is rejoiced at the prospect of death, because death, which he calls dissolution, is a deliverance from what he elsewhere calls the "body of this death," that is, the corruptible body in which we now live, with all its troubles, infirmities, pains, and ailments, and all the hindrances with which it besets the soul. "For the

* Philipp. i. 21—26. † 2 Tim. iv. 6—8.

corruptible body," says the Wise Man, "is a load to the soul, and the earthly habitation presseth down the mind that museth on many things." The body in which we live is marvellously made, but, after all, it is in our present existence often a prison and a house of bondage and even of torture, and among all its great capabilities there is none more striking than its capability of suffering. We begin to die as soon as we are born, a great part of our life is suffering and pain, and, the older we grow, the more do we rehearse our death, time after time. Again, another motive which may be assigned for welcoming death, is that it not only puts an end to our bodily miseries, but to our dangers, our temptations, the life-long struggle between matter and spirit, reason and concupiscence, the lower and the higher parts of our nature, the continuance of which struggle implies our continual danger of sinning. And it is only foolish and thoughtless persons who can undervalue this danger, and who in consequence can think it a light blessing when it comes to an end. The saints of God, though they are the persons who have had the largest experience of His goodness, who have known best the power of His grace, who have practised themselves the longest and the most successfully in resisting the devil and in conquering themselves, though they are thus the persons of all others who might be ready to despise all spiritual danger, as they despise all spiritual enemies when they are engaged in the work of God, the saints are the persons also who know best what are God's rights, how severe is His holiness, how keen His judgments, and who therefore are always fearful of the danger of sin. They have such a horror of any offence of God, that the tidings of their release from the possibility of committing it cannot but be tidings of joy.

There is a letter extant of one of the English martyrs in our own days of persecution, a man full of apostolical zeal, a man who loved, as God gave such men in those days to love, the life of external misery which those then had to lead who worked for the Catholic Church in this country. He was a truly apostolic man, and yet he desired death for this very reason, that he might be safe not to offend God. "If you really love God," he said, "nothing can be so dreadful to you as even the least offence against His Divine Majesty. You would desire nothing in the world so much, as some security that you would never offend Him more. And as there can be no such security in this life, surely you will say with the Psalmist, *Heu mihi, quia incolatus meus prolongatus est!* "Yes," he said, "it is a great thing to labour for the love of God, to undergo sufferings and tortures. It is a great thing to gain souls, it is a great thing to live on in religion with a perpetual victory over yourself, but, if all these things cannot be done without my offending God, I would rather leave them all and die quickly, than do all these great things with the slightest daily fault against my God. For it is better that the world should go to ruin, than that God should be offended." That is the martyr's deliberate view about the danger of sin for a man like himself, and then he goes on, in the same letter, to say what his wishes would be if he knew the will of God to be that he should not die. "But," he says, "God knows my misery, and if He who knows it chooses to prolong my life, and to exercise me longer in this vale of misery, then let all come, toil, prisons, torments, the cross, the rack, the wheel, let all things come to me that can come— yes, rather, O my Lord Jesus, I pray that they may come, I pray by Thy wounds, and by the sufferings of Thy saints, that this may be my lot from this moment at which I write to the end of my life. Let me be tortured, and cut to pieces, and scourged, and beaten, and racked. I refuse nothing, I embrace all, I will endure all, not that I, dust and ashes that I am, have strength enough for this, but because I can do all things in Thee, and nothing without Thee." And yet a man, even of that courage, was desirous of death, simply that it might free him from the danger of sin.

And there is yet a third motive to be assigned for this desire of death, which rests on many a passage and hint in the writings of St. Paul. The motive is the desire to be freed not only from the miseries of the body, not only from the troubles and vexations and occasional disappointments of human life, and of what we call the world. My brethren, I do not think it Christian to rail against the world, in the way in which satirists and cynics rail against it. There have been and are many gloomy, angry, self-centred, self-opinionated men, men of dark, saturnine, fretful, malignant minds, who find no occupation so congenial as that of perpetual fault-finding with everything around them, and this temper and character sometimes infects half a generation, in consequence of the prominent influence of some poet or prophet of despair, sometimes it gives a tone to literature, especially newspaper literature, which is neither healthy nor Christian. These men are angry with God for making the world, and they are angry with all the world for not making gods of them. The Christian temper, even in the world, is that which we see in the writings of St. Paul of which I am speaking—cheerful, thankful, joyous, ever ready to find out, even in the human world as it is dashed and spoilt by sin, a thousand reflections of God's goodness and beauty, a thousand provisions of His love, a thousand hints and promises of far better things which He has in store for us hereafter. But with all that, St. Paul says, " If in this world only we have hope, of all men we are the most miserable," and the general tone of Scripture and of the Saints is to consider this world and this life in themselves as shadowy, vain, false, as impostors, as deceivers, as liars, promising what they cannot perform, piercing the hand that leans upon them, kingdoms in which selfishness and covetousness and evil passions reign over the mass of men, systems in which nothing is good, nothing true, nothing capable of satisfying the needs and cravings of immortal souls.

V.

This is not too dark a picture of this life, and it might be drawn in darker lines than these, but this is enough. We have hearts and minds and instincts of love, yearnings for companionship, longings for unmixed and ineffable good, thoughts which must be fed, intellectual and spiritual cravings which madden us if they are never to be satisfied, and all these things here are without the objects which alone can satisfy them. If we grovel in the pleasures of sense, we find them begin with a momentary sweetness and end in a lasting pang. If we throw ourselves into the activity of temporal things, it is weariness and labour, and it ends in vexation. The bustle of the political world, the commercial world, the professional world, the world of gaiety and pleasure, the world of literature, and art, and science, the highest mental occupations apart from God as well as the lowest—what are they all in the end but restlessness and disappointment, the dashing ourselves against the bars of a cage, like a bird or beast in confinement, attempts to fly from ourselves and find the peace we have not? Nay, I will say more. God has made us for the society of one another, and there is no happiness in this world like that which we can find in the innocent and holy enjoyments which our love for the other open to us. but after all, there is a veil and a wall between us, our sympathies imperfect, our intelligence clouded, our communications inadequate —for there is only one Being who can read our hearts, and that is our God. And I am speaking of death now as it comes to us in the present Providence under which we live, and so it is arranged, by God's mercy, that even that partial happiness which we can have in the society of one another is dashed to pieces by losses, and estrangements, or separations, or bereavements, by the fleeting fickle instability even of what is best. Those who live the longest know the most truly how uncertain, how unsatisfactory, is life, and they long, as the Apostle did, for the sentence which is to set them free.

My brethren, these are the thoughts of the saints concerning the happiness of death—these are some of the reasons which have made them long for it. In thinking of this matter ourselves we are at a great disadvantage, because we can only partially realize one side of the great question. I mean this—the saints of God have not desired death to be free from the troubles of the body, the danger of sin, the miseries of human life. This is all the negative part of death—it is what death puts an end to. But death is not an end so much as a beginning, for this reason—that all that is good and noble and truly great and sweet and happy in this life, does not come to an end with death, but begins again then under new conditions of intensity and purity. Our Lord spoke of going to the Father, St. Paul speaks of "being with Christ, which is far better." Our nature does not come to an end in death, we are to be the same hereafter as now, soul and body, mind, heart, affections, faculties, death takes away the old shams, on which these parts of our compound nature have sought to feed themselves, and puts in their place divine and eternal realities. It opens the doors to the new life, in which a glorified body will take the place of this mortal body, in which the indefectible service of God will take the place of the employments of earth, in which Heaven will become our home, in which our Lord, our Lady, the Saints, the Angels, will become our companions, and all the enjoyments of the Kingdom of Christ take the place of the poor delights of this wicked world. These are matters of faith, not of sight, but they are true, real, and substantial, and above all, my brethren, they are eternal. It is the thought of these realities that has made this life seem an exile to the Saints, an exile which can be borne in obedience and hope, but which cannot be loved, an exile the end of which, when it comes by the goodness of God, must be welcomed with joy and thanksgiving and rapture and extasy.

SERMON XXI.

OUR LORD AND DEATH.*

Ecce ascendimus Jerosolymam, et consummabuntur omnia quæ scripta sunt per prophetas de Filio hominis. Tradetur enim gentibus, et illudetur, et conspuetur; et postquam flagellaverint, occident Eum, et tertia die resurget.

Behold, we go up to Jerusalem, and all things shall be accomplished which were written by the prophets concerning the Son of Man. For He shall be delivered to the Gentiles, and shall be mocked and scourged and spit upon, and when they have scourged Him they will put Him to death, and the third day He shall rise again.

(Words taken from the 31st, 32nd, and 33rd verses of the 18th chapter of St. Luke's Gospel.)

I.

THE Church has set before us these solemn words of our Blessed Lord as part of the Gospel of the day, because on the eve of her great penitential season of Lent she seems to desire to direct our thoughts to the Passion, for the celebration of which Lent is our preparation. And they come in most happily for us, at the end of these considerations on Christian Death, because, without the Passion of our Lord, we should have but little right to console ourselves, as we have been trying to console ourselves, by those thoughts which make the prospect of death happy, bright, and full of joy.

* Preached on Quinquagesima Sunday.

We have seen that death has about it the threefold character of greatness, of sacredness, and of happiness. But if it has these features and characters, it owes them, as far as we are concerned, to Him Who died for us. If our life can be happy and holy and full of hope, we owe it to His Life, if our death can be happy and holy and full of hope, we owe it to His Death. And so now, before we take leave of this great subject, we are to take our stand at the foot of the Cross, of which our Lord speaks in these words to His Apostles, we place ourselves on that holy mountain by Mary His Mother, St. John, and the blessed Mary Magdalene, and we look up to Him Who has just commended His Soul with a loud cry into the hands of His Father, and we ask, "What is it that Thou has done for us, dear Lord? Greater love, Thou didst say, no Man hath than this, that a Man lay down His life for His friends! Thou hast drank the chalice to the dregs, and now Thou art passed to the Father—what is it, O Lord, that Thou hast done for us by dying?"

To give a full answer to this question would take us far beyond the immediate subject of our thoughts this afternoon. For we are not speaking now of the Atonement, the reconciliation between God and man, the satisfaction to God's justice, the eternal Redemption of which St. Paul speaks. We are speaking of what our Lord has done to death itself, what the effect of His Death is upon ours, and although we cannot, in such a consideration, set aside the truth of the Redemption of the world which was wrought by His Death, still this is not so much our direct subject, as a truth which is so large and far reaching that it is mixed with and underlies all subjects which can interest a Christian. So I shall take a few thoughts out of the many which are suggested by the various truths connected with the Death of our Lord, which have some immediate bearing on ourselves. For instance, when St. Paul says, "He died for our sins, and rose again for our justication,"* he speaks of an aspect of the Death of our Lord which properly belongs to His Death alone. On the other hand, when St. Peter says, "Christ suffered for you, leaving you an example that you should follow His steps,"† and goes on to speak of the meekness and humility of our Lord in His Passion, he speaks of something which we not only can imitate, but which we are bound to imitate, whether in life or death. Again, when St. Paul says of our Lord, that "He hath destroyed death and brought life and immortality to light through the Gospel,"‡ he speaks of a part of the effects of our Lord's Death which may be considered by itself—the destruction of death. Again, he says in another place that He was "made a little lower than the Angels for the suffering of death, and then crowned with glory and honour, that through the grace of God He might taste death for all." And then after speaking of the fitness of the Passion as the way of making perfect the Author of the salvation of those whom God was leading to glory, he adds other things which tell us still more about the effects of our Lord's Death. "Because the children," that is, those whom our Lord

* Rom. iv. 25. † 1 St. Peter ii. 21. ‡ 2 Tim. i. 10.

does not disdain to call brethren in one place of Scripture, and children in another, "are partakers of flesh and blood," of this poor frail human nature of ours, "He also Himself in like manner hath been partaker of the same, that through death He might destroy him who had the empire of death, that is to say, the devil, and might deliver those who, through the fear of death, were all their lifetime subject to servitude."* And again, not to multiply too much these passages of the Apostle, we find St. Paul also telling us that though our Lord has in one sense already destroyed death, yet death still remains to have its destruction accomplished, as "the enemy death will be destroyed last of all."†

II.

Here then are a number of statements by the Apostles of our Lord concerning the effects of His Death, and we must select some of them to answer the question which our Lord has done as to death by dying. Now in the first place I will remind you of what we mean when we say that our Lord died for us. We use that expression of others besides our Lord, as when St. Paul says that "perhaps for a just man, one would be ready to die."‡ We say the martyrs died for their faith, or that so and so died for some good cause. No language that we can use of this kind with regard to men can at all mean the same thing as that which we mean when we say that Christ tasted death for all. First of all, all men are now mortal by a law of nature, and therefore

* Heb. ii. 9—15.   † 1 Cor. xv. 26.   ‡ Rom. v. 7.

when a martyr lays down his life for the Church, or for a Christian flock, or in defence of the truth, he does indeed a great and heroic thing, but after all, he lays down a life which has of itself to come to an end, he lays down, as far as lies in him, a few years, perhaps, of life. The other day we kept the feast of St. Simeon, the son of Cleophas, who was Bishop of Jerusalem after St. James, and it is said in the Office for that martyr that all marvelled to see an old man of one hundred and twenty years so bravely bearing the torments which were inflicted on him. In a case like that, martyrdom was the sacrifice of a life already doomed. But our Lord was Life Himself, and the Source of Life, His Human Nature had in it no inherent need of decay, He lay under no law of death for the sin of Adam, except that He made His Father's will the law of His life, and He laid down for us on the Cross a life over which death had no other claim save what He gave it. Again, when we say that a man dies for a cause, or the faith, and the like, we mean that he dies nobly to bear witness to its truth or its goodness. But no man by dying for others has the power of redeeming them, of obtaining for them the remission of sins, reconciliation and pardon from God, no man by his death can cancel guilt or open the gates of Heaven, or reverse the law of eternal death. This is what our Lord did by dying, and this makes His Death unique and unapproachable in its glory and its efficacy. And again, it may be said of the glorious deaths of the martyrs, certainly they benefit the Church, they are the seed of the Church, they are the appointed means, one might almost say, of the propagation of the Church, but they have all their efficacy from the Death of our Lord which has gone before. Again, if they benefit others, those who gain the most by them are the martyrs themselves. No one has gained so much by the triumph of St. Stephen, St. Laurence, St. Alban, St. Thomas, and our own army of Catholic martyrs, as themselves. But our Lord could gain nothing, what had He to gain? He gave Himself altogether for us, for us He lived, for us He died. From the first moment of the Incarnation His Life was ours. It was drawing down blessings on us every single instant that it lasted, up to the Death on the Cross. When He took it again, it was for us, and the Life which He now lives as Man at the right hand of the Father, that Life is for us and benefits us, as His Death was for us.

Now let us see a little more particularly how our Lord, as we may say, dealt with death. Our Lord came, as St. Paul says in a chapter which I have already quoted, to be the author of our salvation. He found man fallen, under the sentence of death, on account of original sin, under the bondage of sin also, on account of the misery and weakness by which original sin had infected his nature, disordering its condition, setting the lower parts of it in revolt against the higher, and because the world had become more and more, in a certain sense, the kingdom of darkness, on account of the prevalence of sin, the ignorance of God, the superstitions, immoralities and cruelties which not only reigned in it, but had almost the authority of law, custom, tradition, and religion on their side. And in consequence men were under the tyranny of Satan, and they looked forward to death with fear and misery, because all their degradation did not suffice to stifle the voice of conscience and the law of nature within them, they felt themselves guilty, on the way to judgment, with a weight around them for which they were responsible and yet of which they had no means of ridding themselves. This is a part at least of the meaning of St. Paul in those strong words which I have quoted to you, "that on account of the fear of death men were all their lives in bondage." And the meaning of those other words of his which occur in the same place, that Satan had the empire or kingdom of death, before our Lord died, seems to be, not that Satan had any lawful right or dominion over men, or over death, but that it had come into the world, as an execution of the sentence of God's justice, in consequence of Satan, for he was the instigator of the sin of Adam, of which death was the penalty, and so that every time a child of Adam died it was in that sense his triumph. Moreover, as the fall introduced disorder into man's condition, and set his concupiscences in revolt, this disorder, though it was not absolutely sin in itself, but the occasion of multitudes of sins, tended to hand men over more and more to him, and thus the death which had been originally the penalty of the fall of Adam alone, became in another sense the triumph of Satan, because it sealed in so many cases a life of guilt, and opened the door to everlasting punishment.

AA

Now as I have said, all these enemies have been destroyed by our Lord, and especially in His death. We know well that Satan and sin and death exist now, as they existed before the crucifixion and resurrection of our Lord. Satan is an intellectual spiritual creature of God, and God has not in the government of His creation absolutely destroyed anything that He has made. Sin is the perversion of the created will, choosing itself rather than God, and, as long as the created will remains in a state of trial and probation, it must have the miserable liberty or capacity of imperfection which we call sin. Satan remains, and sin remains, and death remains,—how has our Lord destroyed them? When St. Paul uses this language, he uses always the same word, which signifies destruction in the sense of bringing to naught, depriving of all power. This our Lord has done to Satan, by conquering him in His own Person, by taking away his power over souls, by destroying his works in the world, by depriving him of the immense power of delusion and tyranny which he had usurped. He allows him still to molest and tempt and deceive, but on the other hand, by His example and precept, and His abundant grace by which He has elevated and strengthened man, He has made him, if he chooses, more than a match for Satan, and the proof of this is in the thousands of millions of souls who have triumphed over him since the Gospel was preached. As for sin, that has been cancelled as to its guilt and as to its pain by Jesus Christ, and though the disorder of concupiscence remains, that also has been made tolerable, and the occasion of immense merit, by means of the copious grace by which the human will is now reinforced to resist it.

And what has He done for death? He has done just what St. Paul says, He has brought it to naught and deprived it, as he elsewhere says, of its sting. I dwell upon this more than on the other two destructions of which I speak, because it is our peculiar subject to-day. Our Lord, as I have said, owed death nothing. He was the author of life, life itself, and the Sacred Human Nature did not lie under the sentence which had been passed on Adam. He chose to die, and as by dying for sin He conquered Hell and sin as to their power over others, so by dying also He conquered death, made it His own, took possession of it, spread His dominion over it. It was said to Josue, the type of our Lord, when he led the chosen people into the promised land, "Every place that the sole of your feet shall tread upon, I will deliver to you." Those words belong, by right, to our Lord. Wherever He is, He is God, Lord, and King. If He comes to earth He is Lord of earth, if He takes human nature He is the Head and King of Humanity, if He touches human life He is Lord of human life, if he goes down into the place of the departed He is Lord and King there. If He lays down His life and dies, He becomes Master and Lord of death. "For this He died and rose again," says St. Paul, "that He might be Lord both of the dead and of the living." He broke and took away the power of Satan and of sin, and if He left death to exist until the time comes when the end of the present state of things closes the history of the world, still He has taken away from it all that is fearful and hurtful to man. It is as if a great sovereign had gone away from part of his dominion, which had been usurped by his enemies, and then had come back and reconquered what was his own by right, and after chasing away the usurpers and restoring his own throne, had found some tax, law, or rule or custom which they had set up in their tyranny, and had allowed the same thing to continue in force, with all its harmful and cruel elements extracted, for a time, for the purposes of his own rule. Death, as I have already said, did not alter the law of human existence in so far as it is simply a termination of our state of probation, that state of probation which would have come to an end with Adam, if he had never fallen, only it would have come to an end without that dissolution and corruption which we call death. As our Lord has not restored our nature in its original integrity and justice, in which there was no interior conflict between concupiscence and reason, as He has left the internal penalties of the fall in us, only taking away its consequences as excluding us from Heaven, and adding immense forces of grace in our regeneration to enable us to cope with our foes, interior and exterior, so He has not given back again, instead of death as it is now, that happy tranquil passage into the next world, without corruption and dissolution, which Adam would have had if he had never sinned. He has removed neither the precursors of death, nor the causes of death, nor death itself. But He has taken away all the disgrace, all the danger, all the fearfulness, He has made it, as we have seen in our former considerations, sacred, happy, meritorious.

III.

And now, my brethren, we see how in leaving us death as our passage in the next world, our Lord has done only what it was natural for Him to do, unless He had altered at once, by virtue of His sovereign power, all the conditions of our present existence. A life like ours, in which the disorder of our nature remains, though we have immense graces given us by means of which to cope with that disorder—a life which, in consequence of the fall, is still a scene of trial, conflict, suffering, physical and moral, in which all the penalties which have come into the world by sin still survive, although we are healed and strengthened and enlightened and filled with hope, so that they are to us occasions of virtue instead of suggestions of despair—a life which is still a passage through the valley of darkness, though we have the rod and the staff of our Lord to comfort us, such a life as this naturally ends in decay and death. Indeed it is a history of decay and of death from its first moment to its last. Our Lord has done with death as He has with all other things which we ordinarily call miseries—He has touched them all, gilded them all, taken the sting out of them all, transformed them all, made them radiant with grace and merit, given them back to us as the flowers and gems out of which we are to weave for ourselves immortal crowns by His grace. Poverty! He touched it, and it became the matter of a beatitude. Mourning! He was a mourner all His days, and He made mourning also happy and blessed. Labour! He was a labourer Himself, He was destitute Himself, He had no where to lay His Head—and all these miseries, as people of the world term them, became beautiful, honourable, noble, glorious. If He had taken the best things of the world for Himself, His Gospel would not have been the Gospel of His poor, God would not have anointed Him, as He said in the synagogue of Galilee, " To heal the broken of heart, to preach deliverance to the captives, and sight to the blind, to set at liberty those that are bruised." It is His way always, not so much to take away physical evils and all sufferings short of sin, as to turn them all into good, poverty into spiritual wealth, hunger and thirst into fulness, slavery and labour into the freedom of the children of God, mourning into joy. So only would He heal the world without altering its fundamental conditions, so only would He tame the concupiscences, and bring in the reign of charity, and make the Church what she is, and heal the nations by the leaves of the Tree of Life. And so He has done to death. He has taken away its sting, He has destroyed sin, He has brought life and immortality to light, and so, by teaching men and enabling men to live holy lives, and putting this hope and expectation of immortality into their hearts instead of the despairing anticipation of endless misery, He has made death in itself no longer terrible. It is a violence to nature, and so nature shrinks from it, as He allowed His own human will to shrink from it. But He has overwhelmed nature with grace, and it is now only one of the physical evils of our condition, the end of all, the door of a better life. The world beyond the grave is not a blank to us, still less is it a prison, a place of darkness, a solitude, a punishment, an exile. It is peopled with all that is bright and glorious in humanity, our friends are there, the saints are there, to have known but one of whom for a day or two would have been enough to brighten a lifetime, they are all our brethren and our sisters, and the Angel hosts also, all watching us, praying for us, helping us, longing for us. We are one with them already, they are one with us. "We are come already to mount Sion, and the city of the living God, the heavenly Jerusalem and to the company of many thousands of angels, and to the church of the first-born who are written in Heaven, and to the spirits of the just made perfect, and to Jesus the mediator of the new covenant, and to the sprinkling of blood, which speaketh better than that of Abel."* The blood is the blood of Christ with which we are sprinkled, and by virtue of it, and in union with His death, our death is meant by God, not to be the simple payment of a debt due by a law of nature, but an act of virtue, an act of faith, hope and charity, the crown of a holy life, a sacrifice and act of religion of immense worth in His sight. Could we have the choice now, between dying and being translated, in all Christian prudence, in consideration of the glory we may give to God, the likeness we may bear to our Lord, the merits we may gain for Heaven, we ought to make our choice for death, to have, as St. Paul

* Heb. xii. 22—24.

says, "the sentence of death in ourselves." As it is better and nobler, and happier, in a Christian sense, to die for the faith, to die for charity's sake, rather than simply to die, so it is far better for us, being what we are, and with the prospect of Heaven before us, to die rather than not to die at all, and thus it is that this enemy is kept by our Lord, as it were, to be executed last. Death has become the servant of God and of His children, the gloom has been taken away, the fearfulness destroyed, the penal character changed into an occasion of merit. He will remain in the kingdom of God as long as there is need of him. When the end shall have come, and the succession of generations closed, and the time of conflict over, and the kingdom of eternal life set up, and the books of judgment closed for ever, and Satan chained, then death shall be swallowed up in victory. "Behold the tabernacle of God with men, and He will dwell with them, and they shall be His people, and God Himself with them shall be their God, and God shall wipe away all tears from their eyes, and death shall be no more, nor mourning, nor sorrow, shall be anymore, for the former things are passed away."*

IV.

But there is yet one more thing which must be added, before we part from this question of what our Lord has done for death. It is not only that if He has left us under the law of death, He has taken away from it all that is painful and hurtful, and turned it into an occasion of infinite blessing, but still more

* Apoc. xxi. 3, 4.

than this, He has taught us how to die. If there were no other value to us at all in His Blessed Passion, there would be in this alone enough to make it our greatest treasure. Well may we spend our Lent in the study of His Passion, and I say that among the thousand teachings and instructions that it contains concerning God and man, and the world and time, and the soul and sin, and grace and virtue, there is not a step in the Passion of Jesus Christ, from the beginning to the end, which is not a special lesson to the Christian how to die, how we are to look forward to death, how to prepare for it, what we are to do when it is yet in the distance, what when it draws nigh, how we are to fit ourselves to meet our God, how to take leave of the world, of our friends or of those who are not our friends, of worldly goods and duties and relations, and all around us, how we are to bear the pains which precede it, how we are to pray, and fortify ourselves by the sacraments and the other aids of the Church, what acts of faith and hope and forgiveness, and humility and contrition and conformity and resignation, we are to exercise. I say all these are written for us in the book of the Passion, from the moment at which our Lord, remembering that He was now to pass out of the world to His Father, took the towel and the basin, and girded Himself and washed the feet of His disciples, to that last strong cry, "Father, into Thy hands I commend my soul." The crucifix is the treasure of the Christian life, because there we read all that we have to do to live well, but above all things it is our treasure, because there we read how we are to die. There are many

Christians who turn away from it in the hey-day of life and of enjoyment, almost as if they thought it a reproach which our Lord addressed to them, to remind them of what they have cost Him. Yes, the crucifix is a reproach to the sinner and to the thoughtless, who either are ready to trample on the sufferings which it records, or care little for them so long as they can have the benefits purchased by them. But no one who thinks seriously of death can love anything better than the memorial of his Saviour's love, which will not only teach him all that he requires to know, but will also bring him, as he studies it, the strength to act up to its teaching.

So then, my brethren in our Lord, with this new glory which He has shed upon death by His own last hours in Jerusalem and on Calvary, may we not say in very truth, that He has turned death into life, or at least He has made death the light and the beacon of life? Yes, indeed He has made it a beacon, but no light that human skill ever kindled and maintained, for the aid and salvation of the storm-tost or perishing mariner, can be compared to this which death now sheds on the raging waters through which we have to make our way to the haven, "where," as the Psalmist says, "we fain would be." Yes, indeed there is a brightness here, a range of light, which turns night into day. Death lights up the angry waters for us, and shows us where are the dangers with which we are threatened, dangers greater by far than the breakers or the shoals or the sunken rocks which lie in wait for the frail barque that has so difficult a course to steer. Death shows us more, for it marks out our way in a broad path of light before us. It shows us unerringly the point for which we are to make, the mouth of the harbour within which all is peace and security. Nay, still more it does, for it reveals to us what no earthly light can show, it shows us the blessed home that awaits us when our course is over, the streets, the palaces, and the gardens, and the groves of the heavenly city of our God, and the fair land around, and those blessed companions who have gone before us thither, holding out their hands to us in welcome, while at the same time they are pouring out their hearts in the tenderest supplication for us, that we also may have the grace to reach without shipwreck that blessed shore, where we shall abide for ever and for ever with them and with our God.

END.

www.ingramcontent.com/pod-product-compliance
Lightning Source LLC
Chambersburg PA
CBHW030542300426
44111CB00009B/833